# Björk

## Wowandflutter

# Björk

## Wowandflutter

MARK PYTLIK

ECW PRESS

Published by ECW PRESS
2120 Queen Street East, Suite 200, Toronto, Ontario, Canada M4E 1E2



NATIONAL LIBRARY OF CANADA CATALOGUING IN PUBLICATION DATA

Pytlik, Mark, 1977-
Björk: Wow and flutter / Mark Pytlik

ISBN 1-55022-556-1

1. Björk. 2. Singers — Iceland — Biography. I. Title.

ML420.B526P98 2003 782.42164'092 C2002-905430-3

Editor: Jennifer Hale
Index: Dana Cook
Cover and Text Design: Guylaine Régimbald/Solo Designs
Production and Typesetting: Mary Bowness
Front cover photo: Richard Phibbs/Outline/Magma
Color section photo credits in order of appearance: Chris Buck/Corbis Outline/Magma; Björg Sveinsdóttir; Richard Phibbs/Corbis Outline/Magma; Shooting Star; Christina Radish; Christina Radish; Bembaron Jeremy/Corbis Sygma/Magma; Björg Sveinsdóttir
Printing: Transcontinental

This book is set in Sari

The publication of *Björk* has been generously supported by the Canada Council, the Ontario Arts Council, and the Government of Canada through the Book Publishing Industry Development Program. **Canada**

DISTRIBUTION
CANADA: Jaguar Book Group, 100 Armstrong Avenue, Georgetown, ON L7G 5S4

UNITED STATES: Independent Publishers Group, 814 North Franklin Street, Chicago, Illinois 60610

PRINTED AND BOUND IN CANADA

ECW PRESS
ecwpress.com

**For Sara: "Always, in some way, to pieces."**

# Foreword

I deliberated long and hard over this undertaking before I signed on not because I had reservations about my subject, but because I had reverence for her. Over a lifetime of consuming music like air, Björk has remained a sturdy beacon, one of the precious few who's been consistently great and giving, especially when I've needed it most — late at night and deep in hunger for consolation, connection.

As is the case whenever respect bleeds into admiration, my reverence for Björk extends beyond her as an artist, but also into what I know of her as a human being. My initial reservations, however small, were borne from that. Out of sympathy to what she endures as a public figure, out of deference to her privacy, and out of a desire not to further contribute to the ongoing headache incurred by public misrepresentation and journalistic dishonesty, I told myself that the only way I could write this book is if I felt that it could be honest without being salacious, insightful without being exploitative, informative without being redundant. If I've done that with this book, then I consider it a success on all counts.

There are no words to describe the gratitude I have for the numerous interview subjects who agreed to meet with me and contribute to what gradually ballooned into a vast undertaking. I'd like to extend warm and appreciative thanks to all who participated by lending their carefully considered thoughts and words: Leila Arab, Markus Dravs, Stefan Edelstein, Guthmunda Eliasdóttir, Paul Fox, Friðrik Þór Friðriksson, Jónatan Garðarsson, Kormákur Geirhardsson, Bjorgvin Gislason, Evelyn Glennie, Michel Gondry, Martin Gretschmann, Gudmunder Gunnarsson, Corky Hale, Hilmar Örn Hilmarsson, Gunnar Hjálmarsson, Eyjólfur Johansson, Ásmundur Jónsson, Nietchka Keene, Thomas Knak, Oliver Lake, Graham Massey, Árni Matthíasson, Einar Melax, Gudlaugur Ottarsson, Bogdan Raczynski, Guðmundur St. Steingrímsson, Netty Walker, and Vibeke Windeløv. Thank you, one and all.

More gratitude to those unsung workers on the frontlines who helped facilitate various interviews: Amro, Cyril Merle, Barbara Marcus, Louise Smith, Caroline Blanco, and Carla Gawthorpe. A hearty cheers to those who graciously augmented my press collection with their own welcome contributions: James Graham and Ole' Martin Hackney.

Special and heartfelt thanks go out to the gracious Jen Hale – as patient, forgiving, and warm as any editor could possibly be; the generous peturiceland@hotmail.com – an endless source of information and a brilliant tour guide; the inexhaustible Suzanne Kingshott – who transcribed and translated more running tape and chirrupy Icelandic accents than I care to tally; and finally, the esteemed Mark Sinker – I may not always see, but I do I bow down to your (always urgent and key) advice, even if you run intellectual rings around me in transmittance.

Props to the choicest circles from the Interweb massive are also in order: the entire Björk Internet Community (for never losing your enthusiasm, for being real fans), Sheikh at Absorb.org (for still caring 'bout the good stuff, damned be everyone else) and, most importantly, the entire ILX community (a more uproarious, thought-provoking and violently embittered group I have never known).

I don't know what I'd do without the support of my dearest friends, whose collective presence and encouragement helped see me through some very difficult times: Sara Chan ("Look no further!"), Patrick Currah (I love ye, wee skidmark that ye are – holy), Dave Edwards (for endless patience in my absence), Jonathan Hale (I'm speechless – you're just the best), Laine Pond ("you need *another* day?!") and Christina 'Veg' Vardanis (for always listening, sometimes buying coffee to boot). I honestly don't know what I'd do without you all. Life-savers, each and every one.

Finally, thanks to my wonderful family for everything. Much love to Mom and Dad for endless support and to Mike and Danielle for being the best siblings a brother could possibly have.

# PRONUNCIATION KEY

Wherever possible, I have opted to use native spellings and characters when discussing Icelandic names and places. What follows is a brief guide to the pronunciation of characters that may not otherwise be familiar. Be warned: since many recognizable letter sets are pronounced entirely differently in Icelandic depending on their proximity to vowels and placement within the word, this overview will not fully bridge the language barrier. What it will do is help to approximate some of the more seemingly impenetrable words.

**Pronunciation key:**

ö — pronounced "ur" (as in "urge")

Þ — pronounced "th" (as in "thick")

ð — pronounced "th" (as in "father")
ei — pronounced "a" (as in "amy")
Sj —pronounced "sh" (as in shine)
á — pronounced "ou" (as in "mouse")
é — pronounced "ye" (as in "yelp")
í — pronounced "ee" (as in "screen")
ó — pronounced "ou" (as in "soul")
ú — pronounced "oo" (as in "moon")
ý — pronounced "ee" (as in "green")
æ — pronounced "i" (as in "file")
au — pronounced "ou" (as in "round")
ey — pronounced "o" (as in "omit")
hj — pronounced "hu" (as in "human")

**For example:**

"Björk" is pronounced "Byerk"
"Örn" is pronounced "Urn"
"Þór" is pronounced "Thor"
"Þeyr" is pronounced "Theyr"
"Friðrik" is pronounced "Frith-rik"
"Einar" is pronounced "Aye-nar"
"Sjon" is pronounced "Shawn"

Like English, Icelandic is a complicated language with many anomalies and conditions; as such, this key should only be regarded as a basic primer for some of its most commonly encountered patterns.

# Introduction



There is a brief scene in the *South Bank* Björk episode that has always struck me as the perfect encapsulation of everything she's about.

Filmed on location in Spain during the recording sessions for 1997's *Homogenic*, the scene depicts a spectacularly clad Björk trundling in solitude along a rugged Marbella beach with headphones on her head and a portable sampler in her hands. The sun's rays beaming down on her are either the beginnings of a glorious morning or the last remnants of dusk settling on a glorious eve. Either way, the weather is verging on something, and Björk is basking in it.

Clouds of sand rise up behind her as she stomps down the otherwise isolated beach in perfect time to the rhythms she's fastidiously manipulating with her thumbs. Later, while sitting down, she timidly describes her latest mechanical toy (a Yamaha SU-10, for the trainspotters) with the hushed tones of a child presenting her most prized possession at show-and-tell. "It's so incredibly convenient," she gushes. "You put the batteries in and you can write on the airplane, in your gran's house, on top of a volcano, in a club, in a tube. . . ."

This vignette eventually cuts to another shot of Björk, headphones back on, this time turned away from the camera. She's still on the beach, now steps away from the gushing tide and pogoing on the spot to some frenetic, double-timed rhythm. As she turns around and begins her hike back to the studio, we notice that her shoelaces are untied.

It is no coincidence that descriptions of Björk as a young child are often easily interchangeable with descriptions of Björk as a full-grown adult. Dating as far back as her early days with the Sugarcubes, this basic precept — of thirtysomething as five-year-old and five-year-old as thirtysomething — has been central to most of the pieces written about her.

For the better part of the 1990s it was virtually impossible to read an interview with Björk where a journalist wasn't pulling literary backflips in an attempt to convey how deeply enigmatic she came across in conversation. The cumulative effort of all those befuddled column inches was an endless string of platitudes, which eventually, by sheer force of repetition, undermined our collective image of who she really was.

No doubt evinced at least partially by her youthful spirit, nearly all of the ensuing clichés implied some sort of otherness or, worse, cuteness. Sometimes, by way of some ill-advised wordplay, they did both. A brief sample: Elfin, The Elf Child, Herself the Elf, The Elfin Alien, A Pixie, A Deranged Pixie, Pixie-Faced, The Icelandic Pixie, Impish, The Icelandic Imp, The Worldly-Wise Imp, The Quirky Flighty Icelandic Imp, The Otherworldly Icelandic Diva, Playful Sprite, Media Kook, Extraterrestrial, Bonkers, Bjonkers, Nordic Child-Woman, The Girl Who Fell To Earth, Björk The Dork, Lunar Astronaut, The World's Only Cheerful Techno Surrealist. It goes on and on.

The words became meaningless after a while, stripped of their intended effect by way of overuse, but none of that altered the fundamental truth of the matter: at the center of Björk's enormous appeal is really, truly, a heart in arrested development, perpetually threatening to combust with the sheer force of so much wonder, so much emotion. To even begin to understand the rest of her, you must accept this truth first. Once you do, then everything else — the exotic teardrop eyes, the adventurous ear, the musical virtuosity, *that* voice — will fall into place as almost incidental, certainly separate: the reaped rewards of an across-the-board sweep in the gene lottery.

To call Björk a pixie is to undermine so much. Better to think of her as a raw nerve in an aesthete's body, empowered by hopefulness, embracing of love, and enabled with a breadth of talent so far-reaching that it's difficult to imagine her as anything other than a performer.

Got that? Good. Now remember this: Björk sometimes either forgets or refuses to tie her own shoes.

Believe it or not, that's half her story, right there.

# one

One's immediate impulse after locating Iceland on a map of the world is to suggest that it is cruelly detached from the rest of civilization. One's immediate impulse after spending a significant amount of time there is to suggest that, as a whole, Iceland probably prefers it that way.

Some history: widely acknowledged to have been discovered by Vikings in the late 800s and settled by Norwegians soon after, the nation of Iceland is one of the world's most recently colonized countries. Its proclamation of independence from Danish rule didn't come until 1944, meaning they're only just verging on their seventh decade as an independent state.

Iceland's youthfulness extends to its very geography. Carbon dating places the earliest rock formations of the country's gnarled terrain at a comparatively green 14 million years old, making it, geographically, a land still in its infancy.

The land knows this, and behaves accordingly. Iceland's natural marvels seem in a constant state of motion, as if still acclimatizing. The geysers gush, the mud pots burble, the volcanoes hiccup, the hot springs steam, the glaciers trickle. The sensation, even in isolation, is of a landscape permanently engaged in a state of mental chatter, accelerated self-advancement.

Some facts: in spite of a land mass roughly analogous to that of Great Britain, Iceland has roughly 1/1000th the population. Its capital city, Reykjavik, is also its largest by far, accounting for nearly half of the country's 270,000 citizens. The next populous city is a northern town named Akureyri, inhabited by approximately 15,000 residents. The remainder of the country's inhabitants live scattered across the expansive land, occupying smaller seaside villages and mountain-shielded farming habitats.

Iceland's proximity to the globe's northern tip means that it is perennially engaged in a prolonged game of hide-and-seek with the sun. As a result, days during the height of summer are marked by no more than three hours of total darkness. Conversely, closer to Christmas, the sun typically tends to rise at around 11 a.m. and set by 4 p.m., casting a swath of darkness over the nation's chilly winters.

Perhaps by extension, Icelanders are notoriously extreme people, equally as prone to sudden fits of inspired drunken lunacy as they are to carefully considered debate. They acknowledge and understand the values of industry, environment, and culture, but never sacrifice one at the peril of any other.

People born in Iceland are self-sufficient and independent in much the same way that people born in England are English. This universal characteristic is often described as a by-product of their relative isolation, but the intensity of their implicit self-belief somehow seems more inbound than that.

As a population, Icelandics are as exacting and as hard-working as they are vibrant, boasting a well-established social system, a progressive political lean, and an emphatically bustling cultural overground that teems with homespun literature, visual art, and music.

Some anecdotes: each year in Iceland, there is roughly one new book published for every 200 inhabitants. In Reykjavik, there are more art galleries than movie theaters, more coffee shops than video rental outlets. Kids skip school to go to museums.

In spite of its rich history in the oral tradition, Iceland rates among the world's most technologically progressive nations; the inhabitants rank highly in Internet usage per capita and adapt to new technology with lightning quick reflexes. Yet they remain a profoundly spiritual nation. While no single organized religion can claim dominance, there is a heavy history of paganism interwoven into their cultural fabric. Also, most Icelanders really, truly do believe in elves.

As a final point of interest, it might be helpful to know that Iceland's prime minister can be reached at any time by a simple ring of the doorbell. This is best not advised, however, if one happens to be drunk in Iceland, because to be drunk in Iceland is to be three times as drunk as one anywhere else in the world.

Björk was born in Reykjavik on November 21, 1965, to mother Hildur

Hauksdóttir and father Guðmundur Gunnarsson. Since Icelandic etymology inferred a newborn's last name from their father's first, she was christened Björk Gudmundsdóttir ("Guðmundur's daughter").

For the first year, the trio lived together in Reykjavik as a struggling but relatively happy family. Once a spate of minor health concerns subsided, Gunnarsson remembers his baby daughter as serene and rarely temperamental. "She was very difficult the first year because she had stomach problems and it was always a very big problem getting her to sleep," he recalled. "Many nights, we had to walk around with her on our shoulder and keep her steady. After that, she was never a problem."

Even in the early stages of their marriage, it was evident that Gunnarsson and Hauksdóttir possessed drastically different philosophies. By nature, Guðmundur was more traditional — not conservative, by any means, but firmly believing in the value of hard work and discipline. In many ways, he was the more stable of the two parents, a classically Icelandic father: independent, generous, and warm-hearted, but with a fiery temper if provoked.

As the current head of Iceland's electricians' union, Gunnarsson has needed to make his fair share of unpopular decisions. He cites his willingness to stay sturdy and go against the grain as a quality that's been passed on to his daughter. "For me, it's no problem to make a decision," he contends. "It doesn't matter if I have to swim upstream if I'm certain that the decision is right. She is exactly like that."

In contrast, the young Hildur was freewheeling, always questing, and prone to prioritizing her sudden flights of fancy above matters of practicality. While Gunnarsson had enrolled himself in school, she'd gone looking for something more immediate and adventurous; she eventually ended up working in a string of bustling nightclubs.

With their ideological gap growing wider, it quickly became apparent to Hildur that her marriage to Guðmundur was not destined to last. It was 1966. Newly inspired by the burgeoning hippie ideal, she left her husband and set off in pursuit of a different scene. "My mother became a feminist, a rebel, and left her husband to become a hippie and lead a very free lifestyle," Björk said. "It was the '60s and everyone was doing it."

"Me and her mother divorced when [Björk] was around two," Gunnarsson explains. "For the years after that she was more often with me than her mother because her mother was working in the afternoon and on the weekends."

Björk lived in a house with Gunnarsson and his parents until she was about four or five years old. Gunnarsson realized during this time that his daughter had been born with an innate touch for music. As an infant, she responded to melodies; as a toddler, she was replicating them naturally. "If she heard a new song on the radio she could sing it without problems," he says. "From very early on, you could see that she had a musical ear at a much higher level than almost everybody else. My mother had a piano and she started on it very early. It was very easy for her to find out which note to push to get the tune."

Björk's virtuosity as a child was matched only by her emerging penchant for showmanship and imagination. By the time she was three, she was treating audiences at family gatherings to her own special performances, where she'd arrive with the good grace to set up her "stage" in advance. "She would take a cloth and put it on the middle of the floor," remembers her father. "Whenever she stepped on that cloth, she'd put on some show."

As she got older and braver, Björk extended her impromptu performances to anywhere that offered a captive audience. "She was always going around singing," Gunnarsson says. "At that time I was in school and I didn't have a car, so I used the bus. Often she would stand on the seat by my side and put on a show for the people sitting backwards on the bus."

Björk's trajectory was laid out like another cloth on the floor, even when she was a toddler. Upon turning five years old, she enrolled in the Icelandic Conservatory of Music; as Gunnarsson notes, it was something that she had long been determined to do on her own. "It was not something that was decided," he laughs. "She went into music school as early as she could go in."

By that time, both Hauksdóttir and Gunnarsson had remarried. Shortly afterwards, Björk went to live with her mother and her new stepfather, a musician named Sævar Árnason, in a shared space populated by a group of fellow bohemians. "They all had long hair and listened to Jimi Hendrix all day long, and everything was painted purple, so I'm allergic to purple now," Björk joked. "They had all these dreams and wild plans — you know, 'Let's live on an airplane!' and things like that, which is brilliant for a kid. Can you imagine being brought up by seven grown-ups who all hate work and all they want to do is play games with you all the time and tell you stories and make kites? It took me ages as a child to learn to be interested in other people because my own head was so busy and so interesting."

Much has been made of this scenario; the abiding notion of Björk as the direct product of a hippie commune is part of her longstanding mythology. The reality is that while this was an important component of her upbringing, it was one of many elements that existed within her overall circle of influence. Unlike virtually every other kid her age, Björk was never constrained to home; in fact, she was encouraged to explore. "My mother had a strong father who was really sexist, who beat her down," she explained. "Her solution was to give me all the freedom she couldn't have. She let me do whatever I wanted — probably more so because I was a girl."

This independence led to self-sufficiency, with Björk often fulfilling many of the tasks normally reserved for the mother figure by herself. "When I was five or so, I had a key around my neck, and I took the bus myself to school and I did all my homework, and dressed and fed myself," she said. "I became by own mum very early, and I developed a relationship to myself where I was the mum *and* the child."

It could've been a fragmented, marginalized existence, but the young Björk seemed to thrive on the independence. Between school, her two sets of parents, and her four sets of grandparents, she always had somewhere to go. The varying dynamics of each environment offered something completely different, and Björk happily fluttered amongst them all, gleaning something unique from each. "When I visited my father and stepmother and their children, I was the odd one out, the freaky one," she said. "At the commune, I was the straight, organized one. When I went to the classical music school, I was the jazz freak, and I enjoyed that."

She also realized, early on, that any of the traditional motherly type things that she couldn't give herself could be obtained elsewhere. In her grandmothers, Björk recognized judiciousness and stability — both qualities that a young Hildur had sometimes lacked. "One granny used to put me in a chair and comb my hair, because it was down to here," she said. "And it used to get, like, dreadlocks. Another granny, my stepfather's mother, used to take my socks off and darn the holes. I was not very tidy because I just took care of myself. My mum was like a kid. When I was three, my relatives saw me look left and right and take her across the street."

Because of her unorthodox vantage point, Björk developed a slight critical distance from her mother's freewheeling lifestyle and cultivated an early appreciation for her grandmother's simpler ways. "I used to look at my mum, who was this madly over-excited hippie, really swallowing life," she said. "She was always a bit worried, running around trying to be sexy and trying to be in love and trying to buy a house and trying to have a job, and I just found my grandmother 10 times more charming. When she was about 55 or 60, she used to travel out into the countryside and paint; she'd take a load of red wine and go and sit up by the lava, staying for a week. She had the best time in the world. I think the climax of my life is going to be after, say, 45. But between 50 and 70's gonna be great."

As a child, Björk was precocious and imaginative, not unpopular at school but generally more comfortable by herself or in the company of adults. "My first memory is being in kindergarten and I refused to be one of the kids, I was always helping the ladies out," she recalled. "I remember putting butter and rye bread out for the kids.

"I liked the kids at school, but it was like they didn't really get me," she said. "I thought I sort of got them, but I didn't find them very interesting. I was quite an introvert — but a happy introvert. I made up a lot of stories. It was gorgeous, you know, a lot of songs, a lot of walking. I remember walking between school, my granny, my mother's house, my music school, and my father's house, and sort of singing on the way, making up songs."

She later recounted, "A lot of children I just wasn't interested in. But I always had three or four really close friends; we're talking mental love affairs. They were always the odd ones out: the tall girl who got tits when she was eight; the guy who collected insects and couldn't talk to anyone . . ."

Einar Melax would later play in a variety of bands with Björk as a teenager, but he first encountered her as an adolescent in school. "I always recalled her as unusual," he says. "I remember seeing her as a kid because we lived in the same suburb. She just didn't act like the crowd. When she walked onto a bus, she would sit in the front seat, not go to the back rows and talk with other kids. She just appeared, from the beginning, somehow different to me.

"I'm not saying that she was cast out from others," he clarifies. "She just was kind of special. She told me once when she was a kid that when she had friends at her home, she would cook for them by taking some cereal and then she would add some liver and pasta to it and cook it like a soup on the oven."

The freedom afforded to her meant that Björk's life was dictated only by the limits of her own imagination. When she wasn't camping with Hildur and Sævar, hiking around the countryside, or drawing chalk murals on Reykjavik's downtown sidewalks, she'd spend her time playing with the family cat, who sadly became an unwitting test case for many of her experiments. Once, in an effort to see if he could fly like the birds he spent his days watching, she threw the cat out the window. "It wasn't meant in a mean way," she later protested. "I really felt sorry for him because he couldn't follow the birds."

Having had no prior history with Iceland, the mass media's proclivity upon first encountering Björk was to connect her exotic appearance with her nation of origin, in turn fostering a base assumption that *all* Icelanders looked as alien as she. The reality couldn't be further from the truth.

Although her lineage is derived from hundreds of years of pure Icelandic blood, there has always been something strikingly un-Icelandic about Björk's face. With her downturned eyes, coal black hair, freckle patches, dipped nose, and curled lips, Björk was singled out by her peers as a rara avis from the very start. "When I was growing up, I always had this feeling that I had been dropped in from somewhere else," she said in 1993. "That was how I was treated at school in Iceland, where the kids used to call me 'China girl' and everybody thought I was unusual because I was Chinese."

The slight estrangement didn't bother her; she did her best to take advantage of it. "It gave me room to do my own thing," she said. "In school, I was mostly on my own, playing happily in my private world making things, composing little songs.

If I can get the space I need to do my own thing by being called an alien, an elf, a China girl, or whatever, then that's great!"

The guitarist in a local rock cover band named Pops, stepfather Árnason had a taste in music that was roughly asynchronous with that of the rest of the free spirits that comprised their household. Björk detested rock, but being outnumbered by at least seven or eight meant that she grew up on a steady diet of Jimi Hendrix, Eric Clapton, and Deep Purple nonetheless. Compared to the more adventurous music that she was hearing elsewhere (classical and avant-garde at school, jazz at her father's, folk at her grandparents') the traditional axis of guitar-bass-drums struck her very early on as being deathly boring, chronically unadventurous.

Soon, she'd begun to dream up more exciting parameters for her own music. "My ideal band would be an open-minded group that won't let anything get in the way of creating something new," she later said. "They could use saxophones, teaspoons, drum machines, or anything to communicate a whole concept, whether it be a house track, experimental music, pop, or just a nursery rhyme."

Steered largely by the sensibilities of headmaster Stefan Edelstein, Björk's formative years at music school were spent exploring the realm of avant-garde, classical, and minimalist music. By the time she was six, she'd been exposed to the work of contemporary German composer Karlheinz Stockhausen, avant-gardist John Cage, and a host of other similarly vanguard music.

Fortunately, Björk's early appreciation for experimental music wouldn't preclude her from pop. She recognized early on that Abba and Boney M could scratch itches that the Oliver Messiaens or Arvo Parts of the world could not touch. In fact, the first record that she ever dared bring into the commune was *Kimono My House*, by the American pop duo Sparks. "The hippies didn't really like it, they thought it was too pop, it didn't have cred," she lamented. "They thought it was too comical. That was the first time I was like 'I've got a record and I'm going to play it and now you've all got to listen to what *I* like.'"

By the time she'd turned 10, most of the commune members had dispersed, and Hildur and Sævar moved into a smaller home located in a suburb of Reykjavik named Briedholt.

The grievous Sparks/Deep Purple divide hadn't kept Árnason from actively supporting his stepdaughter's love for music; around this time, he began encouraging her to perform live. Björk got her start soon after when she covered a pop song for a school function. "They used to have an open house every week where the kids had to entertain, read aloud and things like that," Hildur said. "Björk sang a song called 'I Love to Love.'"

Björk's rendition of Tina Charles' disco hit was so impressive that her teachers felt compelled to deliver the recording to Iceland's national radio station, who added

*Growing up, Björk had occasional bouts of pronounced shyness and introversion — this is her in a moment of quiet contemplation. (Photo by Björg Sveinsdóttir)*

it to their playlist without hesitation. The song rendered Björk something of a local celebrity and was popular enough that Árnason secured her a small record deal with the tiny Falkinn Records.

The dearth of recording studios in Iceland at the time meant that there was no industry to support a devoted record label, so other companies had to pitch in where they could by diversifying. "There were some companies that had been releasing records from around 1930, but just every once in a while," explains Icelandic television personality Jónatan Garðarsson. "They were always more or less into something else, like bicycles or machinery — music was just a department within a larger firm."

While this was also true of Falkinn, the deal was still a boon for Björk. With label support, the well-traveled Árnason was able to secure the talents of some of Iceland's finest musicians for the project. With Palmi Gunnarsson on bass, Sigurdur Karlson on drums, and Bjorgvin Gislason contributing additional guitar work, the group set upon Hljdrijinn Studios, Reykjavik's brand new 24-track recording facility.

The resulting album, simply titled *Björk*, consisted mainly of cover tunes and traditional Icelandic songs, all sung by the 11-year-old virtuoso. Impressively, the final tracklisting even included an original song; "Jóhannes Kjarval" was an instrumental track that Björk composed as a tribute to an Icelandic painter of the same name. "A nice little song," Gislason recalls. "They were doing it on a piano, but I think she wrote it on a harmonium."

Being in Iceland's finest studio with some of the country's most seasoned professionals at 11 years old didn't intimidate Björk one bit; although outsized, she readily asserted her presence. Although he was in his thirties at the time, Gislason recalls feeling comically intimidated by her unwavering confidence. "She was quite different from other kids — she knew what she was doing," he says. "She didn't take any bullshit — I remember that."

Björk's fearless interaction with the adult musicians had been informed by her upbringing. Handily, she'd also developed enough talent to hold her own on a strictly musical level. "She knew what she wanted, but it was always in a very nice way," Gislason says. "She was playing a recorder and she did that very well, even in two-part harmonies. She was very fast at learning the songs; some of them were a little tricky. It was no problem for her."

With Hildur designing the album's sleeve (which pictured a cherubic Björk sitting in the center of a room adorned with Oriental tapestries), the album was released in late 1977. Featuring straightforward, well-executed Icelandic covers of songs by artists including The Beatles ("Fool on the Hill"), Stevie Wonder ("Your Kiss Is Sweet") and Edgar Winters ("Alta Mira"), *Björk* ended up being a distinctly more contemporary record than Falkinn was expecting.

Icelandic music guru (and eventual head of Bad Taste Records) Ásmundur Jónsson was a newcomer to Falkinn at the time of *Björk*'s release. He recalls his handlers being acutely worried by the record she'd turned in — they'd done the album because they figured it'd be a big seller with *children*, so where were the children's songs?

"There were concerns from people within the company who thought it was too sophisticated or too grown-up to be a children's record, and I think in many ways, that was correct," Jónsson says. "Björk's record was a bit difficult for the general public to deal with because it was not a children's record and it was not an adult record. Or maybe it *was* an adult record but fronted by a very young singer."

If the album sounded more mature than typical children's fare, it was because Björk had made a concerted effort to steer clear of anything too juvenile. "When you're 11, you're not listening to *Sesame Street* any more," she said. "I wanted to write music about walking down the street, having visits, laughing, having a swim — the things you do every day."

Falkinn's concerns ultimately proved ill-founded. Although it wasn't necessarily a huge hit with the kids in her age group, *Björk* performed decently as an album, garnering a significant amount of radio attention and generating respectable sales.

While it was a solid release, it was in no way the hugely selling monstrosity that mythmakers have since made it out to be. Longtime Icelandic music journalist and official Sugarcubes biographer Árni Matthíasson is one of many local pundits who laughs at the suggestion of it ever going platinum (even if, on Icelandic terms, platinum would've have been a relatively small number). "People look back and say, 'Oh it was a huge seller,' and it wasn't really," Matthíasson smirks. "But it was *interesting*. I remember reading an interview with her then and she was obviously not just doing the child singer thing, which was just to sing something that someone prepared for you. She had input and she was writing songs, so it was a bit special."

The mild degree of fame that resulted was not without its negative side.

Following the album's success, Björk was roundly teased by her schoolmates; kids would taunt her on the bus, others would facetiously sing the melody to single "Alta Mira" whenever she was near. By virtue of her singular appearance and demeanor, Björk had been used to a degree of this since she was very young. This spate, however, proved frustrating, especially when she wasn't crazy enough about the music she was making to defend it.

A year later, when Falkinn requested that she record a follow-up, Björk refused. The experience of being in a studio had been fun, but she wanted to make music *with* kids her own age, not ostensibly *for* them. At 12, she'd grown tired of being a cover artist.

Gunnarsson, who still saw his daughter frequently during these years, was never comfortable with the idea to begin with. "I was afraid she would be made to do things like all child stars — take some popular songs and copy them — and then her creativity would stop," he says. "She would just become a copy machine."

Copying wouldn't be necessary. If anything, the next 10 years would see Björk suffer from an overabundance of inspiration.

# two

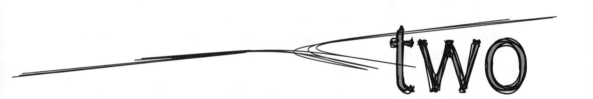

In spite of tidal waves of corresponding activity in England and the United States, punk music and its aesthetic failed to make an impression on Iceland's youth until years after its inception. It finally made ripples at the tail end of the '70s, when it arrived in a slightly adapted form: a localized variant, with small 'p' politics, creative stagnation, and boredom as its mitigating forces.

Reykjavik had remained largely untroubled by anything as ugly as class war, civil unrest, or social insurgency, but a number of local artists and poets connected with elements of the punk ideal nonetheless. Its self-empowering politics resonated deeply with the equally self-sufficient Icelandics, who seized upon it as a tool for inciting a grassroots, youth-oriented uprising against prior generations deemed hide-bound by tradition. By the turn of the decade, a previously dormant Reykjavik suddenly found itself brimming with bands. A bona fide scene had begun, boredom averted, thirst sated.

Icelandic filmmaker Friðrik Þór Friðriksson agrees that the immediacy of Icelandic punk was dictated more by the natural tendencies of teenage rebellion than any hard and fast political ideology. The kids were restless, in search of a new charge, tired of tradition — this thing could be theirs, and theirs only. "Society's always trying to shape their own culture and shape their own art," he explains. "You had people who were teaching other people to contemplate music, but they were playing music that was written 200 years before, so the only thing you could add to that is a feeling. I think these people just wanted to protest this."

These politics were manifested as a crusade against the orthodoxy of tradition: proponents of punk in Iceland strove to narrow the ideological gap between generations, to rail against close-mindedness, to avert the perceived threat of a small-town mentality. Culturally, they weren't at a loss for targets. With few exceptions, mainstream music was pretty terrible, and since Iceland's radio and television airwaves were run primarily by a single governing source, there wasn't much room for a reasonable alternative. The punks had a reason for their malaise — now it was time to challenge it. "People were just tired," said Friðriksson. "Nothing had happened for three or four years."

As the lead guitarist for Þeyr (arguably one of this movement's most crucial bands) and later for Kukl, Gudlaugur Ottarsson knew that disenfranchisement all too well. "You'd get really angry when you listened to the radio for an hour," he said. "We were really fed up with what the public was fed through the radio, in concert, in records. It was all like a mind control to create consumers with no brains. The music was a vital instrument for the market to brainwash people."

Iceland's first wave of proto-punk bands soon emerged, with Björk immersed in the middle of it all. She spent a spell drumming for a band called Spit And Snot, but her first noteworthy contribution to this stable came in the form of a new wave quartet named Exodus.

Exodus was comprised entirely of kids from Björk's music conservatory, and it showed. The somewhat overambitious foursome stood out amidst their comparatively ragged peers as hopeless musos. While their contemporaries were slashing away at tattered two-minute songs, Exodus were busy tinkering with sophisticated time sequences and overcomplicated arrangements. Author of the Icelandic musical tome *Eru Ekki Allir I Studi?* (rough translation: Are We Having a Good Time?) and head of Bad Taste mail order Gunnar Hjálmarsson remembers sharing billing with Exodus early on. "They were sort of like boys who listened to Japan and stuff like that," he smirks. "Good musicians — which wasn't the point. . . ."

"It was a short-lived band," Jónsson offers. "Björk had great charisma but the music that they were doing did not impress me very much." Exodus would eke out a few small successes, including a cassette release and a one-off appearance on local television before folding.

While in Exodus, Björk was constantly courted by other musicians. Drummer Eyjólfur Johansson and his friends had their own fledgling band; they were all so enamoured with Björk that they surreptitiously made overtures for her defection.

"Exodus were more tidy than we were thinking, they were not our cup of tea," Johansson laughs. "They had groomed themselves to be marvelous musicians, but at the time, there was sort of a competition."

Along with friends Eythor Arnalds (guitar) and Jakob Magnusson (bass), Johansson eventually drafted the 13-year-old Björk into their band. United by common musical tastes and a certain voracious spirit, the foursome quickly became friends first, bandmates second. "It was more like a company than a band at the beginning," Johansson recalls. "We hung out together, listened to music, and made some music in between."

The group's first attempts at music-making came under the banner Jam 80, where they goofily peddled a not entirely serious roster of spirited re-interpretations. "Most of our stuff was covers," Johansson says. "I remember doing 'Le Freak' by Chic — disco, but with our influence. Björk was singing, playing the flute and some keyboards."

As with any teenager on the verge of a self-started revolution, the ages of 13 and 14 proved crucial for the still-emerging Björk. Although living at home with Hildur, Björk was overwhelmed by the bursts of creativity surrounding her. Eager to more fully explore the suddenly blooming possibilities, she decided it was time for a change. "She made the decision to [leave] school and start playing with student groups and the others," recalls father Guðmundur Gunnarsson. "It was becoming so much a part of her life that she didn't have time to go [anymore]."

Björk made the most of her newfound liberation and quickly fell in with a wild, left-brained group of kids who facilitated her creative indulgences. The musical dalliances that followed were fleeting, in-the-moment affairs: one-off collaborations, inside jokes, and unconsummated projects derailed by teenage indecision, more bands forgotten than remembered. Local musician Kormákur Geirhardsson has vague recollections of a dicey fusion endeavor: "She was playing with this band from Selfoss which was like a country dance band. . . ."

Although she didn't have much time for boys, Björk lost her virginity at 15 years old. It's an experience she recalls with cherry-eyed zeal: "I had a huge red shirt and big boots — quite punky, I have to say it — and I went on a mission with this boy. We actually went to his friend's house. It was dark and I remember thinking I wasn't sure if that was it or not, but I thought it was ever so exciting."

Suitably distanced from her own halcyon days, Hildur worried about her daughter's feral lifestyle. The resulting tension caused Björk to leave her home in Breidholt. "I left when I was 14 because I got the feeling that time was running out, that there were all these things happening out there and I was missing them," she said. "You decide that you want to rent a flat and cook really bad meals. I had to come home a year later when I was broke."

Björk spent that year bouncing between stations, but most frequently found herself back with her father, still a more lenient alternative to Mom. "She has said that at that time she had very big problems with her mother," Gunnarsson says. "I can understand that, because her mother was very afraid that she would lose her to the dope, the drugs, and she was around that lifestyle, or at least most of it." Gunnarsson didn't entirely approve of Björk's lifestyle either, but he was willing to grant his daughter the freedom she so desperately craved. "She always knew what she wanted to do. In my mind if she came home at 11 o'clock or one o'clock, it was no problem."

The ensuing months were spent in and out of her father's house, where she'd often race in to procure some random item before leaving again in a breathless huff. Although frequently bewildered, her father remained supportive. "I remember one time she came to my home and asked 'Pa, do you have an English book?'" he recalls. "I said, 'Yes, of course I have an English book, what do you want?' She said, 'I need some words to some lyrics.' I said, 'Why do you need *some* English book — doesn't it matter what the words are?' She said, 'I'll take every fifth word from page 20!' And she did that, opened the book and took every fifth word. She said that words didn't matter, it was the *sounds*. I went and heard what she was doing and she was not singing, 'I love you,' she was just making sounds following the instruments that were playing."

Then, of course, there was the matter of her clothes, which were mirroring Björk's more radical, punky outlook. "Sometimes she'd come home after she had bought a piece of cloth, go to the sewing machine, make a dress in 10 minutes and go out the door," her father laughs. Old habits die hard: moments before her gig at 1995's Reading Festival, Björk could be seen backstage, sewing her costume for the evening.

In spite of Gunnarsson's comparatively more charitable outlook, his 15-year-old daughter would not stay with him for long. Björk bounced back to her mother's, before eventually leaving for good and renting a flat with two of her three step-brothers. Eager to prove her independence, Björk cycled through a number of fleeting jobs. Among them was a stint at a Coca-Cola bottling plant. "I had pink hair at the time, and I was supposed to sit in a chair, watching the bottles as they passed to see if they were clean," she said. "Mostly, I just used to fall asleep. I never made the employees' hall of fame."

It wasn't long before Reykjavik's most deserving bands had risen to the top of the scrabbly local scene; by 1981, both Þeyr (pronounced 'theyr') and Purkurr Pilnikk were widely recognized as the movement's finest bands. Led by guitarist Ottarsson (also an accomplished physicist), Þeyr's guitar-heavy sound was frenzied, angular, and strangely mathematic. Theirs was a pained, cosmic music — devoid of any humor, but heavy on philosophy and sweeping intent. Meanwhile, Purkurr Pilnikk's main calling card was a young, bullish insurgent named Einar Örn Benediktsson, who polarized audiences everywhere with his abrasive vocals and combative presence.

Meanwhile, Björk and her Jam 80 cohorts had finally ditched the disco covers in favor of original material. In commemoration, they'd re-christened themselves Tappi Tikarrass, a name derived from an Icelandic expression meant to denote a "good fit" and famously translatable to "cork the bitch's ass." Tappi was a plucky quartet whose frenetic, fidgety pop was frequently maligned by critics; fortunately, what the band lacked in songs, Björk made up for in energy.

Music journalist Árni Matthíasson recalls enjoying their live shows almost in spite of his own critical sensibilities: "Tappi Tikarrass was terrible, but it didn't matter at the time because, as the punk adage goes, it's not what you *can* do but what you do. They were energetic and they were enthusiastic, so you saw them live and you really got caught up in it. You didn't stop and think, 'this is really crap, they can't play shit.'"

"I always thought that she was much too good for Tappi Tikarrass — I never liked that group," agrees Icelandic composer and musician Hilmar Örn Hilmarsson. "I thought the music was shit, but then at the same time I thought there was some incredible charm to what she was doing."

Feisty, charismatic, and joyous, the 15-year-old Björk was the unwitting live focal point, even when she wasn't singing. With her as their calling card, Tappi struck a tiny record deal with Jónatan Garðarsson's label Spor. "We only did one five-track EP, on a 33 RPM record," Garðarsson remembers. "At that time, I was sort of the producer and I released the record. We had a lot of work to do to try to introduce them to the market. These songs were more or less collaborations between the whole group, with Björk doing voices more than lyrics." Partway through these recording sessions, co-vocalist Eythor Arnalds left the band, leaving Björk to assume the role of full-time frontperson weeks before their first release.

Titled *Bitið Fast Í Vitið* (rough translation: "bite hard in your mind"), the ensuing record was comprised mainly of dark, minor-key rock that saw Björk offering restrained vocals still miles away from her trademark elastic growl. The 12-inch barely sold 500 copies, but it helped Tappi further solidify their status as one of Reykjavik's up-and-comers. Encouraged, they pressed on.

"We'd meet several times a week," Johansson recalls. "We had this rehearsal room which was under a car wash. We had these marvelous parties in the basement where we played and then everybody went upstairs, drank, and just had fun. It became sort of like a safe house, the basement of the place. Everybody was more or less welcome there." Since Reykjavik's insular setting meant that many different bands were sharing space together — not to mention frequently hanging out, getting drunk, and playing gigs — it wasn't long before Tappi Tikarrass entered into a loose friendship with the members of both Þeyr and Purkurr Pilnikk. If either band needed a place to crash, they'd look to Tappi for the keys to their space.

Across town, Hotel Borg was proving to be another of the scene's more popular hangouts; every night, kids on the periphery of the local arts subculture would converge upon Borg's upscale lobby and gather to discuss trends, music, and philosophy. This was where ideas were hatched, side projects born, and lasting friendships forged. "It was sort of the hangout for the punk rock new wave staff back in the early '80s," Gunnar Hjálmarsson says. "I remember coming out here with some friends for a Tappi Tikarrass gig and my friend saying that Björk was special and she would be big one day."

Burgeoning filmmaker Friðrik Þór Friðriksson had originally been introduced to Reykjavik's teeming punk subculture by his good friend, Hilmar Örn Hilmarsson. Once exposed, Þór Friðriksson developed a fascination with the movement; it wasn't long before he decided to base his next film around Reykjavik's music scene entirely.

Conversations with members of both Purkurr Pilnikk and Þeyr over the course of his research led Friðriksson directly to Tappi Tikarrass. The filmmaker tracked them down at their rehearsal space, where Björk and her bandmates made an immediate impression. "The first time I saw [Björk] in person was at an old barrack and Tappi Tikarrass were rehearsing there," Friðriksson says. "Immediately, I was in some kind of a weird atmosphere — not only the group, but also the people around them were very special. I said to myself that this must be in the film.

"They were very funny and extremely nice, like elves. Whenever I saw them I was always laughing, but not in a negative sense — it was just happiness and joy. They were very positive about everything."

Filmed primarily during the winter of 1981 and aptly dubbed *Rokk I Reykjavik*, Friðriksson's documentary depicted a cherubic Björk joyously howling through two complete Tappi songs. In a nod to German director Volker Schlöndorff's film adaptation of *The Tin Drum*, Björk is shown clad in a yellow baby-doll dress with giant red circles painted on her cheeks. Even now, with the benefit of hindsight, one can see from that footage how she might have elicited such bewildered admiration from her peers. Of the few girls in the Reykjavik rock scene, there were none who possessed Björk's combination of femininity, ferociousness, and talent.

*Rokk I Reykjavik* was received well, and helped solidify the notion that something special was indeed happening musically in Iceland. Being elevated into this movement also proved to be good for Björk; the added exposure helped her permanently transcend her long-held standing as pre-teen, radio-friendly cover artist. She was becoming a star in her own right; despite the fact that bigger bands such as Þeyr and Purkurr Pilnikk featured heavily in the documentary, Björk's impish pose — yellow dress and all — was used for the film's cinema posters, video cover, and soundtrack artwork.

*A teenaged Björk catches a breather between shows in England. (Photo by Björg Sveinsdóttir)*

The film may have signaled a sort of ascension point for Björk, but not for Tappi Tikarrass as a whole. Creatively, the band had stalled. In the meantime, Björk did whatever she could to keep herself amused, lending her name to any musical peculiarities or experiments that seemed remotely intriguing. One of these distractions saw her team up with Icelandic jazz outfit Stifgrim to take part in Iceland's bid to break the Guinness World Record for longest ever continuous live performance. At least 80 bands are said to have participated; although the ordeal went on for weeks, Björk and company ultimately failed to break the mark. Other nights, to earn money, she would contribute keyboard duties to a barroom cover band named Cactus, who'd earn a decent wage by bellowing out vastly re-interpreted '70s classic rock hits to a largely inebriated and forgiving audience.

During the summers of 1982 and 1983, Björk followed the customary path of many Icelandic teens and left Reykjavik to go work on a farm. Her employer was a man named Labbi Thorarinsson, who owned a farm called Glora in a northern town named Hraungerðishreppur. In addition to being a farmer, Thorarinsson also happened to be a successful local musician, most notably with a popular band called Manar. Glora was always bursting with music, and had a recording studio located on-site. In between doing the housework and tending the animals, Björk would join in on the impromptu jam sessions by singing, playing piano and sometimes flute. She was even a member of a half-serious pickup band named Karma, who recorded some material but never released it.

Björk next found herself in a recording studio in 1983, when Bjorgvin Gislason – one of the musicians who had accompanied her on 1977's *Björk* – requested her presence on an album of his own. Gislason, widely considered to be one of his generation's best local guitarists, recruited Björk to salvage a track that he had long relegated to b-side status. "She came into the studio at two o'clock in the afternoon and the guy who was writing the words was sitting at the typewriter still writing because it wasn't finished yet," he recalls. "She came in, she had the paper, she had never heard the song, but she learnt it. I think she sang it in one take but there was a slight one-note mistake in that taping. We fixed that and then she did a little harmony at the end of the song and off she went, that's it, four o'clock. Learned the song, sang it, did a two-part harmony." Because of Björk's contribution, the song, entitled "Afi" (translation: "grandfather"), made the record's final cut. Twenty years later Gislason still refers to it as "probably the most played of all my songs."

With no band to keep her busy, things may not have been particularly fruitful on a creative front, but Björk's personal life was blooming. Thanks to a mutual friend named Sjon Sigurdsson, she'd been introduced to a boy named Þór Eldon, and in no time she'd fallen hopelessly in love. "When I was 14, I thought boys were only good for being in bands with," she said. "I thought one of the most horrible things that could happen to me would be to get a boyfriend, as all my girlfriends had just lost the plot when they got one. Then I met Þór when I was 16 and it was love at first sight. I moved into his house the same evening."

The ensuing months saw the once lively underground slowly dry up. Purkurr Pilnikk had unceremoniously parted ways, as had the once formidable Þeyr, and Björk was largely absent from the scene. Where once things had seemed so promising, now there was a tremendous void. Suddenly, the high-flying days of *Rokk I Reykjavik* felt light years away. "Þeyr terminated after our last Scandinavian tour in spring 1983," recalls guitarist Ottarsson. "I think it happened also that Purkurr Pilnikk was non-existent, so there was a very strange situation in Iceland: all the great bands had ceased to exist – you had all these musicians almost idle. Something had to be done."

The addition of a second radio station to Iceland's state-run airwaves in December 1983 meant that many of the music-minded DJs from Station One were either being re-assigned for duty or outright released. Among the unfortunate casualties of this reshuffling were Jónsson and Gulli Hjálmarsson, hosts of *Afanger*, an exploratory program dedicated to the avant-garde and the underground. As one of Iceland's woefully few remaining media for vanguard and marginalia, *Afanger* had come to be regarded over the years as a hugely significant show. Some even credited it with helping to germinate Iceland's punk and new wave scenes.

"In the early '70s it was a lot of Velvet Underground, The Stooges, and then some great jazz like that we were putting together," recalls Jónsson while rifling through a mental playlist. "All different types of music — world and some classical pieces like Satie. It was like a mixture of interesting music, or we thought at least, and then it developed more and more into introducing this new wave within the pop music scene. In '77–'79 we had Einar Örn feeding us with this new stuff that we were actually turned on by . . . it became a channel for introducing the New York and the London scenes."

"They were the only ones that played any sort of avant-garde music," Hilmarsson remembers. "They would play everything from Charlie Mingus to Quicksilver Messenger Service. Also, they knew things that were happening. In a way, they were sort of educators for the younger generations of musicians. When radio decided to stop the show, they decided to go out with a real bang."

Having long enjoyed established relationships with all the musicians they once nurtured with new music, Jónsson and Hjálmarsson hit upon a brilliant idea: one by one, they began to call up their friends from the local scene. "For our last show, we asked them to do something special for us," Jónsson smiles. "They got together — Siggi [Baldursson, formerly of Þeyr], Birgir Mogenson [a local musician], Gulli [Ottarsson] the guitar player, Einar Melax [Þór's best friend], as well as people like Sjon and Þór." Invitations were also extended to Björk and Einar Örn Benediktsson; soon, a veritable Icelandic supergroup was born.

The original intention was for the outfit to disband after the completion of a one-off show to be aired live on the final *Afanger*, but a persistent Einar Örn had other plans. "That one gig turned out to be quite a fun party," Garðarsson recalls. "Most of those who were in the studio at the time continued working together; this was not planned. I think it's mainly Einar's fault that it carried on because he was always the most aggressive. He's like a force.

"I remember Einar at a very early age in 1978 when The Stranglers came to Iceland to play a gig. This young kid came into the office and said 'Okay, I'm here. What can I do? Can I hang up some posters?' He was, I don't know, 14 or 15 years old, but very aggressive. . . . Later on, he became the agent for [Icelandic band] Utangardsmenn; he was not old enough to be in those places but he went on tour with them to Scandinavia and Holland. He was always into doing whatever needed to be done — he never questioned if it could be done, he just did it. I think the same thing happened with Kukl. He found that this was quite fun, more fun than being with Purkurr Pilnikk, and so he went out and put them all over Europe."

With a final lineup that featured Einar Örn, Björk, Ottarsson, Birgir Mogenson, Einar Melax, and Siggi Baldursson, this one-off supergroup quickly morphed into a real band. Without ever really forming, Kukl (Icelandic for "black magic" or "sorcery") had unwittingly begun.

Einar Örn had the connections to match his ambition – impressively, he even had a plan. While studying media at a London Polytech in England, he'd formed a working relationship with U.K. anarchist record label Crass, and figured he could lure them to Iceland to headline a self-started festival. He did so, and then added Kukl to the bill; within weeks of their impromptu debut, the makeshift sextet were playing to nearly five thousand people. "Kukl had their first official concert appearance the following month, on the 10th of September, which was for a festival we created called We Demand the Future," recalls Jónsson, who was working for Bad Taste Records by that time. "We invited Crass from the U.K. to come over, we published a magazine and all of these people were participating in street theaters, so it became quite a big event."

Tappi Tikarrass, meanwhile, were still officially together, but had been rendered dormant for months. They'd undergone yet more lineup changes – the absence of a steady, reliable drummer proved to be a nagging problem – and seemed to be sagging under the weight of an internal malaise. In spite of their increased profile post-*Rokk I Reykjavik*, Björk was beginning to outgrow their music. "At that time things were changing with her," Jónsson says. "She did not feel very comfortable with what she was doing with Tappi, or that was my feeling at least."

Nonetheless, Tappi had committed to doing a full-length LP on Bad Taste Records before the end of the year and, despite her hesitations, Björk intended to honor that promise. Fraught with tension and anxiety, the album's recording sessions (done in a London, England, studio) marked the beginning of their doomed finale. "Everything was delayed and we were very frustrated about that," Johansson said. "We came too late to the studios, so London was actually quite edgy. I remember that the boys in the band had a physical fight out of frustration."

The resulting album, titled *Miranda*, took roughly two weeks to finish. In addition to singing lead on most of the tracks and playing various instruments, Björk also supplied the album artwork and wrote the liner notes. In the end, hers and the band's efforts went largely unrewarded; the quartet unwittingly sealed their own fate by releasing the record a mere two days before Christmas. "It shows how things were operating at the time," Garðarsson joked. "We weren't really into marketing or anything, we were just doing it. Even though it was the night before Christmas, it didn't matter! It was still about having fun and doing whatever we wanted to do.

"The first 500 pieces came out, as we know, on the 23rd of December and we had like six hours to sell it. It was a horrible time. We were not thrilled with the album, but it was okay."

The release of the Tappi record also followed the unveiling of Kukl's debut recording. Clocking in at roughly three minutes, the band's debut single "Songull" (the b-side was "Pokn") marked a definitive shift of direction for Björk. Finally, there was a different energy here, something gut-level. Perhaps in accordance, her singing style had also changed; in place of the trebly, girlish yelps that had punctuated so much of Tappi's work was a more robust, sensual vocal. This was the Björk capable of eliciting goosebumps with ease.

Even though it was becoming apparent to everyone around her that Björk's future was with Kukl, she dutifully continued to carry out her commitments to Tappi Tikarrass until there were none left. It wasn't until then that she officially severed ties with the band. "She talked to all of us and said she wanted to move on and do something else," Johansson says. "But it was obvious at the time."

"She felt responsible for promoting that record for us, which she did, even though you could feel that she had already left that music," Jónsson adds. "When you listen to Kukl you can see how different the music was. In *Rokk I Reykjavik*, you obviously notice the context of her personality with the rest of the Tappi people. Compare that to the people that actually became Kukl later on and how different they are. Creatively, this was an important step for Björk to take. Tappi's music was very poppy and in a way not very exciting, a very standard type of pop music."

In contrast, Kukl's music was gravely discordant, perpetually distressed. Their moody stabs of angular punk had positioned them as the antithesis of accessible pop and earned them a reputation for unyielding intensity. Inherent in what they were doing was a sort of controlled desperation, likely the result of having so many dominant personalities within one band. Deathly serious, they filled their artist bios and album artwork with obscure, metaphysical texts espousing the virtues of true freedom and non-conformity. Philosophically, they had surpassed the regional confines of punk's politics and graduated to something more universal. "In a way it was political, but at the same time it was, well, cosmic," Hilmarsson agrees. "The issues were always huge."

"Kukl was a bit strange in a way because we were gathered together without really knowing each other," says keyboardist Melax. "Two of the guys had been playing together but all the others had just come into a group. It made this group special; that's why maybe everybody in the band seemed a bit shy because they didn't know the others and were trying to work together. [Björk] was really just into the material. I think she was the most punctual one."

If the band were timid with each other at first, they made up for it with their fiery arrangements. Kukl's music often evinced the sensation of internal struggle – it was as if they'd learnt to find joy in discord. "You only have to listen to a few songs to notice that you cannot hear any standard chords," recounts guitarist Ottarsson. "In Þeyr, we had this mandatory rule that you were not allowed to play a chord or a melody that had been done before. There were a lot of strange harmonics. Kukl was the vehicle to really develop this strange music and I think it's very obvious. Nobody else was ever able to play a Þeyr song or a Kukl song. If you combine this strange music with our almost hatred of the current scene . . . we wanted to demonstrate for people that you don't always have to play two chords with always the same melody."

Suitably encouraged by their live performances and invigorated by each other's presence, Kukl crystallized in late 1983 with a lineup that counted six official members. Björk and Einar Örn traded lead vocal duties and various other instruments, Ottarsson played guitar, Siggi played drums, Birgir Mogenson added bass, and Einar Melax filled in wherever he was needed, usually on keys. The band struck a record deal with Crass shortly after their second gig, and by January 1984 they were hard at work on a full-length debut at London's Southern Studios.

Titled *The Eye*, the album was completed by the end of that month. Aside from a few select dates in Europe, Kukl kept a low profile until the record's release later that year. During the downtime, most of the band members either pursued other projects or toiled at day jobs: Einar Örn was a media studies lecturer, Einar Melax maintained a church, Siggi and Birgir built roads for the city. In addition to working in a fish factory, Björk supplemented her income by self-publishing a small handbound booklet. Only 100 copies of *Um Urnat* are reported to exist, each containing 16 pages of original prose and hand-drawn artwork. The prose loosely braids together to tell a story of a creature emerging from hibernation and rediscovering his surroundings. Björk created and sold all 100 books and used the money to help pay for her rent during Kukl's downtime.

The absence of a distribution deal in their homeland meant that Kukl's eventual debut was scarcely available in Iceland upon release. When it was issued on Crass in England, *The Eye* was heard mainly in punk circles where, not surprisingly, critics zeroed in on Björk. Some likened her vocals and the band's bleak, gothic sound to Siouxsie & The Banshees; others marveled at her on-stage charisma. "Boy and girl charging around, shouting and screaming, while four others contrive to make one hell of a racket, lapsing into occasional bouts of melody," went one live review in *Sounds*. "I'm not sure that it was their intention, but I found them jolly entertaining, and they should be seen if only to witness the extraordinary performance of that manic little girl."

"A spunkish drunkish short set of Bow Wow Wow sounds, the words coming from the plainest boy in history and a girl with the most unsightly pageboy cut since Skafish," barked the *NME*. "The guitar was groovy and the drums were bendy, and I could have listened to them for at least another 12 years if duty had not called."

In support of the album, Kukl shot a spooked, low-budget video for lead single "Anna" and embarked on a European tour with stops in Denmark, France, and England. Full of energy and contradiction, this period was an interesting one for the band. Their live shows implied an almost nihilistic outlook, but in reality, Kukl were buzzing with tempered positivity and promise. "I always felt that we were representing hope and optimism that you can do things yourself," Ottarsson says. "There's something you can do to alter what's currently empty; you can affect people and their values. I felt people found something in us. But of course there were a lot of hardcore scenes, it was very intense, with a lot of violence and fighting at the concerts. We were trying to put out optimism — 'the future is an unwritten page, you can mold it, you can even create your own.'"

In the tradition of many Crass artists before them, Kukl's optimism was often obscured by a cloud of recklessness or worse, outright disdain. Partly in accordance with their own philosophy of self-reliance, partly in deference to their self-assumed role as agitators, they were infrequently accessible to fans and even less so to the media. "I used to be in a punk band that was so hardcore that if someone came to us and asked for an autograph," Björk said, "we'd just tell them to fuck off and get a life."

This prevailing attitude made it easy for Kukl to hold their own with the rest of the Crass collective, to whom they probably felt as if they had something to prove. "We don't have any cults, we don't have any classes, we don't have any differences really — Iceland is a very social country," Garðarsson says. "So what do you do to become different? You aggravate. You piss on someone or you shit on the table or whatever. You use bad language, you try to dress differently, you give them the finger. That's exactly what they did. There's never been really any doubt in my mind that they were doing this more or less out of fun."

"[They were] trying to shock people," concurs Gunnar Hjálmarsson. "All in the good name of having fun in an artistic way and drinking red wine and stuff! I think that was the scene that Björk got into when she met Þór, and that was basically the feel of Kukl, some kind of joyful artistic expression."

With her bowl-shaped haircut perched atop her Inuit eyes and tightly pursed lips, the young Björk was part wallflower, still emerging. At only 18 years old and the lone female in a male-dominated scene, she was prone to moments of painful introversion, especially when not on stage.

Fortunately, with a host of strong personalities in the band, Björk's shyness didn't matter as much. In Kukl, Einar Örn cut his teeth as a masterful provocateur — once tales of his outlandish persona began to circulate, he compulsively fed back into it, furthering his dubious reputation. "Einar's always been difficult," Garðarsson smiles. "He has this aura. If you meet him alone, he's quite nice, but if there is a group of people, he's like the devil's advocate."

At the conclusion of the European tour, the band returned home to Iceland in dire need of rest and time to decompress (save Einar, who went to London). As rewarding as everything else had been, the mere task of simply being in Kukl had proven to be a drain. The discord, the darkness, the wrenched emotions — night after night — had taken their toll on most of the band members, many of whom were not naturally that intense. "One thing that the people don't really realize is that Kukl was incredibly funny and humorous as well," Hilmarsson says. "There was always humor attached to everything, even when they were doing the most outrageous political things." That may have been more evident behind the scenes, but where their audience was concerned, "Kukl" and "humor" were not words oft uttered in the same breath. This affected their standing at home; the prevailing consensus around Iceland was that the supergroup was almost too intense to invite enjoyment. "A lot of people admired [Kukl] because of their integrity and because of their commitment, but generally, people didn't *like* them very much," Árni Matthíasson explains. "It was so tiresome, seeing them live because you came out of there and you were just finished, you'd want to go somewhere and lie down."

If the audience felt that way, Kukl felt it tenfold. As a result, during the ensuing downtime, Björk indulged her lighter side; the majority of her side projects during this lull were desultory, short-lived jokes between friends. The most mysterious of the lot was probably Rokha Rokha Drum, in which Björk actually played drums. Fronted by local poet and longtime friend Sjon Sigurdsson (known to the public as Johnny Triumph), and rounded out by Þór Eldon on guitar and Kukl alumnus Einar Melax on bass, the band only played a handful of gigs before expiring. An oft-rumored eight-track demo is said to have been cut and subsequently lost.

Hilmar Örn Hilmarsson recalls being involved in similarly off-the-cuff endeavors with Björk during this period: "We had this trio with Gudlauger [Ottarsson], the guitarist, where we decided that we would take old Icelandic nursery rhymes and do a rap performance," he says. "It would start with me doing a boring, tedious talk on how Iceland really originated rap music and then we would just do this mad performance and take all the money we would get from that and buy alcohol and get gloriously drunk. It was all about having fun and probably taking the piss as well."

Björk's other project with Ottarsson was more serious than that. With Siggi Baldursson occasionally filling in on drums, the duo wrote a collection of moon-drenched, uneasy lullabies and performed them under the name Elgar Sisters. Although they only played live occasionally, the Elgar Sisters possessed a fairly deep catalog of songs and provided Björk and Ottarsson with an ongoing songwriting vehicle outside of Kukl. "We had a coalition because she was this natural musician with natural, simple scales," Ottarsson says. "She had this ability to put a thousand melodies into a single note — that was very interesting to me. It's also how I tried to be minimal; a single note can tell a much richer story than if you try to spread it into a thousand."

Along with Siggi on percussion, Björk also performed a few slipshod, largely improvised shows. Although some of them were spotty affairs, these gigs contained hints of brilliance that foreshadowed the Sugarcubes' later triumphs. "He played the drums and she vocalized," recalls Matthíasson. "It was interesting. Really, it was good, but it was a bit unrehearsed and large parts of it were just crap because they weren't connecting. But when they connected, it was beautiful. And to me that always has been the prototype of 'Birthday.' That's when it started to me, because when you heard 'Birthday,' you heard that coming back."

"When those performances were taking place," says Jónsson, "they were definitely side projects because, basically they were trying to develop something, doing something while Einar was away and the band was not together. They were always quite interesting shows, but it was very different from Kukl because it was a more acoustic type of music."

For their second album in 1984, Kukl decided to fully explore the theme that their newer songs had hinted at. Although no tracklisting was officially included, each of the eight songs on this followup was named and inspired by a specific European city which they had previously visited while on tour. Bookended with in-flight announcements taped from Icelandair, the band conceptualized the album as a sort of audible travelogue and named it, appropriately, *Holidays in Europe (The Naughty Nought)*.

True to form, *Holidays in Europe* came loaded with tomes of dense, nearly impenetrable metaphysical theory attached. A press release for the record read as follows: "*The Naughty Nought* pertains to the insignificance of the individual as being nothing but a numb number in a computer game of loss/profit good/evil black/white binary parts. You are taken from quintessence to the four elements from the holy trinity to duality and then from monism to the naughty nought. In this process the music breaks the seals by thundering trumpets and pouring vials of wrath together with subtle musical poetry. The naughty nought is the source of all creative energy and is manifested through whirling cyclonic motion from the very shatters of matter to the spiralling galaxies. By contemplating the kinetic aspects of this naughty-ality, you gain your former potence as the master and creator without mutilating your fellow beings."

They lived like this, every day.

More unhinged than its predecessor, *Holidays in Europe* saw the band stretch their tentacles further outward to incorporate another set of gonzo sounds into their already chugging cauldron of textures. Synths burbled, trumpets brayed, toy boxes tinkled — they even threw a few samples into the mix. As if a sign of things to come, Björk and Einar's vocal interplay had also become more pronounced: a few tracks on *Holidays* had screaming matches to rival any of the Sugarcubes' oft-maligned calls-and-responses.

*Holidays in Europe* was impressively more ambitious and more obtuse than *The Eye*, but listeners met it with emotions ranging from casual warmth to blatant indifference. Part of this audience reaction was attributed to what was perceived as a decline in the band's trajectory — half a year off the circuit had undone any of the strides they'd made. Along with Crass, fellow anarchists Flux of Pink Indians, and legendary punkers The Fall, Kukl gamely toured Europe again.

Unfortunately, the new material and the time off had not done much to eradicate their creeping sense of discomfort. The initial creative buzz of their interband dynamic had been replaced with a sense of stagnation. The six strong personalities within were slowly succumbing to the crushing weight of simply being in Kukl. "Crass was extreme punk music and it never really got big here," Matthíasson explains. "I remember buying those first albums, and they were enjoyable in a way, but it was such a blind alley. You can go this far, but what are you going to do next, turn up the volume a bit? Play a bit faster? There's nothing more in it. With Kukl, it felt a bit like that — like they'd taken it this far and then it was obvious it couldn't go any further, so it had to end."

Meanwhile, Björk had learnt some news that would cast more doubt over the band's future. Father Guðmundur Gunnarsson remembers when she became pregnant with Þór Eldon's baby in September 1985: "She was living in a small room somewhere downtown," he says. "I talked to her and told her that it doesn't work like that with a child; you have to live in an apartment or something like it, and you have to change your life a little bit. Þór was a little bit afraid — they were both afraid that they would fall down by the tracks and that with an apartment, child, and work they would lose everything they had."

Iceland's progressive outlook on teenage pregnancy meant that the 19-year-old Björk wasn't in any real danger of being stigmatized by her peers or the rest of society. Nonetheless, Gunnarsson knew that his daughter would require more stability, and he helped Björk and Þór buy a downtown apartment. "She had said to me that she was so much in love with Þór it hurt," he smiles. "She wanted to be with him and live with him. It's exactly like the love we fall in when we are 18 years old; we get so much in love that our body is aching with love all the time. Sometimes we stop thinking and we just think about the heartache — she was going through that at that time."

The pair soon married. In spite of how strongly she felt about Þór, it's a union that Björk insists was just as motivated by convenience as it was by love. "It's a different thing to marry in Iceland," she said. "We are not married in a church. You get more rights if you're married. For me and Þór, it just took 10 minutes. And then we could get money from the state to buy contact lenses for him."

Matthíasson explains: "To get young people to be more responsible with financial matters, there was this law in Iceland that part of your earnings were put into a special account [until later]. There was also a provision that if you got married before you were old enough to [access the account], you could get the money right away. So it was reasonably common to get married to get that money.

"It was a mixture of things," he concludes. "Yes, they were very much in love and wanted to be together; it was also a bonus in that you could get all that money."

Although she was only 19 years old, Björk heeded her father's advice and began to prepare for her new role as wife and mother. Hilmarsson marvels at how capably she handled her situation. "I remember when she and Þór bought an apartment," he says. "It was Björk who handled all the practical things; she went to the bank managers and made sure that the loans were paid on time and stuff like that. She has always been the practical one. If she commits to something, you know that she will do it no matter what." Of course, Björk had committed herself to music long before anything else; rather than sacrifice it (or any of her other creative outlets), she proudly adapted so as to accommodate them all.

Things did slow down, however — by the beginning of 1986, it became painfully obvious to nearly everyone involved that the band was no longer working, and Kukl folded as unceremoniously as it had begun. "In the end we were criticizing each other so much that there was nothing left," Björk said. "Instead of putting more into the band, we were sort of . . . throwing out. Until there was nothing left except seriousness. So there was an eruption or something like that. And we decided to do something just to have fun."

Björk remained in close contact with many of her bandmates, a few of whom were part of a larger clique that saw each other frequently. On some nights, people would gather at her and Þór's place to socialize and discuss matters of the day, which ranged from politics to philosophy to, inevitably, music. Once Einar Örn returned from another brief stint in England, he started coming round as well. That's when things began to move forward. "Einar and Þór got to be really good friends," Matthíasson says. "[They were] drinking a lot of cheap red wine and discussing things. Soon they started Smekkleysa — the Bad Taste collective."

The formation of Bad Taste had been something that Einar Örn had wanted to facilitate for some time; the idea was to establish a base of people who could help foster the growth of art and culture in Iceland. Bad Taste would publish music, poetry, art, literature — anything — as long as it abided by the organization's two presiding tenets. Derived from Pablo Picasso's famous rumination that "good taste is the enemy of creativity," the first of these chartered tenets explicitly stated a desire to "fight everything that can be branded 'good taste' and 'frugality.'" The second was equally seditious: "In the fight against the above ('good taste' etc.), Bad Taste will use every imaginable and unimaginable method, e.g. inoculation, extermination, tasteless advertisements and announcements, distribution and sale of common junk and excrement."

*The Sugarcubes perform in the basement of the Icelandic State Radio station, 1987. L-r: Björk, Einar, Bragi. (Photo by Árni Matthíasson)*

"We question what people would call good taste," Einar proclaimed. "And we try to find out who are the 'tastemakers.' We question why so-called bad taste should be called that by the people who think they are in good taste. It's in everything — clothing, furniture, house colors . . . toilet paper even."

With Björk, Þór, Einar, Bragi Ólafsson (Purkurr Pilnikk, Kukl), Siggi (Kukl), and longtime co-conspirator Ásmundur Jónsson at the forefront, Bad Taste was established in the spring of 1986. The collective had no idea what their first project would be until a perfect opportunity dropped into their collective laps.

On the heels of a successful meeting the year prior in Geneva, it was announced that American president Ronald Reagan and Soviet leader Mikhail Gorbachev had earmarked Reykjavik as the site of their next summit. Altogether inspired by Studmenn, a long-standing local band who subsequently wrote and rush-released a song ("Moscow Moscow") about the summit, Einar and company decided to follow suit. Bad Taste knew that the compressed time frame of the event meant a dearth of summit memorabilia, so they commissioned artwork from associate Friðrik

Erlingsson and used it as the basis for 5,000 black-and-white commemorative post-cards. To Bad Taste's churlish delight, the souvenirs sold out almost immediately.

Meanwhile, the absence of a stage and a captive audience had done nothing to quell Bad Taste's impishness. Ever the opportunists, and in accordance with their charter's guidelines ("to [award medals] to those who succeed outstandingly in bad taste and dissipation"), they turned the satirical publicity stunt into something of an art form. Jónatan Garðarsson recalls one of their most famous ambushes: "They appeared on the most popular radio show at the time, which was a variety show, and Jakob Magnusson — the main man in Studmenn — was there as well. They handed him the Bad Taste award for the song 'Moscow Moscow.' He didn't know it was coming and he was not happy with it. He didn't say anything but he had this funny look on his face. Everyone knew then that there were people in town doing something new."

The punk era in Iceland may well have been over, but Bad Taste and the Sugarcubes were poised to start another.

# three

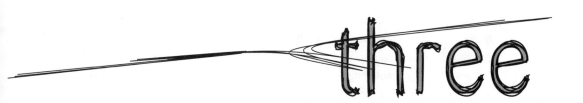

Nineteen eighty-six had proven to be a landmark year for Björk. The darkness of Kukl had yielded to the joyous camaraderie of Bad Taste, she'd settled in comfortably with Þór, and she was excitedly preparing for motherhood. New musical possibilities had also begun to bloom. Eager to revisit and properly record the Elgar Sisters' material, she spent a few weeks in the studio with Ottarsson, where the duo committed a ghostly 11-track album to tape. The songs proved a weighty counterpoint to Björk's accumulated catalog of spasmodic punk, with the former Kukl foil supplying the churning guitar motifs and Björk the broody vocals. It marked the first time in her career that she'd expressed a romantic, starry-eyed sentiment with any degree of effectiveness.

The album never got a proper title or release, but untouched versions of a few of these songs would later turn up as b-sides on a few of Björk's *Debut*-era singles — "Stigdu Mig" appears on "Venus as a Boy," the slightly more upbeat "Sidasta Eg" on "Violently Happy." That Björk thought to release these pieces almost 10 years after their genesis is testimony to the Elgar Sisters' work — even today, it remains one of her most significant side projects.

By working together again, Björk and Ottarsson opened the door for a handful of Kukl reunion shows, one of which was broadcast on Icelandic television. This appearance famously depicted a very pregnant Björk flailing about the stage with armpits unshaven and bare belly exposed. Björk's performance sparked a minor controversy. An elderly woman who happened to be watching reportedly suffered a heart attack as a result; a few others wrote angry letters to the local newspaper, complaining that there was something inherently distasteful about an uncovered pregnant stomach. To the rest of the nation, it was a non-event. "Everything she does is natural," Ottarsson shrugs. "Obviously she was just feeling healthy and this was the most natural thing to do. She was not sick — why lie in bed if you're not sick?"

That live television appearance, bulging belly and all, was to be Kukl's swansong. Correspondingly, Bad Taste's in-house band had started to become more serious about music, even if they remained resolutely noncommittal about their future. "They really hadn't performed as the Sugarcubes because it was a looser collective," claims Matthíasson, author of the Sugarcubes' official biography, *Skyurmolarnir*. "You have lots more people coming in and drifting out and so on, so it wasn't really a band. It was a bunch of friends playing instruments."

The band's core lineup (which usually consisted of Björk, Einar Örn, Þór, Siggi, Bragi, and Friðrik Erlingsson) started to perform the occasional live show. As they developed a small repertoire of original songs, it became more and more obvious that something was bubbling underneath, that a full-time band was inevitable. Halfheartedly, the collective began to toss around ideas for band names. "The first name for the Sugarcubes was actually Thukl," laughs Hilmarsson. "It means 'big stuff' — a piss-take on 'Kukl.'"

The advent of the band ultimately coincided with the final days of Björk's pregnancy. One summer afternoon, she gave birth to a healthy baby boy, whom she and Þór named Sindri Þorsson. Demonstrating a flair for the poetic, the Sugarcubes marked their own inception from that very same day. For Björk, June 8 had yielded both a newborn son and a brand new band.

The Sugarcubes steeped their music and image in broad strokes of color, humor, and self-effacing irony, mirroring Bad Taste's modus operandi. Having emerged a bit battered from the bleakness of Iceland's punk scene, Örn wanted the Sugarcubes to position themselves as the complete antithesis of their collective alma maters — in other words, joyous, bright, and completely clichéd. "I guess they had just gotten fed up with the pretentiousness of Kukl," Hjálmarsson says. "It also had something to do with Þór's vision of music; even though he was Björk's husband, he didn't like Kukl that much. He just wanted to play pop, or some kind of special version of pop music."

"There was a festival in a tent near the university where the Sugarcubes did their first performance," remembers Jónsson. "It was done in quite a rock and roll way. If I remember right, people were a bit drunk and the band came to the show in this big old American car. You could see it had this humor in it and that it was just meant to be fun."

"We had all played before, but with the Sugarcubes we decided to play pop music and totally disgust ourselves," Einar Örn said in 1989. "We looked at each other and said, 'Can we play this — it's such a cliché?' And we said, 'Fuck it, we can, because we're the Sugarcubes. We're a pop band, a living cliché!'"

Even though they'd finally given themselves a name, the Sugarcubes (officially comprised of Björk, Einar Örn, Þór, Bragi, Siggi, Friðrik, and Einar Melax) weren't in any particular hurry to accelerate their careers. The majority of the members still regarded the band as a jokey diversion at best, something that took a distant back-seat to other ventures and projects, not the least of which included the ongoing upkeep of Bad Taste.

To her credit, Björk proved handily that she was more than capable of juggling the strain of being a teenage mother with the demands of her career. Weeks after giving birth to Sindri, she'd jumped back into the swing of things with Bad Taste and even found herself vying for a role in an independently made film.

Based on a Brothers Grimm fairy tale, *The Juniper Tree* was the brainchild of American-born director Nietzchka Keene, who'd won a Fulbright scholarship to shoot the project in Iceland. Keene, who had been busily prepping the film in Reykjavik for nearly a year, was two weeks away from shooting when potential disaster struck. The 13-year-old girl that she'd originally cast had violated the terms of their agreement; now on the eve of production, she suddenly found herself in the unenviable position of having to swiftly replace one of her lead actresses.

Although she was a comparatively ancient 19 years old, Björk's youthful appearance made her a viable candidate for the part. Keene was already on friendly terms with the singer, and had strongly considered her for the role before she'd gotten pregnant. With only days to spare and nothing to lose, she offered Björk an audition. "She was very interested in it," Keene recalls. "She said absolutely and just very seriously, 'Yes'. She came over the next day and I had her read with the other lead actress. We rehearsed some scenes just to see how it worked and it was clear it worked very well, so we started shooting a week later.

"I knew she was a performer — that was really important," Keene continues. "And her looks and the aura she gave off made me feel like she was right for the part because it's a very withdrawn part — a lot of it is reacting to what is going on around the character. When I rehearsed her, she was very quick at taking in the emotional state and incorporating it.

"She [also] had a great sense of humor. She has a very funny way of skewing things and talking about things. . . . [She was] really quite quiet, but very observant, very pleasant to be around, and completely professional about doing the film. She

*Top: Filming for The Juniper Tree began mere weeks after Björk had given birth to her first son, Sindri.*
*Bottom: Art Director Dominique Poulain shares some of her wisdom with Björk during the film's downtime. (Photos by Robert Guillemette, copyright Nietzchka Keene)*

took it very seriously and was always prepared, very easy to work with – she wanted to do what I wanted her to do."

Despite her lack of experience as an actor, Björk proved instantly at ease in front of the camera. She intuitively developed her own acting methodology, part of which dictated an almost complete immersion into the part. It's the same technique that would earn her critical raves 13 years later for her role in Lars Von Trier's *Dancer in the Dark*, an experience so emotional that it would sour her completely on the notion of ever acting again.

"She doesn't work like a technical actress," Keene explained. "When she did *Dancer in the Dark* and was talking in interviews about being miserable and how draining it was – a professional has senses against that. That's part of the training, because you are going deep down into emotions and, yes, parts can be draining but you don't necessarily experience it so fully.

"When we would work, she would sometimes say things like, 'I haven't made this scene my own yet' and we would go through a couple more rehearsals and work on that so that it became her own. In many ways, she was working like a method actor without knowing that she was working like a method actor."

Keene soon discovered that the best way to elicit results was to rouse Björk's imagination, and she began to draw parallels between being a musician and being an actress to help Björk negotiate this unfamiliar terrain. "We had conversations fairly early on about the similarity of being on stage performing music or poetry and acting in front of the camera," Keene says. "I was saying that you're you up on stage but you are also *not* you – you're choosing the persona that you are putting out. She was very aware of doing that. She said, 'Yeah, you know, that actually makes being on camera easier . . . I am me but I'm choosing what parts of me to expose.'

"At the end of the shoot we were driving back from somewhere in my car and I found this bag of odd clothes that I knew weren't [mine]. I said, 'Oh my God, what is this, part of wardrobe?' and she said, 'No, no, no, that's just my Björk costume!'"

Filming for *The Juniper Tree* took roughly five weeks to complete, but the new mother didn't spend a single day of it away from her son. Aided by her 14-year-old stepsister, who babysat Sindri while Björk was filming, Björk made sure that her month-old son was on-hand for the entire duration of the project.

Once her day was over, Björk would take Sindri home to Þór, often in time for dinner and whatever else they might have planned for the evening. She had learned to re-prioritize to keep the most important things in her life intact, but she certainly wasn't living the life of a carefree, unburdened teenager anymore. "[Sindri] changed the decisions she was making," her father agrees. "She always had to think about where Sindri fit in. I'm sure that her life would be very different today if she hadn't had him."

As is common for independent films of this scale, a myriad of post-production

*Even though she was a comparatively ancient 19 years old at the time, Björk was very believable as the film's 13-year-old Margit. (Photo by Robert Guillemette, copyright Nietzchka Keene)*

and budgetary delays slowed the release of *The Juniper Tree*; the prohibitive cost of shooting a film in Iceland certainly didn't help. The movie eventually premiered in 1991 at The Sundance Festival — a popular independent showcase — and was met with largely favorable reviews. Mainly by virtue of its association to Björk, it has since enjoyed a steady audience, including a theatrical run in Japan as recently as 2001.

The end of that summer brought with it new opportunities to make music. Bad Taste suddenly had a modest pool of money at their disposal, thanks in no small part to sales generated by the Summit postcards. In the absence of any other interesting local music worth releasing, the Sugarcubes went into the studio together and recorded two original songs in Icelandic: "Kottur" (translation: "Cat") and "Afmæli" ("Birthday").

Einar Örn personally delivered the finished master tapes to Crass in England, who indulged him by pressing 500 copies of two-track vinyl. Immediately upon touching down in Iceland, a jittery Benediktsson bolted directly to the state radio station, where Jónatan Garðarsson happened to be in the middle of his weekly reggae show. "He came in with this newly pressed vinyl and he wanted it to be played but no one was ready to do it, so I just put it on," Garðarsson recalls. "We didn't play 'Afmæli,' we played 'Kottur' because that was the song that they were sure would become a hit. Everyone liked it, so it was played a lot and from there it took off."

Dubbed *Einn Mol'a Mann* ("one cube per person"), the vinyl was released by Bad Taste, who adorned it with the characteristic personal touches. "A lot of the originals were hand-colored," Matthíasson says. "There's this stylized picture of a sugarcube on the front, and the eyes were colored red by hand on a lot of the original copies." Since a large portion of the vinyl had become damaged in transit, the band spent nights coloring, assembling, and finally testing each item by hand.

Largely due to scarce supply and heavy radio play, the vinyl sold out quickly upon release. The Sugarcubes' charmed life was only beginning, though; the band were as surprised as any when, in the new year, radio spins for the single's *other* song began to suddenly pile up. "'Afmæli' took off after the new year and was being played [a lot]," says Garðarsson. "It even entered the chart, which was more or less a listener chart than anything else."

Not only had the Sugarcubes become a minor sensation without really trying, they'd done it while some of them weren't even in the country. Einar Örn had been dividing his time evenly between Reykjavik and England, still in the process of completing his media studies degree. Although unable to capitalize on the consistent radio play, the band's absence from the live circuit didn't diminish their appeal one bit. "They were playing very few gigs but everyone liked the songs," Garðarsson says. "It was almost like something new had happened. Nobody was expecting this from this lot. There was a relief in it because both songs were aggressive but also melodic."

If the Sugarcubes' music could reasonably be deemed pop, then it was a very skewed take on pop indeed. From its introductory swirl of seasick horns to Björk's strangely guttural chorus, everything about "Afmæli" was just left-of-center enough to feel completely spontaneous, utterly fresh. Local Icelanders weren't the only ones to be struck by the song's peculiarly engaging subtleties — Derek Birkett, former bassist for Crass act Flux of Pink Indians, had become similarly enamored of it. His interest piqued, he told the band that if they recorded an English version, he would release it on his own recently envisaged label One Little Indian, established in the wake of Crass' demise. The band obliged, but didn't figure that much would come out of it. After all, they were each seasoned musicians who'd tested the competitive waters of the British music scene before — what impact could one single possibly have?

It all happened within days.

Derek Birkett and One Little Indian released "Birthday" in August 1987 to a largely nonplussed audience. Weeks passed without occasion, and just as the single seemed poised to drop off radar screens completely, Britain's then-influential *New Musical Express* magazine declared it Single of the Week. Einar Örn was in a meeting with his employers, Gramm Records, when he got the word. "He got a call from the U.K. — it was Derek telling him that the single was Single of the Week, and the only thing he said was, 'Oh, fuck,'" Matthíasson laughs. "They were stunned. Immediately there was this pressure for Björk and Einar to go to the U.K. and do interviews."

Although in many senses a conventional pop tune, "Birthday" was off-kilter enough to be positioned as the perfect antidote to the prototypical British indie chart fare. The band, newly canonized, were bemused by the attention; the label was unprepared; and in the time-honored fashion of U.K. music media, the press were head-over-heels, full-on, completely in love.

By October, the band that considered itself an elaborate joke on pop music were somewhat reluctantly gracing the covers of the U.K.'s most prominent pop music magazines. These cover features would mark the beginning of a turbulent relationship with the media and signal the advent of an insidious trend. "Like It or Lump It!" proclaimed the *NME*, somewhat awkwardly, over an accompanying photo of a vaguely untamed Björk with band members cowering in the background. "It's Your Birthday!" trumpeted *Melody Maker* over a similarly obvious cover shot — Björk front and center, the rest of the Sugarcubes peering out from behind a stairwell.

After one only single, the media's lust for Björk was on. The band, led by Einar, gamely tried to communicate a democratic front, but the press outlets were relentless in the specificity of their requests. "The media just wanted Björk," Matthíasson says. "They wanted pictures of Björk on the cover, which would have ruined the band a lot sooner than it did."

*The Sugarcubes blast through one of their many sets at Reykjavik's tiny bar Duus, the 'disco' referenced in their song "Blue Eyed Pop." L-r: Einar, Siggi, Bragi, Björk. (Photo by Björg Sveinsdóttir)*

The saving grace ultimately proved to be Einar Örn, whose presence and involvement in the band's dealings (including press obligations) helped give the media another person to fixate on. "He planned everything," Matthíasson explains. "He controlled it, and the rest of the band were very happy to let him. He wasn't controlling them, but he was controlling the media a bit."

The massive hype begat a wave of public interest, with press and fans both eager to learn more about this exotic-sounding pop band and their extraterrestrial lead singer. Arrangements were soon made for the band to meet their overseas admirers. "We had Derek phoning from England saying, 'You're playing a concert next Friday,'" Þór said. "We said, 'No, we're not.' He said, 'You have to because there are all these journalists coming over.' Then we had to play again because all these record companies came over. They made us a lot of silly offers; the whole process was silly."

As puckish as ever, the Sugarcubes performed every single song at the ensuing media showcase in Icelandic. While it would be the first of many exploits to earn them a reputation as "difficult," no act of self-sabotage would've been grave enough to squelch the bidding war that followed. Lost in the scrum of the media madness was the fact that a handful of major labels were suddenly approaching with pens out and checkbooks wide open. With glazed eyes and confounded grimaces, the

Sugarcubes — a self-made cliché, a *gag* — suddenly found themselves turning down hundreds of thousands of pounds. "They forget," Einar said of the labels, "that the Sugarcubes may be daft, but we're not idiots. And we're not young — we've survived for eight years in Iceland without a major deal. We now notch up the number of record companies we've seduced."

A bidding war between Warner and Polygram ensued. Eager to retain their autonomy, the band stressed that any deal they signed had to leave them with complete creative control, but in the end, nobody was willing to give them that kind of power. They did come close, however; they were mere hours away from signing with Warner before the label reneged. Warner's refusal to give the band the power to dictate their own single selection and order proved the deal-breaker.

Flummoxed by the silliness of it all, Einar and his bandmates decided that their best course of action would be to record the album themselves for One Little Indian. Birkett had been working at London's Berry Street Studios to offset rent while he got his label off the ground, and he'd struck a deal that allowed him access to the facilities when they weren't in use. With Birkett and friend Ray Shulman at the production helm and only a handful of poorly-recorded but promising songs to work with, the band flew to London to record their debut.

If there was pressure on the Sugarcubes to follow-up the success of "Birthday," they weren't showing it in the studio. The Berry Street recording sessions for this first album yielded some of their finest work, even if they did take an inordinate amount of time to complete it. Countless hours were spent polishing up some of the recordings that they'd already cut at Reykjavik's Studio Syrland. Sung in Icelandic, and not recorded at suitable quality, these rough cuts eventually formed the backbone of many of the songs on record.

The Sugarcubes always composed in an entirely democratic fashion; they felt that doing things any other way would undermine everything that they stood for. This collective working method kept the entire band rooted in creative soil, their music underpinned by a faint whiff of impending collision. Unfortunately, as it meant no member would have any room to grow or exercise creative precedence, it also doomed the Sugarcubes to a built-in expiration date. In many senses, the music they were making was less important than the collusion of personality and spirit at the core of their work. "It was a joke band," Björk concluded in retrospect. "Bragi would never have brought a three-page poem for us to use, it would just be ridiculous. It's like, you wouldn't go to your grandma's and discuss your sex life — it wasn't the place for it. We would never discuss music, that was like the bottom of the pit!"

Joke or not, the notion of the Sugarcubes as musical republic was one that each member took very seriously. Although they were intensely loyal to one another, certain relationships invariably outweighed others. "You had Einar, Bragi, and Friðrik on one side because they were really close friends after they played in Purkurr Pilnikk," Matthíasson explains. "And then you had Björk and Þór, but they had some problems in their relationship that were intensifying. [Siggi] and Björk were quite good friends and always have been, so it was like three groups with two of them overlapping.

"To me, a lot of the melodic ideas came from Friðrik," he continues. "I don't know because I never was in the rehearsals, but Friðrik and Bragi were more or less the musical machine. Then there was Björk with her special vocals and Einar with his . . . equally special vocals, but in a different way. It was a bunch of friends and it never really felt like a band, not until after the first album."

Some of those friends wouldn't be around long enough to see the record through. Disinterested with the prospect of bona fide international pop stardom, Erlingsson parted ways with the band during the recording sessions. Not long after, and still early in the process, Kukl keyboardist and reluctant founding member Einar Melax also left, leaving the band a player short. To compensate, Björk assumed the role of studio keyboardist long enough to see the record through.

Titled *Life's Too Good* — an optimistic exhortation lifted from a poet friend's response to being handed a coffee and a cigarette — the Sugarcubes' ensuing debut was a vibrant gush of zany, sun-drenched pop and spiky angles. Its churlish humor, wryly satirical tone, and ham-fisted whimsy also rendered it a decidedly Icelandic album — unarguably the first of its breed to have an impact elsewhere in the world. Although it failed to properly sustain the momentum established by "Birthday," it plays like a greatest hits album in retrospect.

*Life's Too Good* was released to largely glowing reviews in August 1988, and prompted a hailstorm of tours, press obligations, contractual hagglings, and fame-induced headfucks that altered the band irrevocably. Throughout it all, the band stubbornly positioned themselves as a vanguard art collective intent on subverting the notions of pop by embracing it with open arms. The unfolding truth was much more damning: in the most crass, commercial sense of the phrase, the Sugarcubes were slowly on the road to becoming the one thing they'd always secretly despised — a real pop band.

Forget drugs or egos — the quickest, dirtiest way to put a band through the wringer is to foist America upon them.

While recording *Life's Too Good*, the band had struck up a friendship with an Elektra Records A&R man named Howard Thompson. There was a mutual trust between both parties from the beginning. "They felt that they could work with him, and they needed something in the U.S.," Matthíasson says. "At that time there weren't many decent independent labels that you could actually trust to do things. I know that Rough Trade wanted to sign them but Einar had had some dealings with

Geoff [Travis] from Rough Trade and didn't really want to work with them."

Thompson orchestrated a licensing deal with Elektra Records, and *Life's Too Good* was released in the U.S. around the same time as in Europe. To the band and label's delight, America quickly proved just as vulnerable to "Birthday"'s charms. The track saturated U.S. college radio before crossing over to mainstream radio stations, where it quickly imprinted itself onto the brains of the nation's tastemakers. The U.S. media followed the Brits' lead by also seizing upon Björk as the band's true star, which frustrated the band once again.

Before they could tour, the Sugarcubes needed to address the vacant keyboardist position. A few months before the release of *Life's Too Good*, they approached Margrét [Magga] Örnólfsdóttir, keyboardist with popular Icelandic band Reptile, and asked her to join the band full time. On the counsel of Benediktsson's sister Arna, Magga quit her job at a local Chinese food restaurant and became the Sugarcubes' new sixth member. The band promptly chucked her into the fire: her first live performance came that very same day.

Björk and Þór's relationship had been on a steady decline for months, with separation imminent. They had gotten married for the wrong reasons, and had been drifting apart for a long time. Upon their eventual divorce late in 1986, the band held a state-of-the-union meeting to discuss whether it would be possible to continue. Neither Björk nor Þór wanted to be responsible for ending the band, so, as a group, they decided to press on.

Their practical outlook on marriage made this process a little easier to endure. "I think one reason divorce is so common in Iceland is marriage is not taken seriously," Björk said. "You love a person — if you don't love that person anymore, you don't live with that person, because why suffer? All my ex-lovers . . . they're all mates of mine."

Nevertheless, for the short term, there were still obvious fractures within the band. These were further complicated by Magga's sudden presence; she and Þór had begun to flirt. The pair's ensuing relationship, marriage, and baby would add another wrinkle in the band's already complex weave of relationships. Despite it all, Björk and Magga struck up a solid friendship, their cosmic link superseding any potential animosity. The similarities between the two of them are profound: they share the same birthday and the same husband, and years later Björk would give birth to her second child on October 4, the same birthdate as Magga's first child.

The big money treatment being lavished on the band by Elektra certainly made it easy to forget everything else. Granted, there really wasn't much money to be *made*, but the perks that came with being on tour — free drinks, swish hotels, constant attention — appealed to the band's hedonistic side. Subsequently, the first American tour at the end of 1988 went down like one extended, disbelieving celebration. "It was

*Top: The Sugarcubes, sans Einar, singing Christmas carols and children's songs at Reykjavik's Tunglid in December 1989. L-r: friend Siggi Bjorns, þór, Magga, Björk, Bragi, Siggi.*

*Bottom: The band cavorts behind the scenes during a filming session for Spanish music television, 1988. L-r: Einar, Bragi, Einar Melax, Björk, Siggi, þór.*
*(Photos by Björg Sveinsdóttir)*

like a holiday," Björk said in 1993. "Free limos, free food, free drink, and you could bring all your friends. It was like an endless holiday. It was brilliant."

As they'd routinely done from the beginning, Björk and Þór brought Sindri along for the duration of the tour. The toddler's presence kept the rest of the band a little saner; each took turns playing surrogate uncle or aunt to the four-year-old boy. "There were always a lot of Icelandic people traveling with us, sort of like a family," Björk said. "When I think about it now, I can't believe it. I had one suitcase with winter clothes, one with summer clothes, and another full of toys. But it was quite magical to discover the world with a child.

"We kind of had a schedule," she added. "He'd wake up at about 7:00 a.m., and just gently shake me. And while the other people in the band were maybe partying quite hard, fair enough, and waking up in the tour bus around noon, he and I would be off to three amusement parks and four gardens, and we'd be drawing maps and making up games. For a while we toured with a bicycle that had a little kid's seat attached. We'd just throw it in with all the equipment. Outside of the bus we'd ride around, and he'd wear his little helmet. We wouldn't know where we were, so we'd just have to find our way together. And then after the concerts, I would climb all sweaty into bed with him. So I always felt like I was the lucky one, to have a partner who would do it all with me. I guess we're like sister and brother in a lot of ways."

That sense of stability proved integral: for this group of pragmatic Icelanders, magic America was proving to be a confounding place. "When we were on *Saturday Night Live*, me and Siggi were going back to our hotel after the rehearsal and this guy came running towards our car and asked for our autograph," Einar said. "Siggi said, quite rightly, 'Do you know who we are?' 'Yes, yes,' he replied, 'you're that famous band, The Sugarkings!'"

What was initially conceived as a short American jaunt had morphed into a veritable international tour; as long as the record kept selling, there appeared to be no end in sight to the work ahead. The extended holiday had a profound impact on certain members of the band. "In the beginning, it was a joke with them but then they sort of got comfortable with the routine of being pampered and being drunk on the road and groupies and seeing new places and stuff like that so it became something that they wanted to maintain," Hjálmarsson said. "Well, some of them. I think that from the second album on, Björk had started to feel uncomfortable."

She wasn't letting on, but Björk had become increasingly disenchanted with the limitations of guitar-led pop. Her predilection for vanguard sounds was pulling her in different directions, directions that some of her bandmates would never have approved of. Hip-hop, jazz, and, most crucially, the found sounds and digital scribbles emanating from Britain's burgeoning electronic scene were secretly exciting her much more. "I remember being at this bar one day," Hjálmarsson says. "She had a walkman on and she let me hear some impossible music, you know, for that time. She said, 'Listen to this!' I said, 'Uh, it's *okay. . . .*'"

The few attempts Björk made to interest other band members in her broadening palate proved similarly futile — in the end, only Siggi shared her enthusiasm. Her most outspoken opponent was Þór, who made no bones about the fact that he despised a lot of the music that she was listening to. "[She] would always bring in dance or rap music and she would want them to listen to it, and they just *wouldn't*," Matthíasson recounts. "Or if they did, they would all just sit there stone-faced while she played it and not remark. But Þór never listened, he always got up and went for a walk. There wasn't any understanding of what she was thinking about, and they didn't want to approach it in any way."

Björk was starting to fall out of orbit with her bandmates in musical terms, but she still prized the camaraderie and friendship that came with being in the Sugarcubes. Since the band was constructed in such a way that made it prohibitive for one member to make any exorbitant suggestions, she had no choice but to quietly kept her passions to herself, or leave.

Ironically, the mounting interview requests for Björk — and only Björk — during this time helped perpetuate the growing perception that she was the main creative force in the band. She'd done nothing to encourage the notion, but she found herself compromised nonetheless. "When you've got 300 requests for interviews you just can't stick it on one person, and everybody wanted to speak to her," Matthíasson says. "She always had to do more than she wanted to do, and that was a big problem."

Meanwhile, spurred on by the media's antipathy towards him, Einar became increasingly more nettlesome. The band had countered Björk's mounting popularity by letting him do still more interviews, and he was making the most of the opportunity. "It was almost like Tourette's Syndrome," Garðarsson laughs. "He probably wanted to be nice, but still he couldn't do it. That's his way . . . be a punker."

The grind of the major market mechanisms took its toll; slowly, the band's resolve began to crumble under the weight of so much detritus. "It was obvious to anyone that it wouldn't last," Matthíasson says of the group at this point. "I'd say that the dynamics changed. They became more of a band, they became more of a touring machine . . . it died a bit, to me anyway. The camaraderie changed."

The relative commercial failure of the second single, "Coldsweat," meant that the Sugarcubes never got an opportunity to properly build on their momentum while on tour; they spent the remaining months on the road with "Birthday" as their sole calling card. Once the hailstorm of "Birthday"-inspired press, touring, and attention subsided, the Sugarcubes found themselves struggling to find a foothold in a brick wall of media-mongered bias.

*Top: Björk and Einar while performing live favorite "Deus" in a makeshift outdoor venue for the 1990 Reykjavik Arts Festival.*

*Bottom: Taking a mid-song breather during a guest appearance in a Battle of the Bands contest at Tonabaer, Reykjavik in March 1990. L-r: Bragi, Björk, unknown, Einar. (Photos by Björg Sveinsdóttir)*

Exhausted by Einar Örn's antics and sensing a band on the ropes, the media began to tender the idea that the Sugarcubes were nothing but hacks, first-time lucky. Others landed the blame for the band's stalling squarely on Einar's shoulders, with some vociferously demanding his extradition. "People started saying, 'Björk is a good singer, she's a great vocalist and what she needs to do is get rid of Einar,'" Garðarsson laments. "That started quite early."

Confrontational in nature and perceived by many as an attention-seeking annoyance onstage, Einar Örn was roundly chastised by critics, many of whom felt he was hindering Björk's emergence as a true star. Some even questioned his overall relevance to the band, demonstrating a clear misunderstanding of the Sugarcubes' genesis. In retrospect, his agitating, rabble-rousing presence probably generated just as many column inches as Björk's charged shrieks. Without his input, the Sugarcubes may well have been another dime-a-dozen girl-fronted pop outfit.

Producer Paul Fox, who worked with the band for their final studio album, believes Benediktsson was essential: "I got to understand the dada of [his performance]. It's almost like in the old theatrical sense of the antagonist and the protagonist, her this beautiful elfin singer with this fantastic voice and then this guy interrupting and trying to disrupt what's going on.

"It's almost in the same way as Fred Schneider from the B-52s," he continues. "Here's the guy who's more like the common person, the person who doesn't have the talent to really sing with a great voice, but sings along and has this different function and role and viewpoint that makes it more of a universal experience for listeners."

"It was not only about Björk's vocals and her ability to become quite a great singer, it was also Einar's attitude, Einar's driving force, Einar's ability to talk to the press all around the world at the time," Garðarsson contends. "He had been studying media in England at that time so he knew his way around, he knew the press people, he had all the right connections, but they had no more songs, no more basis to work on, and they couldn't care less, I think. When it came to the second record, I think they felt that they should be improving, they should have gone further and they weren't prepared for the building-up and tearing-down situation in England, which always happens there. They said they didn't care, but they did."

*Life's Too Good* had conveyed a certain doe-eyed spontaneity, the sense that a flash of bounding energy had somehow been captured on tape. For their second record, the Sugarcubes had to somehow find their way back to that place. Only now, there was pressure to answer to — Bad Taste were depending on them, the media were eager to pounce, and the whole of Iceland was gunning for their triumphant comeback.

Understandably, the band found themselves in an entirely different headspace when they went back into the studio to record their sophomore outing in 1989. Their friendships remained intact, but they had to face certain realities: that the public wasn't going to blindly embrace anything that they did, that Einar was perceived as a hindrance, and that Björk was the band's real draw. The band denied it, but combined with the post-tour haze that still hung over them like a monstrous hangover, these precepts handicapped them creatively.

Further contributing to the Sugarcubes' creative slump was the growing realization that they were inadvertently becoming that which they once spoofed. By selling over half a million copies in North America and England combined, *Life's Too Good* had compromised the band's once subversive, utilitarian view of pop music as "a living cliché." "Þór, who wrote the poppiest songs, wasn't into writing more because this was basically against everything that they had been working for," Garðarsson says. "They weren't going to sell out." These obstacles proved insurmountable; the resulting record (the wryly titled *Here Today, Tomorrow Next Week!*) was not up to the standard of their first album.

"It was totally not a good record," moans Hjálmarsson. "It was just done on the run and they had trouble with the producer who left in the middle of it. Too many songs . . . too many bad songs."

"When they were recording the second album, it was like they were stuck in something they really wanted to get out of," Matthíasson agrees. "I didn't feel that they were at all comfortable with what was going on and I don't think it was about the backlash — it was about the constant pressure of touring."

The cumulative effect of the stress, creative uncertainty, and sudden scrutiny had quite naturally resulted in a loss of spontaneity. Spanning across a total of six recording studios, the sessions for *Here Today, Tomorrow Next Week!* were just as spotty and fractured as the album itself. Although Birkett was once again on hand as producer, the number of participating engineers, co-engineers, mixers, and masterers had run into double digits. The band eventually found themselves at odds over the final outcome — they argued about everything, right down to which songs to include and which final mixes to use.

"The mixes weren't coming out right," Matthíasson says. "It was mixed on the fly with Petur [Gislason] mixing a song, flying out to meet them, and then going back to mix it a bit more, so it was more or less a disaster waiting to happen. It didn't have the veneer that the other one had. It wasn't as smooth, as polished, as personal. . . . When Friðrik left, some of the balance went out of the band and it never really regained that."

The underwhelming response to the forgettable first single "Regina" proved a sign of things to come; upon its eventual release in late 1989, the album was universally panned. Maintaining a spiky, unified front in the face of disapproval, the band attempted to justify the album's failure with post-haste, revisionist logic. Their spin on the record's muted response was one that Björk knavishly echoed years later in a 1993 interview. "The Sugarcubes were a bit of a clique, you know," she said. "We had been going for years before people in Britain discovered us. When we became so famous, so talked about after our first record, we said 'Fuck the world,' and decided to make the most unpredictable album we could."

A few plum touring opportunities arose, the best of which included a string of gigs opening for Public Image Limited and New Order (on the so-called Monsters of Alternative Rock Tour). After that, more tours in Europe, Japan, and Australia kept the band busy until the end of the year, at which point they retreated back to Iceland for lengthy rest and reconsideration. Their future together was a giant unspoken question mark; rather than search for an answer, they took an indefinite hiatus.

"To me it seemed that they had more or less decided to quit," Matthíasson says. "There was this feeling that it was over, but nobody came out and said it. They did all sorts of different things. A lot of people thought that there was enmity in the group and that they were angry and bitter with each other. But it wasn't so — they started a jazz band [Konrad's B Jazz Group] where they all played together under different names. They all were in that group, so they were still friendly and keen on doing things together. They just weren't keen on the Sugarcubes."

"By that time," Hjálmarsson agrees, "I think Björk started to seriously think about the future."

In stark contrast to prior homecomings, Björk had more than just the rent to consider; for the first time in her life, her own creative impulses seemed more urgent than the band's. The notion of going solo had always been a silly joke to her — now, it seemed an inevitability.

# four

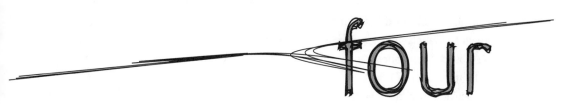

Most of the Sugarcubes spent the better portion of 1990 toiling away happily at endeavors outside the band. Einar Örn was busy with Bad Taste, Bragi devoted time to his true love — poetry — and Þór and Magga prepared for the birth of their first child. Björk wiled away the months by spending time with Sindri, who was now four, and by taking various odd jobs, including one at an antique shop and another at a record store. Once removed from the stage, Matthíasson recalled her as a painfully timid record stork clerk. "When you were just interacting in a normal way — telling a few jokes or bantering and so on — she wasn't very comfortable," he said. "But talking about music was perfect because she was really, really into listening to new stuff; at that time I was listening to African music and music from Asia and she was very into that."

Björk contributed musically wherever she could, lending vocals to a track by a local Bad Taste band called Bless. She'd also taken the first steps to realizing her ambitions as a solo artist. Armed with a handful of songs, which she'd mostly arranged in her head, she met with an amateur Icelandic brass outfit in a local studio to sketch out some rudimentary demos. It was obvious from these spotty rough cuts that her vision needed guidance and refinement, but the spirit of what she was trying to achieve — evident in gloriously tangled versions of "The Anchor Song" and "Aeroplane" — was present from the outset.

Björk played all three songs from that demo tape for Bad Taste manager and mentor Ásmundur Jónsson, who immediately noticed their emotional gravity. "Those demos felt quite isolated," he recalls. "The atmosphere was like a person standing alone somewhere. I got that feeling from 'The Anchor Song' when I heard that the first time — it must have been some kind of a process that she was going through."

Björk now had time to further develop her obsession with the music that the Sugarcubes wouldn't dare touch. Intrigued by the pulses and hiccups of keyboards and drum machines, she'd tuned into electronic music just in time to catch the first rumblings of a minor revolution. Rave was already beginning to happen in England, and thanks in no small part to Britain's pioneering electronic label Warp and their essential *Artificial Intelligence* compilations, a headier offshoot of mainstream electronic was bubbling right underneath.

Björk's early exposure to the electronic *sturm und drang* of pioneering experimentalists like Stockhausen meant that she wasn't prone to the same errors of prejudice that plagued some of her guitar-clutching contemporaries. Everything but the most dunderheaded dance music excited her immensely, and she plunged headfirst into everything from the brave to the rave. Speedy J's manic drum and bass, the immaculately programmed touches of Black Dog, the considered experimentalism of Manchester's 808 State — all of it was all tickling her in some new and glorious way.

Björk knew that if her solo ventures were going to be truly representative of her varied aesthetic tastes, she would need to eventually step out and find a way to involve herself with this scene. She knew that the songs she had stored in her head could work with these elements, but without the equipment or the programming knowledge, she had no idea how to make it happen. Acting on pure intuition, she decided to call 808 State's Graham Massey — whom she'd never spoken to or met — near the end of 1990.

"She didn't say who she was, she didn't mention the Sugarcubes," Massey recalls. "She just said she was an Icelandic songwriter, but I kind of suspected it was her. She had been listening to our music and was interested in finding somebody to program beats to work on some tunes, and asked would we be interested in meeting up?"

Massey obliged, and as fate would have it, Björk happened to be in London while 808 State were there to fulfill press obligations. The pair met for the first time in a British TV studio, where Massey and his cohorts had just appeared on a show called *The Word*. "At that first meeting, she played a tape, and it was some of the songs that later appeared on *Debut*, but all recorded with a brass quartet," he says. "I think there was a saxophone, trombone, and trumpet — if you heard the tape now I don't know if you'd recognize them as the tunes."

Massey was intrigued by Björk's idea — to braid seemingly antiquated instruments such as brass and harps with the forward-thinking chug of drum machines and keyboards. Knowing that it might turn out to be a disaster, he agreed to collaborate with her nonetheless. In the end, there was something about her character that reassured him. "When you meet people you either feel like you don't know them or you do," he explains. "I think the initial impression was that somehow I knew her personality quite quickly. She was very good at putting herself across and had a look of 'I am going to do this.' Though she was very shy, there was a lot of confidence there. But she wasn't arrogant with it, it was just kind of something you would sense."

The duo's original agreement was to reunite once 808 State had completed their next record. They parted ways, but Massey couldn't get her out of his head. "She was due to fly back to Iceland and I woke up the next morning with a funny feeling about the situation," he recalls. "I felt like it was worth a try to try something out and see how it was."

Operating on a hunch, Massey invited Björk back to Manchester to spice up the recording sessions for 808 State's forthcoming album, *Ex:El*. He had no idea what to expect from the collaboration, but figured it would give him an opportunity to get to know Björk a little better. "It was an experiment," he shrugs. "The thing that came across was that she was quite brave in experimenting in that situation. We were pretty much a techno band, and vocals weren't a thing that we had in techno at that point. There was no blueprint for that. It's very different these days as there's been a lot of vocal collaborations on dance music, but there wasn't too much of it around other than the sort of American R&B style. Certainly not in the realm of what we used to consider indie. It felt like an unusual thing to do."

Massey previewed a handful of rough 808 sketches for Björk and encouraged her to explore any ideas she might have along the way. Björk had long made a habit of singing her own vocal lines over electronic songs while at home, and she had no problems with the exercise. Her careful reverence for the tunes also impressed Massey; instead of trying to wring them into pop songs, she simply bobbed and weaved along with the music, like a jazz singer improvising.

The pair worked on a number of tracks together, but the one they kept coming back to was a throbbing, minor-key banger named "Q-Mart." With its bulging synth lines and frantic, staccato percussion, it wasn't the most obvious candidate for a vocalist, but Björk had come up with an equally rhythmic scat that seemed to fit it perfectly. Her performance here left Massey — a jazz aficionado himself — with a newfound respect for her talents and sensibilities. In Massey's eyes, the only thing that rivaled her impressive instincts in the studio was her considerable knowledge of electronic, world, and jazz music. Over time, he realized that they had something very special in common — they were both impenitent, hardcore music geeks.

Once a successful take on "Q-Mart" was in the bag, the duo moved on to the other 808 State song that had piqued Björk's interest. With its strummy acoustic guitar opening and housey horn flourishes, "Oops" had a more conventional verse-chorus-verse song structure to it; there also seemed to be room for a complete vocal line. Björk took a walkman containing the song's rough cut out into the Manchester rain and came back an hour later with complete lyrics. The pair had sparked the beginnings of their second proper collaboration.

Massey's immediate sense upon completing the song was that they'd just recorded something very special. "You have to remember the time span, where certainly [dance music] was the dominant culture at that time even in places like Iceland – it was getting to be a phenomenon at that point," he explains. "Nobody knew what we were doing, and I certainly had a sense of freedom in making those records at that point that wasn't to do with 'this is how you make dance music.' Nobody knew what this music was – there was a great freedom within it to do what you wanted, so it was with that sense that we made this record."

Thrilled with the results of their first collaboration, Björk left Massey and returned to Iceland days later, where another too-good-to-be-true opportunity was waiting to present itself. Unbeknownst to her, a local jazz trio fronted by pianist and jazz luminary Guðmundur Ingolfsson had been commissioned by state radio to commit a live set of popular standards to a two-track reel. The idea sounded brilliant to the threesome, but they figured it would be better if they could procure a singer.

Björk's previous appearances on a local jazz radio program called *Godravina Fundur* had made an impression on drummer Guðmundur St. Steingrímsson (otherwise known in local circles as "Papa Jazz"). He also had passing memories of her from way back when she was a 16-year-old jazz obsessive hanging around his recording sessions at Labbi Thorarinsson's farm Glora. "We were recording one of the first of Guðmundur Ingolfsson's records," St. Steingrímsson recalls. "She was in the countryside then and she was always coming in. She was very interested because she liked jazz . . . she liked every kind of music." Upon St. Steingrímsson's request, the trio asked Björk to participate. She had never had the opportunity to work with proper jazz musicians before, and jumped at the chance.

With the help of legendary Icelandic poet and singer-songwriter Megas (commonly regarded as the nation's Bob Dylan), Björk set out to select the program's setlist. Björk trawled through an enormous selection of local jazz standards under Megas' well-schooled guidance, eventually settling upon a small clutch of rousing tunes. She brought them back to the trio, who quickly learned the few that they didn't already know.

Rounded out by bassist Þordur Hognason, the newly-configured quartet debuted on August 30, 1990, at Hotel Borg, where the audience's reaction was immediate. Ásmundur Jónsson was in the crowd, and later raved to St. Steingrímsson about how fantastic their performance had been. St. Steingrímsson's reaction: "Isn't this worth recording?"

Jónsson didn't need much prodding. Not long afterwards, the quartet found themselves in Reykjavik's Studio Syrland, recording live off the floor at a breakneck pace without almost any overdubs. Dubbed *Gling Gló* (an Icelandic onomatopoeia meant to signify the sound of clanging bells), the resulting record was completed in an astonishing two days. "Fourteen tunes, 17 hours," St. Steingrímsson laughs.

It's an accomplishment made all the more impressive by the album's exquisite, note-perfect performances, of which Björk's was arguably the most memorable. Until this point, the sheer ferocity of her vocal prowess had been well documented, but her command and utilization of vocal expression had not. Leaving a gymnastic trail of giggles, squeals, and vocal backflips in her wake, Björk positively danced through these 14 songs. There may not be another album in Björk's entire discography that showcases her vocal ability as convincingly as *Gling Gló*.

With hundreds of sessions already under their belts, the Guðmundur Ingolfsson Trio had years to establish a rapport with one another; yet here was Björk not only keeping up, but in some instances, completely outshining them. "I remember almost laughing out loud when we were taping because she was passing through the bars like nothing," St. Steingrímsson nods. "Wow. And then always on that time — it was *amazing*. That's instinct."

*Gling Gló* was released during Christmas 1990 to almost instant acclaim; it was played to death on radio and quickly went platinum in Iceland. Its subsequent success ingratiated Björk with an audience upon which she had previously failed to make an impression. So wide-ranging and extensive were her many different ventures that suddenly everyone — even the culturally exclusive middle-aged mothers — knew who she was.

Björk's native universality, her potential for anythingness was a weapon that she was still learning to wield. Nonetheless, her simultaneous success with projects as divergent as the Sugarcubes, 808 State, and *Gling Gló* had only confirmed what her intuition was already suggesting: that the key to her creative growth would lie in her ability to embrace and celebrate this rare versatility.

More gigs with the Guðmundur Ingolfsson Trio — about 10 to 15 in total — followed right up until Guðmundur Ingolfsson's death in 1992 from cancer. Ten years removed from its original recording date, many of the songs on *Gling Gló* are still commonly regarded as definitive jazz standards. With tongue planted firmly in cheek, Jónsson bemoaned the record's continuous impact on Iceland's older, less adventurous set. "A lot of people prefer listening to her doing the standards, which is kind of annoying," he sighs. "She has done all of this great music and then it's, 'Why don't

*Björk gets jazzed up for one of her live appearances with the Guðmundur Ingolfsson Trio. (Courtesy Guðmundur St. Steingrímsson)*

you sing "My Funny Valentine"?'" By virtue of numerous re-pressings over the years, *Gling Gló* is still in circulation, and regarded by the majority of Björk fans as an unimpeachable treasure.

With no end in sight to the Sugarcubes' extended hiatus, Björk had more time to warm to the idea of a solo album. The more she thought about it, the more she wanted her friends' support, but when Björk finally revealed her plans to the Sugarcubes, some of her bandmates were more supportive than others. Irrational as it may have been, certain members couldn't help feeling betrayed by the fact that she'd seemingly abandoned punk for something as inscrutable and as passing as electronic music.

In a way, the favorable response to 808 State's *Ex:El* had made things even more difficult on Björk. The eventual single, "Oops," had become a bona fide smash; although she only appeared on two of the album's 18 tracks, Björk suddenly found herself being talked about in a way that the Sugarcubes hadn't been for months, maybe years. Naturally, she was thrilled, but her excitement was tempered by an overwhelming desire to share this good fortune with friends.

808 State were due to play a gig in Iceland that year, and they'd asked Björk to do a cameo with them onstage. In a last ditch effort to try and help them understand where her head was at, Björk invited the Sugarcubes to attend the show. The result was a disaster. "Her friends in the band came to watch this phenomenon that she had been talking about for a while and putting energy into instead of being with them," Hjálmarsson says. "The gig was horrible. There was a delay and some breakdown in the equipment and so on. After this gig, or maybe it was the day after, Þór came to her house and it was just crazy. [He was] saying stuff like, 'If this is what you want to do, fuck off! Why do you spend your time on this and not thinking about us?' Just being very angry, screaming at her."

The split between the two didn't mend easily, and for a long time, it appeared as if there was no hope for a third Sugarcubes album. Unfortunately, since the band's pact with Elektra had expressly called for another record, it wasn't going to be easy to fold up and walk away either. In the end, the band's familial bond proved too strong to sever, and they set about planning their return. Although her desire for a solo career was now common knowledge, Björk eventually relented as well. By winter 1991, the Sugarcubes had begun to seriously discuss the details of their third — and final — studio outing.

Believing that the Sugarcubes were still fully capable of re-visiting past commercial glories, Elektra did everything they could to facilitate a hit album.

Inspired by his work behind the desk for XTC's seminal *Oranges and Lemons*, Elektra A&R man Howard Thompson placed calls to producer Paul Fox to ask him if he'd be interested in working with the band. "I actually liked a lot of the second

*Despite the fact that they were growing increasingly tired of the stress and attention, the Sugarcubes always tried their best to maintain a sense of fun and frivolity. Clockwise from bottom: Björk, Siggi, Einar, Magga, þór, Bragi. (S.I.N./Corbis/Magma)*

record but it wasn't as big a success in the media and commercially as the first one," Fox says. "This was the record company coming in and saying 'Okay, we're going to bring in an American producer who has been fairly successful at taking bands that are fairly left of center and have a core audience and trying to bring them to a larger audience without damaging their credibility.'"

Already a longtime Sugarcubes admirer, Fox accepted the proposal without hesitation and flew to Reykjavik to meet them in the new year. If there was a nasty fracture in the Sugarcubes' resolve at that point, he didn't notice it. "My first impression was that this was just a magical country and a magical little city and here were these incredibly talented and really sort of zany, bright, creative people who all lived in what was kind of like a band but also seemed like a big extended family," he says. "[In] bands, there are some people who are kind of loners and tend to be by themselves, some who are very outgoing, and sometimes there's one person who clearly is the focus. In their case, while Björk was clearly the top of triangle, I have to say that each one of them was a real separate entity in terms of their personality and contribution to what was going on. I just found them a delight to be around."

Fox spent time with each band member individually, and ended up forming friendships with all of them in the process. His first recollection of Björk is one that has since been echoed by many: "I got the impression that this was somebody who was truly special," he says. "I don't think I've ever met anybody quite like her in my life. She seems so in tune with what she's doing at the moment that she's doing it, there's this duality of extreme childlike enthusiasm and this incredible sense of sophistication and self-knowledge. I got very excited by the prospect of working with her just because she really seemed like a true artist.

"When we first met we were waiting for a table at this restaurant and when we finally got a chance to talk a little bit I got that sense of awe that she seems to have, like she's looking at everything through a magnifying glass."

True to form, Fox's first meeting with Einar wasn't nearly as peaceful. One evening, while famished, the embattled producer made the mistake of blindly accepting unidentified meat from Benediktsson. This, of course, was a mistake. "I was eating it and I was like, 'Oh it must be like fresh seafood, fresh scallops or something.' Einar starts laughing and says, 'So how do you like your food?' I say, 'It tastes great and I'm quite hungry, so anything will do right now.' He goes, 'Well, congratulations — you've just eaten your first sheep's testicles.' I thought 'Oh, you *bastard*.'"

Fox and the band fostered a mutual admiration over the course of these meetings, and within time, they agreed to work together. Recording sessions for this third album were basically conducted in two parts — the first half at Reykjavik's Syrland Studios, and the second in New York's famed Bearsville Recording Studios. By all accounts, the New York sessions ranked among the most stressful in the band's lengthy history. "Recording *Stick Around for Joy* was very hard," Matthíasson says. "Relations within the band were quite bad at that point and they more or less didn't speak, so everything was on a very formal, cold basis."

Gunnar Hjálmarsson spent years of his life in a band with Þór Eldon called Unun; before that, they'd been friends for a long time. "I heard it was a very intense situation," he says. "In the studio, Þór didn't speak to her for the whole time. I know how he is, feeling abandoned — he has a little bit of a personality fault. He's 50/50 — great and then totally horrible."

"There was no knockdown," Fox clarifies. "There were no fights at all . . . they were pretty aware that she was leaving the nest [but] at the same time they were also a band that was making this record. There was a bit of inner tension from that and also from the fact that you have two actual real family dynamics going on, with Þór, Magga, Björk and the kids all there in Bearsville at the same time."

The experience was especially emotional for Björk, who felt torn between loyalties. "It was bittersweet, like this excitement of her being aware that she was starting to hear something new that she was going to go after, and at the same time that this was so much her family and she didn't want to hurt her family," Fox says.

"There must have been some kind of an internal dynamic that was confusing to say the least — between doing the record that she was there to do and also knowing where she saw her life going at that point."

The mediating presence of longtime friend Sjon Sigurdsson at Bearsville saved these sessions from completely derailing. By maintaining a sense of humor, Sjon, a constant member of the entourage, kept the band completely grounded, and in a way, helped them remember why they were doing this in the first place. As her own coping mechanism, Björk seized upon the music and threw herself into the record with typical zeal.

"I've never seen anybody give themselves over the way she gave herself over," Fox says. "I'll never forget this as long as I live — she started singing the song 'Gold' and she was literally knocking stuff over in the room. The lamp got knocked off the table! Her enthusiasm, the way she threw herself into the music — my engineer and I were looking at each other like we'd never seen anything like this. She remained incredibly focused on that record throughout."

By the end of the sessions, Björk had begun to confide in Fox about her own ambitions. She'd already played him her demo cassette and the pair struck a bond over their mutual love for music on the periphery of the mainstream. "There's not that many people around who like the Art Ensemble of Chicago," he smiles. "She was such a big fan of that music and she just thought they were so brilliant. I happened to know the names of those people and I knew what kind of music they made and so that was something that we could talk about."

With the Bearsville sessions, the band all but completed the album. The only remaining adjustments to be made were in the form of vocal overdubs; since the Sugarcubes always wrote their songs in Icelandic first, Björk still needed to come up with English translations for certain songs. She flew to Paul Fox's Los Angeles studio to finish the process. While in L.A., she'd often turn to Fox's wife Frannie for help. "A lot of the time Björk would translate them from Icelandic to English and they wouldn't really translate," Fox recounts. "She would come up with certain phrases that she felt uncomfortable singing or she didn't think were as strong as they could be so she'd turn to Frannie to get some help as to how to make them more poetic."

While in Los Angeles, Björk took Sindri on a day trip to Disneyland, where through a friend she met burgeoning British DJ Dominic Thrupp. There was an immediate chemistry between them, and Björk returned to the studio feeling the familiar strains of love tugging away at her insides.

Previously called "Smooth Intender," the album's first single "Hit" had long been a point of contention for Fox, mainly on account of Björk's inability to come up with a proper English lyric for it. They were one week away from mixing the finished product when Fox desperately requested that Björk write something — *anything* — so that they could record her vocals. "She said, 'This song hasn't happened yet!,' meaning that she hadn't lived it," Fox says. "[Then] she came in one day and said, 'I have it for you!'" It was easy — "Hit" was about the sudden impact that Thrupp had had on her.

Fox wondered what the media would make of a first single called "Hit," but Björk didn't even consider the implications. "She wasn't naming it that because of any sense of commerciality, it was more that it was just what she felt had happened to her," he says. "She was just hit by this person she had met."

Strange as it may seem, the tension-fraught Bearsville sessions ultimately yielded a much more focused, joyous record than album number two had been. Titled *Stick Around For Joy* (a title inspired by some ill-translated soda sloganeering), it was met more warmly by critics and fans than their previous album had been. Many of the sticking points that had previously dogged the band seemed to have suddenly melted away — the media were no longer obsessed with what the Sugarcubes could be. As ever, the band still had their detractors, but the ripostes weren't as searing, nor the criticisms as vicious.

"Hit" and the followup single "Walkabout" both performed reasonably well for the band (the latter even garnered Single of the Week plaudits from the *NME*), so the Sugarcubes once again found themselves fielding a variety of interesting offers from various parties. Unfortunately, these tour propositions — including one with the celebrated Lollapalooza Festival — had to be rejected. Björk wasn't interested in them. Her commitment to the band was finally fulfilled, and for the first time, she felt like she was ready to step out on her own.

Then U2 approached the band and asked them if they'd be interested in opening three weeks worth of shows for the U.S. leg of their 1992 Zoo TV tour. As a final act of goodwill towards her bandmates, Björk embraced the idea. "She said yes, probably just to make the wealth, or to make peace with everybody," Hjálmarsson jokes. "Give the boys a glimpse into rock and roll high life."

"She felt that, in a way, 'These are all my pals and I'm deserting them,'" Matthíasson says. "I think it was her idea to wrap things up and finish it on a positive note."

It was to be their farewell. Although they remained coy about it with the press — most Cubes publicly referred to their split as a "hiatus" — the band members knew that the Sugarcubes were finished. Some handled the breakup better than others. "There was an acrimonious split in a way because Þór actually wanted to keep on touring," Matthíasson says. "He loved his job. Touring, lots of free drinks . . . okay, not so much money but a decent amount of money. He wanted to keep on doing that."

"Einar was very frustrated even though he said he wasn't," Garðarsson adds. "You can hear in Icelandic interviews that he's a bit pissed. This is something I heard both from him and people around him."

*On tour with U2 in 1992, at which point it had become impossible to conceal the fact that most of the band were miserable together. L-r: Einar, Bragi, Siggi, Björk, Magga, Þór. (Photos by Björg Sveinsdóttir)*

Spearheaded by Björk and Siggi, a Sugarcubes remix album surfaced in December 1992. With the title serving as the band's final rejoinder to the oft-posed question ("are you still together?"), *It's-It* featured dance remixes from Todd Terry, Marius De Vries, and Graham Massey, among others. In private circles, most of the other Sugarcubes grumpily took to referring to this record as *It's Shit*.

Björk didn't mind much. She'd finally given herself the gift of being in a situation where music came first over camaraderie. "The Sugarcubes were attracted to each other because we were all extreme people," Björk said. "We always had a good time, even if we were stuck in a boring German suburb eating cold hamburgers. The music was secondary, so we didn't have this big musical ambition to be brilliant. I could be in the background and write my melodies and lyrics and then watch how the music turned out."

After being in a variety of different Icelandic bands for the previous 13 years, Björk had been in the background enough. She had a splash of sounds wandering around her brain and an overwhelming need to excise them. There were possibilities to be explored, risks to be taken, rules to be broken. Her heart churned, her belly bubbled, her ears rang with excitement. "I realized I could have an easy life in Iceland, just have a glass of Cognac and good books and two jobs and do my songs in the evening, but I would be such a consumer, taking it all in and not giving anything back," Björk said. "I thought: Okay, I'm 27. If I don't go on a mission now and make some sacrifices, as these people did, I will never forgive myself."

The sacrifice meant leaving home and moving to London. For the moment, Reykjavik had nothing more to offer.

Having long ago approached Derek Birkett with her demo cassette (which she prefaced with the warning of a similarly uncompromising and unconventional record), Björk had secured herself a deal with One Little Indian. Such was Birkett's loyalty to the Sugarcubes that she probably didn't even need to play him any music in advance. "That was always unwritten — it was just there," says Birkett's then personal assistant Netty Walker of Birkett's continuing relationship with the Sugarcubes. "If any of them did anything then Derek would most likely be involved, he was that deeply connected with the band. I don't think there was any question. [But] from the record company point of view, Björk was the optimum."

Although London's urban surroundings were proving somewhat counterintuitive to the naturalist in her, Björk's decision to move to England was proving to be a wise one. If Reykjavik represented her history, tradition, and experience, then London was a shining beacon of futures: ambition, possibilities, discovery. She was finally free to do whatever she wanted, whatever pleased *her* most, unburdened by the strain of obligation or expectation. The city's vibrant multiculturalism and bustling musical community quickly seduced her. She'd spend her days record shopping on Berwick Street or downing curries in Little India; her nights dancing at some of the city's trendiest clubs and taking in sets by her favorite DJs.

The culture shock inherent in the move from Reykjavik to London manifested itself in some unconventional ways. The independence bred into her by Iceland's cultural and physical remoteness became an agent in the way Björk interacted with her new surroundings. In a way that few others might, she seized upon her own otherness as cause for celebration rather than castigation. And, although horribly outnumbered, she fancied herself the observer rather than the observed. The resulting anthropological bent of many of the lyrics on *Debut* (namely the Desmond Morris-as-New-Bohemian angle of "Human Behaviour") were a direct result of this outlook; it's no coincidence that she'd spend the next year publicly proclaiming Richard Attenborough a personal hero.

Björk didn't know many people in London at first, but her small circle of friends were close-knit and supportive, almost familial. Her relationship with Dominic Thrupp had blossomed into full blown *lurve*. Over time, they moved in together and he became a sort of surrogate father to Sindri.

Derek Birkett was also in London, trying to sort out details for this first album.

About half of the songs were already written in some form, but nothing had been properly recorded — there wasn't even a producer on board yet. Björk wasn't bothered. She knew Massey was nearby and figured that until the technical things revealed themselves to her, she could spend time writing and hashing out more songs with him. While recording in the front room of a friend's house in Manchester, the pair composed and demoed "Army of Me" and "The Modern Things" in one weekend. Björk loved them both, but had doubts about whether they would fit onto the album that she'd imagined *Debut* to be.

Thanks in no small part to Paul Fox, Björk's vision for the record was crystallizing. Fox had never forgotten how Björk had once told him that it was her lifelong dream to record with a harpist; it just so happened that he knew one of the world's best. After she moved to London, Björk was introduced to Fox's friend, harpist Corky Hale. The pair met for the first time at his own Summa Studio in Los Angeles, but as Hale tells the story, it was an encounter that almost never happened.

"Paul called and said, 'I'm going to bring over a girl from England and she wants to sing jazz with a harp,'" she recalls. "I said, 'That's not possible.' He sent me a tape, and it was pretty weird, I must tell you."

Hidebound by her somewhat classicist roots, Hale didn't know what to make of the demo. Björk's technoisms and strange vocal mannerisms weren't at all in harmony with her own finely-tuned traditionalist bent. Sensing an insuperable generational gap, she planned to politely refuse the offer until her stepson — a Sugarcubes fan — intervened and implored her to take the gig. Trusting his instinct and figuring she should probably work with more contemporary singers anyway, Hale reluctantly agreed and took the job.

"[Paul] brought her over the next week," Hale recalls. "She was terribly, painfully shy. I agreed to go into a studio with her and do demos. They just took my harp up to some old studio up the street and I sat there for five hours teaching her the songs. She was very sweet; she's a darling woman.

"[But] she really didn't know any standards," Hale laughs. "Even her English didn't seem to be great at that time. I more or less taught her how to do it, and I of course thought [the recording session] was pretty terrible and forgot about it."

The experience may not have resonated with Hale, but it marked a giant step forward for Björk. With Hale's glissandos chiming underneath her, Björk learned and performed a handful of standards that evening, including "I Remember You" and an early take on "Like Someone in Love." Neither of them were in consideration for *Debut* at the time, but Björk held on to the demo tapes nonetheless. This session had meant so much to her that she was moved to tears of gratitude for days afterwards. The experience cemented her feeling that she was indeed onto something, that her oddball concept for an album could actually be pulled off, even if her friends and collaborators still weren't quite sure what she was aiming for.

"She'd make tapes that had absolutely nothing to do with electronic music while still talking quite a lot about electronic music, which was kind of confusing," Massey laughs. "'I want it to be like this' — so why are you asking *me*? We were trying to find some common ground. All these tapes had a sense of indigenous music from around the world that was very rootsy, so my perception of what she wanted to go for was kind of a rootsy thing with an electronic element."

Back in London, Björk and Massey focused their attention on two songs from her original demo, "The Anchor Song" and "Aeroplane." They'd made some headway, particularly with "Aeroplane," but something was missing — Björk thought it needed horns. Over time, she began to wonder aloud about the possibility of including a jazz arranger in the writing process.

At this point, a casual observer might have dismissed Björk as too prone to sudden flights of fancy to properly midwife a record with cohesive vision. The actuality is that her constant unease was probably one of her strongest attributes as an artist. The dialogue that occurred between her brain and her intuition was pure, and rarely interrupted by anything as crass as label deadlines or money or public opinion. It was almost binary: Björk would only embrace an idea if it excited her; she would only reject one because it did not. "She's highly intelligent, very driven, and knows exactly what she wants," says Walker. "And in some ways is quite a bit of a control freak to that extent — if she doesn't want to do something, she does not do it. You spend hours trying to convince her that it would be really great if she would."

So here she was, in between doing electronic-based tracks with Massey and jetting off to Los Angeles to record potentially unusable demos of standards with a harpist, still very much consumed by the idea of working with a proper jazz producer. It had to happen somehow, if only because she wanted it to.

Near the tail end of the Los Angeles overdub sessions for *Stick Around For Joy*, Fox had gotten wind of a promising opportunity that had the potential to help Björk realize this goal. A friend in the music industry had approached him about the possibility of producing a solo Björk song for a Hollywood film. The concept was for Björk to record the standard "Life Is Just a Bowl of Cherries" with a proper jazz outfit; in turn, the song would be used for the end credits of a forthcoming John Hughes (*The Breakfast Club*, *Home Alone*) film named *Curly Sue*. "The three of us went to dinner to talk about it," Fox says. "Björk loved the idea. I was going to produce it and I was going to track down Oliver Lake [head of the Art Ensemble of Chicago] for her. We were going to do this song."

The idea was ultimately shot down at Hughes' door ("He just thought it was too far out and he didn't get it at all," says Fox), but the notion of it opened the dialogue on two collaborative possibilities for Björk's record: Fox as producer and the Art Ensemble of Chicago as contributing arrangers and performers. It wasn't long before Björk found herself posing the idea to Lake himself. "She actually called the label to get in touch with the World Saxophone Quartet about appearing on her first CD," Lake says. "When we were approached with that, none of the group had heard of her. We gave her some price and her manager thought it was ridiculous.

"Then they called me and asked if I would possibly do the arrangements using some [session] saxophonists in London," he says. "I said sure. I wasn't at all aware of her, but I like to write music and I like different challenges . . . for me it was a challenge to write arrangements with someone doing a different style of music than what I'm known for doing."

Thrilled with the compromise, Björk sent Lake a copy of her early Icelandic demos to use as a reference point. Lake wasn't sure what to make of the arrangements until Björk called him up one night and explained what she was after. "From that point I started putting it together," he says. "It wasn't so much me hearing it in my head, it was more of me listening to the tapes that she had sent and me trying to arrange it. Instead of it being a saxophone quartet, it was going to be a saxophone trio, so it was me and two other saxophonists in London."

Lake's ensuing encounters with Björk revealed her to be a simultaneously steadfast and gracious collaborator. She would not compromise certain elements of her visions for the songs, but within that designated space she granted Lake the creative leeway to come up with whatever arrangement pleased him most. The democratic give-and-take of their relationship endeared Björk to Lake, and he worked around the clock to come up with satisfactory results. "I was engrossed in hoping to come up with arrangements that she liked, so that was where most of my thoughts were," he says. "She was a very different stylist and that was very interesting to me. That she had even thought of having the World Saxophone Quartet on her CD and had the following that she has for a pop singer — that automatically made her different from everybody else."

Björk loved the outcome — the off-kilter, seasick sway of Lake's vanguard arrangements had cast both "Aeroplane" and "The Anchor Song" into far riskier terrain. There was something potentially polarizing about both tracks that appealed to her. She still didn't have a stated blueprint for how this record should sound, but what they'd done felt too gloriously uncertain to be wrong.

"I was pretty familiar with the World Saxophone Quartet and it was a big thrill to get Oliver Lake, but it did sound like a very odd combination," Massey agrees. "I kind of felt like there was a period of trying to find your ground with what was going on . . . it was very experimental."

Things were falling into place; Björk's disparate collaborations suddenly seemed to be gelling into a more uniform whole. Her relationship with Fox, meanwhile, was still strong, and Elektra A&R rep Howard Thompson had began to tender the idea that they work together for the record. This was setting up to be the likelihood until one day when, through her boyfriend Dom, Björk met producer Nellee Hooper. Best known for his involvement with Soul II Soul and Massive Attack, Hooper had typically aligned himself with artists too credible to be considered truly mainstream, but too glossy to be considered truly experimental. Björk knew this, and was skeptical.

"I was a bit suspicious to begin with," she said later that year. "I had to ask what he had done. I like Soul II Soul, but mainly when they're on the radio. Myself, I like to go out and dance to hardcore or industrial techno, hard beats with an experimental edge. I thought Nellee was too "good taste" for my liking. But then I met him, got to know him, [and] got to hear about his fabulous ideas. . . ."

Björk had never intended to settle with just one producer; one of the early concepts for *Debut* actually had her working with a new producer for each track. But after extended discussions with Hooper revealed very similar attitudes and philosophies, she jumped at the opportunity to work with him. Hooper would be the first of a select group of people whom Björk would speak of with a loving, almost intimate, reverence.

"[Nellee] turned out to be this really exciting, open-minded guy who was on exactly the same trip as I was," she gushed. "Fuck styles, fuck categories – take risks, try anything. We basically just didn't want to make an album that had been made before; it was just by chance that he was the producer and I was the singer songwriter, or whatever you'd call it. It was more about our musical relationship, which was a very, very magical one. I guess it was a bit of a musical love affair between Nellee and me."

As their creative relationship blossomed, it became more and more evident that *Debut* was meant to be Björk and Nellee's honeymoon alone. It became clear to her that the record she really wanted to make was the one she could make with him, and Björk found herself in the unenviable position of having to break off commitments with others. It was a task that she performed with grace and sensitivity.

Fox received a phone call from her soon after. "She said, 'You know, Nellee and I just have this really special thing that we're doing and it looks like I don't know who else I'm going to work with, but I'm definitely going to be doing most of it with Nellee. I hope you understand that,' and I said, 'Absolutely,'" he recalls. "Sometimes a collaboration is so intimate and so intense, it's almost like you become married . . . I thought that she was incredibly adult about [the Nellee situation] and very professional, forthright. She just dealt with it."

"When you were amongst it, there was quite a lot of stuff coming in at all angles," Massey adds. "The harp tunes, the saxophone stuff, and then when she started working with Nellee, the more dub-oriented stuff. It became an odd mix. I know I've been in situations where you're just sort of writing stuff and you leave other stuff behind. I think it turned more into the Nellee record as it went on.

"I guess it was a timing thing," he continues. "She moved to London and was staying at a flat there. Dom was in London, Nellee was quite a good friend of Dom's, and it became her London family. I was still in Manchester and pretty full-on busy with what was going on. I met Nellee at that point. Björk was very considerate of the situation and just said, 'do you mind if I carry on doing this?' She was just in the flow of doing stuff, so it's not like I could say 'wait for me' because I was busy as hell. But we always had this understanding that work would be ongoing."

In the same way that a freshly formed couple might spend the majority of their waking hours together in bed, Björk and Hooper spent countless hours united in the studio. Giddy with the rush of discovery and the newfound promise that lay ahead, Björk felt like this was it; the remaining piece of the puzzle that she had long been waiting for had finally arrived.

*Debut* was completed in early 1993 with all of Björk's impulsive sidebars and collaborative doodlings seamlessly incorporated into the mix. Much of the joy from the ensuing sessions came from the way in which Hooper and Björk had managed to rectify her various creative dalliances into one cohesive whole. From the atonal, tribal rumble of lead single "Human Behaviour" to the gorgeous chimes of "Like Someone in Love," through to the four-on-the-floor technoisms of "Big Time Sensuality," it all amounted to an unapologetically chancy opening salvo.

Having benefited greatly from their numerous reworkings, both "Aeroplane" and "The Anchor Song" had made the album's final cut. Björk also wrote a final batch of songs in the studio near the album's completion, with Hooper's presence and uncommonly high standard as her motivating force. These songs (with eventual singles "Venus as a Boy" and "Big Time Sensuality" among them) infused *Debut* with a very healthy sense of the present, something sorely needed in order to fulfill the album's sense of travel and trajectory.

The prerequisite for any classic album is that each of its songs should contribute to some larger picture in a unique and singular fashion, fostering unity while avoiding redundancy. Within this criterion, *Debut* is perhaps still Björk's finest album to date. Equal parts electronic and organic, joyful and melancholic, London and Reykjavik, wow and flutter, it marked a startling, perfectly formed declaration of intent, a brilliantly molded snapshot of circumstance. Like Björk herself, it was a successful marriage of seemingly incongruous forms and philosophies into something complete, vibrant, and whole.

*Debut*'s emotional breadth rendered most of the other albums from that period strangely one-dimensional. Where many of Björk's contemporaries were sanctimoniously purporting to be dealing with the stuff of everyday life while actually retreading the same tired circles, here was a record that actually followed through on its promise. Strong, wistful, celebratory, vulnerable, wintry, solemn, sexual, melancholic, hopeful: very few albums made during the 1990s that can rightfully lay claim to this range of descriptors. Better yet was how accessible it remained. Unintentionally, Björk had birthed a rare bird — a pop record that united all factions.

"I think pop music has betrayed us," she declared. "Everybody in the world needs pop music, just like they need politics, their pay, and oxygen to breathe. The problem is that too many people dismiss pop as crap because nobody has had the courage to make pop that's relevant to the modern world. Pop music has become so stagnant. This is really a paradox because it should change and evolve every day. I don't think anybody has made a decent pop album in years.

"I want this album to be pop music that everybody can listen to. I think not sticking to any particular musical style makes the album real. Life isn't always the same. You don't live in the same style from day to day, unexpected things happen that are beyond your control. That's this record. One song is about the mood you're in walking to the corner shop, another is about being drunk and out of it on drugs in a club, and the next one is about feeling romantic and making love."

*Debut* also benefited from some fortuitous timing. With dance still only on the cusp of mainstream acceptance and the rest of pop music in the throes of an abusive love affair with the nihilistic, joyless strains of grunge, a gaping void remained. "It just has to be there at the right time in the right place," agrees Netty Walker. "This is what *Debut* was and it exploded because of that. Of everyone who listened to it, some people would say, 'Oh I hate that song but I love that song' — it was like everyone seemed to be able to find one song on the album that they really liked. But they found the album itself quite confusing in some ways because they couldn't love it all. That's great, because life's like that — you can't like all of it."

The blueprint redrawn by MTV in the early '80s meant that artists no longer had the luxury of hiding behind their recorded material; in an increasingly image-conscious media, synthesis of style was proving just as important. Newly untethered by the Sugarcubes' prefab image as peddlers of pop cliché, Björk seized upon her solo career as an opportunity to redefine her brand, and in the process revealed herself to be more canny and media-savvy than anyone had imagined.

Shot by photographer Jean Baptiste Mondino and designed by design group Me Company, *Debut*'s sparkling, pinkish-gray cover marked the beginnings of Björk's self-fashioned, celestial aura. With tousled hair, an imploring gaze, prayerful hands pressed again her mouth and synthetic teardrops bubbling under her eyes, this cover depicted Björk as Bohemian, soulful, and star-touched. Madonna had long ago consorted with high fashion and artfulness in efforts to prolong her career; in her own, less insidious way, Björk revealed signs that she was learning to do the same. Where some music purists might have rejected this part of the job, Björk — ever the aesthete — embraced it through and through. Every artistic detail became an opportunity, a vehicle for collaboration, creation, and discovery.

"She knows exactly what imagery fits the music that she's producing at the time and how she wants to present it as an entire package," Walker says. "She was very careful about what she wanted to present [and] who she wanted to collaborate with. She would find designers who hadn't made anything big, like Hussein Chayalan. She was always looking for discoveries, I think. She's like a collector — out there looking for things all the time."

Although he's now commonly regarded as one of the industry's most pioneering music video directors, France-born Michel Gondry had a comparatively scant résumé when Björk first contacted him in 1993. Ever the talent scout, she'd seen an obscure video he'd done for his own band, Oui Oui, and was interested in meeting up to discuss the possibility of working together on the video for "Human Behaviour." "She was really excited by a lot of things in the same way I was," Gondry says. "Our conversation went very fast [about] all the little details we like . . . I think she was the first one to really understand and love and share my sense of humor."

Gondry's video reels for Oui Oui belied a cartoony surrealistic streak that clicked with Björk. The pair arranged to have lunch together and quickly fell into an instant rapport. "Our references came into the conversation very fast — how we liked certain types of movies, Eastern European animation films, a low tech and high tech combination, handmade stuff. It was very quick," he says. "I remember on the menu [there] was a wood imitation cover and she said 'I like this texture — I see myself in a house with this texture.' We talked a lot like that — detail by detail on her passion for the polar bear."

Their off-kilter, free associative encounter served as the inspiration for Gondry's proposed video treatment. When he braided Björk's ideas into some of his own concepts, they seemed to complement each other brilliantly. These initial sparks led to a mixed aesthetic-surrealistic treatment that involved a starlit forest, a log cabin, and an oversized rampaging teddy bear. "At that time I was really into this feeling of being in a little house in the forest near nature," Gondry says. "We reconstituted a forest or a little nature area on stage just by going into the garden and collecting grass, moss, branches, leaves. It all had this quality of [being] handmade because we were like tree people.

"It was the first time I had a decent budget to do a really original video," he continues. "When I proposed the storyboard to her and she really liked it, I thought, 'Oh my God, she spent all this money on a disaster.' I thought that nobody would like the video – it would be too bizarre, too naïve, too something . . . I didn't know this video would be popular like it was and it would actually be a new start."

Netty Walker was still working for One Little Indian as Derek Birkett's personal assistant when *Debut* first hit stores. She fondly relays how, on the eve of its release, the label had budgeted for the album to sell a total of 40,000 copies worldwide – a figure they arrived at by estimating the Sugarcubes' total fanbase at the time. It's an anecdote that neatly sums up the modest expectations surrounding the album.

Nobody in Björk's camp was at all prepared for what was about to happen.

# five

Buoyed by significant word of mouth and rave reviews, *Debut* sold upwards of 600,000 copies worldwide within the first three months of its release in July 1993. "It just went out the door," sighs Netty Walker. "It was a little bit tentative and then within a month it was, 'We want *more*!' The hardest part was we never got radio play. Radio wouldn't come on board in England — it took until 'Big Time Sensuality' was released for Radio 1 to pick it up, and it's quite hard to promote an album without any of that. We organized a couple of festival shows as sort of runners-up to doing any touring."

Such massive sales straight out of the gate evidently caught Björk's entire camp off guard. It showed: she didn't have a backing band yet, much less any concrete touring agenda. In an effort to maintain the album's momentum, One Little Indian shifted their focus to press and public relations. With hundreds of interviews suddenly staring her in the face and nobody else to pass them off to, Björk realized that she was going to have to be careful about what she was willing to reveal. She discussed the situation with lone One Little Indian PR representative Christina Kyriacou and set about establishing boundaries and guidelines for press requirements.

"She trusted Christina," Walker says. "Christina was a consummate professional about what they picked, but Björk had a very defined idea of how she wanted

*Taken from one of Björk's first promotional photo shoots as a solo artist in late 1992. (Cathrine Wessel/Corbis Outline/Magma)*

to look and how she wanted to present herself. She had realized over the years that she had to leave some of her private self tucked away. It's very easy in interviews to give all of yourself to everybody all the time [but] then there's nothing left. I think, with the photos that she wanted, the way she wanted to present herself, she could at least have a separate person from herself to an extent. Then again, Björk puts 150% of herself into every single thing she does, she just keeps going and she tends not to say no to some things so she gets exhausted by it all."

With this first round of interviews began Björk's paradoxical, often complicated relationship with the press. Her hyperexaggerated, unorthodox personality interested a slightly repressed, fastidiously jaded media. Everything about her was unique and therefore (at first, anyways) invulnerable to journalistic stereotyping; much like her music, the task of reconciling Björk's personality was proving an appealing challenge.

The mainstream media's initial reaction to Björk was mainly one of gawk-eyed celebration. Nearly every new story paraded her otherness, lionized her differences, and positioned her as an outsider operating as a slave to her ever-changing emotional state. Björk had endeared herself to the media in the same way that she'd done with her friends. In turn, the press seemed instinctually protective of her childlike tendencies.

"You get the visual impression immediately," Walker explains. "I know there's quite a few guys that have said it, it's [like] they always want to hug her and protect her. You get the same sort of motherly feeling as a female, [of] wanting to look after her. . . .

"You know the way that you stand and talk to someone you don't really know there's usually quite a distance between you?" Walker continues. "She's actually in your space when she talks to you, so you can't get away from it. She has a knack of becoming very Icelandic in her accent and everything. It's very sweet and very coy and almost like this adult child."

It's a perception that Björk was initially complicit in creating. In her innocent way, she aided the exaggeration of her persona by playing up her status as exotic, punky, and extraterrestrial. After all, still only a year removed from her days in Iceland, Björk was herself engaged in the process of self-definition; this call-and-response was just as crucial to her own private identity search as it was to her public image. The caricature of Björk as breathless, wondrous elf began here.

*Debut* was well on its way to becoming an established success by the time Björk played her first proper solo gig in August 1993. Without the benefit of much rehearsal time or a well-practiced backing band, this first London gig was tenuous at best. But even when things weren't translating properly on stage, there was a prevailing sense that she was on the verge of tapping into something. "People were curious," recalls Árni Matthíasson, who was in attendance that night. "It wasn't really working, but it sounded okay and it was interesting. The feeling you got in the U.K. was that she was becoming this cultural icon; she was on to something."

Some festival gigs followed that summer, and by the autumn of 1993, Björk set out to assemble a proper touring band. Rather than trying to faithfully replicate *Debut* in a live environment, she veered off in another more human, organic direction. Inspired by London's bustling multiculturalism, she recruited a hugely disparate band of players: among them were Indian-born percussionist Talvin Singh (who had supplied string arrangements for "Venus as a Boy"), Turkish drummer Tansay Omar, Caribbean bassist Ike Leo, and transplanted Iranian (and keyboard hobbyist) Leila Arab.

In certain instances, Björk's selection process had conformed with her punk ideology: the overall mix and spirit of the band were just as important to her as their overall level of musicianship. Björk discovered Arab through mutual friends, and while Arab wasn't at all confident in her own abilities as a keyboardist, Björk had specifically insisted on a female keyboard player. Barely concerned with Arab's protestations to the contrary, Björk implored her to give it a whirl. "The first time I spoke to her I was kind of like, 'Look, I'm not being rude, but I think you've made a mistake. I can't read music, I can't write it, and I've been studying film and media studies,'" Arab laughs. "And she was like, 'No, no, no, it's fine, come to the audition!'"

Veteran keyboardist and programmer Guy Sigsworth was already in the band, so Björk promised Arab that she'd leave the difficult stuff to him. "When I went to meet her for the first time, I can't really remember even playing much," Arab says. "On the way home in the taxi I kind of turned to my friend and I was like, 'So what just happened? Have I got a job?' And she said, 'Yeah, I think so.'"

Establishing this sense of family was still critical to Björk — by surrounding herself with friends, or people she thought could become friends, she was reconstructing elements of the Sugarcubes' dynamic. Something in Arab's personality had attracted Björk; despite Arab's limitations, Björk knew that she wanted her along for the ride, just to share in the fun.

Although they were quite clearly Björk's Backing Band, Arab says she never felt that split — there was a unity among everyone that Björk went out of her way to foster. "She would travel with us, she'd be in the same hotels with us, you fuck up [and] it wouldn't be a big deal," she explains. "It *is* a big deal because it was her first solo tour. She could have been really up her own ass about it all, but she was just incredibly gracious with a load of people she didn't know very well at all."

Dauntingly, their second gig as a full band was at London's massive Wembley Stadium. In spite of the magnitude of the event, Arab recalls feeling oddly protected by Björk's commanding presence. "She's such an enormous creative energy that when you are on stage with her, your fear disperses because you know you could all fall off stage and she would carry on and be able to hold it," she says. "With her in front, the barrier is just incredible because you just don't feel any of the fear. If you had said to me, 'Oh your second gig in public will be in Wembley Stadium,' I would have shot myself before the gig. But it doesn't work like that because she just carries the weight so well and so graciously. It just becomes easy."

Walker's best memories of the *Debut* tour relate to Björk's singular way with communication. One rehearsal, while at a loss trying to describe a problem with the mix to the sound engineer, she reverted to a string of Björkisms. "'Can you make it a bit more angular?' Or, 'Can I have it a bit more pink and fluffy?'" Walker recalls Björk saying. "The first time she says that to describe things to people it's sort of, 'What's she on about?' And then you start understanding and you think, 'Yeah, that's right, that's *exactly* what it is, it's more angular.' It was beautiful — I loved it because I had loads of pictures running around in my head all the time."

As the tour continued on through Europe and then eventually to America, there seemed to be no end in sight to the mounting pressures. By December 1993, Björk started to feel the strain incurred from the rigorous demands of her schedule. Although *Debut* had already sold upwards of a million copies worldwide and had been out for six months, Björk's star was still very much on the rise. She was in the midst of crossing over from indie music pin-up to international star, and the pressure of maintaining this momentum while staying creative and keeping in contact with Dom and Sindri proved challenging. Eager to please, and certainly victim to her over-ambition, Björk was suddenly in danger of spreading herself too thin.

"When it started exploding it was like everybody in the world wanted her to talk

*Months after Debut was released, Björk bravely opened the Wembley Arena date for U2's Zooropa Tour — it was only her second proper show. Lack of rehearsal time and broken monitors made this an extremely frustrating gig. (Photos by Björg Sveinsdóttir)*

to them," says Walker, who had quit One Little Indian at the end of 1993 to become Björk's manager. "We tried to do press conferences or whatever to make it easier. Dom was looking after Sindri and being at home — a bit like a house-husband — and it was sort of working, but it was strained because I don't think the stimulation was there. She was realizing that she was going to have to change some things to make it work for her."

Björk's displacement from her home in London had exposed a cruel reality about her relationship with Dom — things between the two of them were no longer working. "When things do go wrong she chews over it for a long time and makes decisions and then tries to work out how to make the split amicable," Walker says. "You always want to leave some good karma. But she was tired, she toured; it was all rehearsals, getting a band together, trying to keep everything going and she was already talking about her next album. The pressure was always there. . . . I know it was very emotional for her with Dominic and I know it was really, really hard for him."

Much of the residual pressure was self-inflicted, the direct result of Björk's own desire and her inability to say no. Her stubborn, unyielding vision for how things should be meant that she had a much closer involvement in her day-to-day goings-on than other artists might. It gave her more control over various dealings, but it also left her with more to worry over. Walker cites tour planning as a perfect example of this recurring syndrome: "When it comes to touring, Björk wants to go to certain places; she *doesn't* want to go to Germany. 'Why does she have to go back to Scandinavia?' is [also] usually a question."

The many facets of her hyper-accentuated personality had become so widely documented that the music media were now responding very differently to Björk's international success. With overexposure threatening to turn Björk into a caricature, there was now a healthy dose of tempered cynicism in the stories being written about her. Journalists were asking different questions.

"At times she got really angry because they can be so obnoxious," Walker says. "I think she was beginning to realize that somehow it wasn't the Sugarcubes anymore – it was much, much bigger than that. Everyone wanted to delve into her private life – it was beginning to invade everything – and she had to try and get some distance back. She was emotionally drained, you don't get any answers out of her, she had to take a break at that point."

Besieged by stress and fed up with finding new ways to answer the same questions, Björk cancelled a bout of press interviews, citing exhaustion. "It was alright the first six months; seven months was a bit tricky; eight months was when I started hitting people," Björk said. "I've been telling this hideously pathetic, stupid joke that the Bible in England is different. God created the world in one day and then he talked about it for eight days."

Björk left music school at 15 years old partly because she resented being forced to endlessly dissect music. After months and months of press, she found the same resentment creeping in again. "If you went out somewhere and had a really good time, you don't wake up the next morning and try to figure out *why* you did," she said. "It's not *because* of anything. It's just the atmosphere, the people, the chemistry of friends, your mood, what happened before, what will happen after. And you can't explain it, and I don't understand why you should. And it's the same with songs."

The resulting disillusion was leading to a minor crisis. Frazzled, she responded to the overwhelming hype by questioning everything, including the quality of her album and the sincerity of the ensuing critical acclaim." If I'd delivered exactly the same album and I came from Nottingham," she mused, "I'd have got completely different reviews, normal, down-to-earth ones.

"This record was a bit of a rehearsal and it's really not that good. I can do much better."

Ironically, Björk's decline in motivation and desperate need for new energy was coinciding with her most successful single yet. More overtly accessible than "Human

Behaviour" or "Venus as a Boy," the straightforward techno-stomp of "Big Time Sensuality" had found a permanent home on mainstream radio and television stations worldwide. Although less ornate than her previous singles, "Big Time Sensuality" had the spirit of Björk's emotional candor embedded within it.

"I've got a lot of courage, but I've also got a lot of fear," she explained. "You should allow yourself to be scared. It's one of the prime emotions. You might almost enjoy it, funny as it sounds, and find that you can get over it and deal with it. If you ignore these things, you miss so much. But when you want to enjoy something, especially when it's something you've just been introduced to, you've got to have a lot of courage to do it. I don't think I'm more courageous than most people. I'm an even mixture of all those prime emotions."

Resigned to the realization that *Debut* still had life left in it, Björk took a brief rest after completing the year's remaining tour obligations. She finished 1993 exhausted, but overall she was content and deeply grateful, still able to keep things in perspective. "I don't believe in astrology, but if it works, it was probably written in my map that '93 was going to be a good year," she said in December. "The whole thing has been so effortless for me. At the same time, I realize that it was something I've been preparing for unconsciously for 10 years, so it's not just come out like that. But it's been 10 times better than I ever thought."

The first months of 1994 yielded a mixed bag of surprises. Following the receipt of two awards from the *NME* for Best Solo Artist and Best Album, Björk enjoyed a bit of a coming-out party at the high-profile Brit Awards in February. In addition to unexpectedly scooping trophies for Best Newcomer and Best International Female, she performed The Rolling Stones' canonized "Satisfaction" alongside another rising female star, PJ Harvey. Many artists had specifically requested to sing with Björk at the awards, but Harvey was the only one that Björk herself had requested.

The visceral thrill of the pair's unlikely union was quickly overshadowed by how well it actually did work. With only PJ's sludgy power chords as backing, the pair lay claim to the song's pangs of frustration and recast them as sexual liberation. Their joyousness in singing those words translated into a feminist act, a subversion of the notion that feminism is equal to attaining dominance over desire.

Björk's curled yelps didn't seem out of place stationed alongside Harvey's low moan and soiled guitar work. Although she fumbled for the words in spots, it was obvious that she was (as ever) singing in the moment, savoring the song. There, on stage, it became abundantly clear that this bask was not solely transmitted by her voice, but through her entire persona.

This performance fed into ongoing public discourse of Björk as anti-feminist feminist figure, a notion which a later *Q* cover appearance alongside kindred spirits

*Björk caps off a memorable Brit Awards by growling her way through a grimy rendition of The Rolling Stones' "Satisfaction." sung with friend PJ Harvey. (Marshall John/Corbis Sygma/Magma)*

Harvey and Tori Amos (along with the headline "Hips! Tits! Lips! Power!") cemented. Rather than disown anything, Björk openly vocalized her every aspect on *Debut*: emotion, vulnerability, independence, sexuality. Björk had unwittingly come to represent a sort of political ideal by totally embracing herself without ever trying to justify her subject matter within the framework of the standard feminist ideology. It's an attitude that she traces back to the ideological clashes she had with her mother as a child. "She wouldn't even go into the kitchen, silly things like that," she recalled of Hildur in 1995. "But I do appreciate that the cage has been opened for my generation and all we've got to do is be active. It's quite easy for us. I don't have to be negative and paranoid — 'I'm in a cage. People are suppressing me.' For my generation to hear women say that, it's like, 'Please! Get a life.' That's what I used to think about my mum."

The afterglow of the Brit Awards triumph didn't last long. A mere three days after her surprise victory, reports surfaced that Björk was being sued by Simon Fisher (stage name Simon Lovejoy), a British musician with whom she'd briefly collaborated in early 1990. Fisher's suit sought damages in excess of £200,000, and contended that he'd had a hand in co-authoring "Human Behaviour," "Venus as a Boy," "Crying," and "Aeroplane." While the case wouldn't go to court for over a year, Fisher's baseless accusation went against an inherent trust that Björk placed in her collaborators. It quickly became a nagging source of stress. "It was constantly at the back of her mind that someone was trying to say 'I did that,'" Walker says. "To say that they had written part of any of Björk's songs to the extent they were claiming, especially when one part of it was actually a sample by Quincy Jones . . . it was sort of, 'Who is this guy, why is he doing it?' [Simon] was on legal aid, so it was all free for him and she was financially getting drained. Derek was backing her all the way, but she had to go into court, she had to sit with musicologists day in and day out. She was trying to get on and do the next album and it was something that kept coming up."

Her plans for a *Debut* remix record had been temporarily shelved, but a handful of London shows (including a pair of seated and standing gigs promoted, respectively, as Björk in Seats and Björk on Legs) and the release of *Debut*'s fourth single ("Violently Happy") soon followed. With Björk back in London and the Brit Award triumph still fresh in the media's mind, public interest in her private life intensified further. By March, the story of her split with Thrupp had broken, complete with accompanying details of a new love.

Parisian native Stephane Sednaoui was a flamboyant and arty photographer/video director whom Björk first met in New York, where he was directing her video for "Big Time Sensuality." Once Thrupp was out of the picture, their friendship developed into an intense relationship. "It was sort of an explosion of two people," Walker says. "Very passionate to start off with. It was very intimate because of the things that Stephane was doing. It sort of worked for quite a while. . . ."

Their relationship was intense and mutually creative, with art always at the center of their focus. The nature of their professions precluded the couple from seeing each other as often as they would have liked, so to compensate they devised ideas for projects that they could work on together. In addition to compiling and directing *Vessel*, Björk's first live concert video release, Sednaoui frequently photographed Björk. The most famous of his pictures appears on the cover of her second album, *Post*.

A round of summer festival appearances began that June. One of the highlights saw Björk dropped via parachute onto a Reykjavik festival ground to perform in commemoration of Iceland's 50th year of independence. She sang her entire set in Icelandic, but the new songs were unmistakable; the long-shelved "Army of Me" and "The Modern Things" were finally getting their due.

The desultory theme to Björk's professional career had become second nature by now. As if constructing *Vessel*, composing songs for *Post*, touring, and continuing to fulfill press obligations wasn't enough, there were constantly other things to worry about. Björk's increased profile had encouraged a variety of weird and wonderful offers from around the world, each one requesting her co-operation in some fashion. Song requests, remix jobs, and ad pitches were pouring into the One Little Indian office at an alarming rate; there was barely time to read them all, much less respond appropriately. "There was just piles of it that you had to say, 'I'm really sorry but we can't do anything at the moment' sort of thing," Walker says. "And in amongst the pile would be a little gem which you would then contact the person and apologize [for not being able to do]."

While the sheer breadth of opportunities must have been tempting, Björk was adamantly against lending her name to anything that might have compromised her stature. "Point of principle for the Sugarcubes and for Björk was not to do anything that was commercial, and particularly not to endorse anything," Walker says. "This is why they never went to South America straight off because the only way of touring there was to actually take on sponsorship. She didn't want to be sold as someone who was branding things."

Of the few offers that were too flattering to refuse, the most outrageous came in the form of a song request from none other than Madonna. Again looking to change direction after 1992's disappointing *Erotica*, Madge had reportedly turned to *Debut* for inspiration or (perhaps less graciously) direction. Madonna had already enlisted both Hooper and Marius De Vries to contribute to her new album; now, she used these connections to make contact with Björk. "Like attracts like in lots of ways," Walker offers. "Musicians attract other musicians and it becomes sort of incestuous at certain points. I used to sort of stand back from it and say, 'You all live on a completely different planet from the rest of us.'"

Björk didn't consider herself a fan of Madonna's music, but she was intrigued by the offer nonetheless, if not a little intimidated. "Whatever anyone says about Madonna, she is someone who just evolves with the changes and controls what she wants to be and how she wants to present herself, but on such a major scale," Walker says. "I think Björk recognizes some elements of that and is in awe of it to a point because she knows that Madonna's never completely sold out — she's still in control of what she wants to do . . . constantly changing, and I think there's an element of Björk that is constantly changing. She was enormously flattered."

Björk figured the opportunity to have her words coming from Madonna's lips was too good to pass up, and so she gamely penned the lyrics for "Let's Get Unconscious" with Madonna specifically in mind. The resulting lyric ("Today is the last day / that I'm using words / they've gone out / lost their meaning / don't function anymore") were borne out of Björk's own criticism of Madonna's aesthetic. "When I was offered to write a song for her, I couldn't really picture me doing a song that would suit her," she said. "But on second thought, I decided to do this to write the things I've always wanted to hear her say that she's never said."

She offered the song in demo form to Hooper and De Vries, who rearranged the composition significantly enough that all three ended up splitting the co-writer credits. Renamed "Bedtime Story" and released as the third single from the accompanying album *Bedtime Stories*, it was not the breakthrough that Madonna was looking for. In fact, it was her first single in years to fail to place somewhere within the American Top 40 chart.

Madonna wasn't bothered — although they still hadn't met, she continued after Björk, at one point requesting that she perform the song live with her at the 1995 Brit Awards. Put off and probably a little suspicious, the Icelandic politely declined. "I was supposed to get her personal number and call her up, but it just didn't feel right," Björk said. "I'd love to meet her accidentally, really drunk in a bar. It's just all that formality that confuses me."

The heaps of incoming offers weren't always related to music. No doubt spurred on by her ubiquity, producers and directors had begun to send in loads of scripts as well. Among the many offers that Björk rejected was a starring role in the film adaptation of cult comic *Tank Girl*. Someone had requested she take on the part of Jet Girl, Tank Girl's sidekick and faux-lesbian lover. Like all her acting offers, she very briefly mulled it over before wisely turning it down (the part was eventually taken by Naomi Watts).

Sometimes, Björk's personal artistic vision took precedence over the commitments she'd made to others. Italian filmmaker Bernardo Bertolucci had written to request original music for a forthcoming film of his named *Stealing Beauty*. Björk agreed and set to work on the tune soon after before promptly reneging. "We got as far as her putting a bit of a backing track down but then we were on tour in Asia for two months," Walker says. "She handwrote a fax, which I still have a copy of, to Bernardo because she'd realized that the music that she was creating she actually wanted to keep herself."

Perhaps, in an environment where everybody wanted a piece of her, a little selfishness was par for the course. "[She] was over-stretching herself, trying to do too many things at once, she was constantly like that," Walker says. "You get to a point — I do the same — [where you] try to do fifty things at once instead of five. She just couldn't fit things in so you would get halfway through the conversation and you'd be almost there on arrangements and everything else and then it would be, 'I'm too tired, I can't do it.'"

Inevitably, the residual problems stemming from Björk's serial careerism began to spill over into her personal life. Things with Sednaoui were strained; his sometimes volatile nature and the nagging distance between the two made it difficult to always come together. As Björk's manager, Walker often found herself brokering their fractured communication. "It was a dangerous position for me because on the management side of things you tend to get caught in the crossfire whether you want to be there or not, and somehow involved in something that you shouldn't really be involved in, but you can't really avoid it either because everyone talks to you."

Things with Björk and Sednaoui reached their boiling point by the summer of 1994, when their plans to vacation together coincided with work that Björk needed to do in order to properly plan and facilitate an appearance on *MTV Unplugged*. With nearly 30 musicians participating, the event had become an enormous ordeal; Björk was compromised between leaving the organizational work to Walker or staying behind and disappointing Sednaoui. "She really needed a break," Walker says. "I said, 'Look, Björk, just go have a great time, have a wonderful time,' but it was fraught because she knew she wanted to get these things underway.

"Stephane had other work pressures and then miscommunication happened. She was supposed to be somewhere and then she had another commitment that she really thought she had to make and he was upset."

Their busy schedules invited more botched attempts at getting in touch: a litany of missed phone calls, hurt feelings, and aborted flights ensued. "I can't remember how it worked," Walker sighs, "[but] I got this guy ranting down the phone at me going, 'She doesn't want to come and she doesn't care and blow this holiday!' and sort of being very French and very dramatic about the whole thing."

The incident marked the final nail in the coffin of their doomed relationship. Maddeningly, Björk quickly found herself under duress from the media. Whereas she'd perhaps been a little too earnest in discussing the details of previous relationships with the press, here were signs that she was learning to cope. "It's a secret," she said of the breakup. ". . . it just wasn't right, that's all."

Had it not been for the offer to film an *MTV Unplugged*, Björk likely would have started work on her second album right away. In the end, the opportunity was simply too good to pass up; the endless instrumental and rearranging possibilities were tantalizing.

"She looked at it and she said, 'Well, it's unplugged, so that means no electricity,'" Walker laughs. "Björk always got incredibly bored playing the same songs over and over again, so she'd throw an extra spanner in every now and again and change the song a bit to try to do something just to keep herself interested. *Unplugged* was like a real opportunity to say, 'Okay, let's strip everything away — how can I portray these songs completely acoustically?'"

The added exposure couldn't hurt, either. With six *MTV* Europe Video Award nominations recently lavished upon her and *Debut* certified gold (500,000 copies) in the U.S., things couldn't have been going better; not even resident MTV metalheads Beavis & Butthead could knock on the video for "Human Behaviour." Knowing that this would be her last gig before commencing work on *Post*, Björk decided to send *Debut* off in style.

"She'd seen something somewhere about a glass harmonica player, so we found a glass harmonica player," Walker says. "She wanted Oliver Lake over so we had to ring and court him. Then she wanted Corky [Hale] over . . ." Before long, the concept for the show had ballooned to include Evelyn Glennie, a deaf musician with whom Björk had begun to collaborate, Talvin Singh on various percussion instruments, and the whole of the South Bank Gamelan Orchestra.

"A huge challenge," Walker recalls. "But it was a fantastic experience, I loved it. I even ended up driving the van to pick the orchestra up and bringing them back to the studio, running backwards and forwards across London ferrying people about. . . . God knows how but it worked."

"When I saw how she put that show together . . ." Lake raves. "She surrounded those same tunes in very different ways and it was then I really realized how talented and creative she is as an artist. I realized it before, but this put the icing on the cake."

Filmed in England at Wembley's Lime Grove Studios, the *MTV Unplugged* experience had proven memorable for everyone involved, a total career benchmark. "There was one point in the rehearsal where she didn't want to sing because she wanted to have her voice for that night, so she got on stage with the Gamelan Orchestra and whistled," Lake laughs. "And the way she whistled, you thought it was a flute playing. I was blown away. I don't know if she's ever recorded herself whistling, but it's incredible!"

"All the orchestra was there, all the other musicians were set up and all happy," Walker remembers. "Björk whizzes in in the taxi ready to go and do the show, [and realizes] 'I haven't got my lucky shoes!' So I get this message — can I go and get them — and I'm like, 'Can I have a runner, can anyone run me over to Björk's house?' And we scream across the highway and all the way back up to Wembley.

"She put them on for the first number and then straight away just took them off and did the rest of the show," Walker laughs. "And I'm standing there absolutely exhausted and thinking, 'Okay, fine.'"

An unqualified success, this singular opportunity gave Björk the chance to put one final exclamation point on what had been a hugely successful year. Now, after 10 years spent creating *Debut,* it was finally time to look to the future.

# SIX

If the extended process of birthing *Debut* had been long and laborious, it was because that record had been analogous to Björk's much larger search for self through creative autonomy. It was just as much about exorcising the amassment of ideas from the past 10 years as it had been about realizing them. Newly unencumbered by any obligation to her past, she was now completely free to rummage around her present for new musical clues for her next album.

As a result, her vision for the album that would become *Post* was much more fully realized from inception. For starters, although she definitely wanted Nellee Hooper back in some capacity, Björk also knew that she needed to be more involved in the recording process. With a great deal of trepidation and doubt, she bravely considered producing the album herself.

This was an especially gutsy idea, considering how crucial Hooper had been to the *Debut* sessions. But just as Björk had learned to recognize and rely upon the intangible magic of true give-and-take collaboration, she had also learned to revere the importance of risk. Maintaining the status quo for fear of change was not an option. "With her, everything has a certain lifetime and once it's finished she seems to be very independent," Ásmundur Jónsson agrees. "Again, we come back to this attitude that was very much a part of the punk scene: take everything into your hands and do what you want to do. Of course the past is there, but she wants to go forward. It is very important for her to always be working on new developments or new music or creative things."

Björk expressed her designs to Hooper, who in turn encouraged her to produce the record herself with the caveat that he'd be willing to back her up if she ever felt in over her head. "That," Björk later said, "was the most generous offer anyone has ever made me."

It became apparent early on in the process that Björk would need Hooper along in some capacity; nonetheless, she remained insistent that he not be the record's only producer. "I think perhaps she felt that she still needed his support for some things as a bit of a lifeline," Netty Walker says. "But she was already evolving, working out her new ideas and plotting how she wanted to put it together musically. She must have had private conversations with Derek about collaborating with Nellee, but I have to say, she was insistent that she wanted to co-produce. He wouldn't be put down as the lone producer — it would be a co-production for her *and* Nellee.

"I think instinctively she knew that she couldn't stay with him through the next album. [*Post*] wasn't 10 years of things she'd accumulated, it was more immediate than that. To make it stay that fresh, she had to think about other people being involved."

For the first time, the task of negotiating with prospective collaborators was also proving to be something of a minefield. With Björk now a proven commercial commodity, the dirty issues of money and ego had become inextricably involved. "It becomes a bit of a business deal," Walker says. "Everyone wants a contract, everyone wants to make sure they're getting their money out of it. But that swamps you creatively because it's not about that, it's about whether the spark works for what you want to produce."

With Hooper on board, ostensibly as co-producer, Björk set about determining a locale. She knew that she wanted to commence work on the record almost immediately, and Hooper had a vague inclination to take the sessions somewhere exotic. After some deliberation, it was determined that they'd head to the Bahamas' legendary Compass Point Studios. "I can't remember why it was the Bahamas," Walker says. "I've got a feeling it was something to do with Nellee. Wacky idea. It also meant that they could have a bit of break in some ways and be away from England in a completely different environment."

Although it proved hugely expensive (with overall costs aggravated by Compass Point's dearth of dance-slanted recording equipment), the decision to record in the Bahamas furnished Björk with a vibrant new energy. Newly enamored of her picturesque surroundings, she encouraged any attempts to meld the recording process with their exotic natural environment. The tales surrounding these recording sessions are appropriately evocative.

"I'd have a very long lead on the microphone and a long lead on the headphones and I'd just sit there at midnight," Björk gushed. "All the stars would be out, and I'd be sitting there under a little bush. I'd go running into the water and nobody could see where I went. In the quiet bits, I'd sit and cuddle, and for the outrageous bits, I'd run around. It was the first time I'd done a song like that in about 20 years. I was crying my eyes out with joy, because it was something I so deeply wanted all those years. Almost like you had sex lots of times and it's gorgeous, and then you couldn't have it for 20 years, and then suddenly you have it." Many of those vocal cuts would make it onto the album, including Björk's awestruck performance on the shimmering "Cover Me," recorded entirely from a nearby cave.

A new record finally gave Björk the opportunity to resurrect the songs she had left over from her pre-*Debut* Manchester sessions with Graham Massey. Since both "Army of Me" and "The Modern Things" had become live staples over the summer, neither of them needed to go through any radical transformations at Compass Point. Massey remembers both songs being written quickly and not differing too drastically from their original demo form. "[With 'Army of Me'] we wanted to try something that was quite hard and techno-y," he says. "I'm not quite sure how she wrote those lyrics so fast but I remember that song being almost instantaneous. If you listen to the music, it is purely one sequence. It's very simple: one drumbeat, one sequence — the rest is like dressing on top. We kind of knocked that off in one day and then started on 'The Modern Things' the same day and finished that the next."

The eventual proliferation of warm, pastoral electronic music in the late '90s (think Boards of Canada) helped to shift the prevailing tendency away from thinking of anything computer-generated as cold, austere, or inhuman. In 1995, however, when the notion of electronic music as earth music was still comparatively alien, it seemed unorthodox for Björk to be playing with electronic elements — the stuff of science-fiction soundtracks, Kraftwerkian teutonics, and Orbital-style blippiness — and using them to express a closeness to nature.

In Björk's mind, the two sides should have never been deemed mutually exclusive to begin with; electronic music wasn't unnatural, people simply perceived it as such. "Electricity is not just a phenomenon of the 20th century," she said. "It's been around before us, it's like thunder and lightning. There is electricity inside us. With acupuncture you're putting a needle on the electrical current that travels in your nerves. Or you walk on a nylon carpet and it pops when you touch the wall. It's just in this century that they made that into audio. Now you can hear it. It's part of our lives.

"People always think the future is alien and cold," she continued. "Just before

Noah's flood they all said, 'The future is doomed, we're all doomed.' It's basically fear of change. People saying 'techno is cold' is rubbish. Since when do you expect the instruments you work with to deliver soul? You do music with computers and get a cold tune, that's because nobody put soul into it. You don't look at a guitar and say, 'Go on then, do a soulful tune.' You have to put soul into it yourself."

The constant interplay between synthetic and natural elements is something Björk frequently revisits — from different angles — in all of her music. On *Post*, this tension was achieved by braiding her bucolic lyrics with a tangle of largely programmed music. On its surface, *Post* is a litany of burbling bass lines, thumping loops, and chiming pads; but dig a little deeper and you'll hear Björk singing excitedly of mountains, forests, and caves. It's an ideological vision that still identifies as uniquely hers.

"She is very much a child of nature," Walker says. "I know when she goes back to Iceland she goes out in the wilderness and just walks. She told me that there's a little place that she goes to sometimes . . . it's out in what I would call the outback in central Iceland. She described it one time — you're on your own and there's nobody else anywhere around you and you can walk out the door and look at the sky and the stars and everything else. That feeling of knowing that you are alone, but *not* alone, and you can do anything you want in your head, create anything you want, imagine anything you want — she's great like that. She loves being near nature, the wind in your hair, the whole bit.

"In New Zealand we went down to the beach one day; Sindri was swimming in freezing ice-cold water and she was sitting on a rock composing. The sun started to fall with me and Sindri splashing about and she's just there, in the perfect environment, letting things flow."

Björk's creative streak did not diminish with the completion of these Bahamian sessions; new songs were still coming quickly and easily. Her yearly retreat to Reykjavik at Christmas, for example, yielded the beginnings of "Isobel"'s melody line, which she worked out and preserved on an old Casio keyboard before bringing it back to Hooper's studio.

Her new unions with other electronic luminaries were also bearing fruit. Intrigued by Tricky's work as a part of Bristolian beatmongers Massive Attack and later by his seminal slo-mo debut *Maxinquaye*, Björk had approached the electronic recusant in the hopes of coaxing him into a collaboration. Already a fan of Björk's voice, Tricky complied, albeit with one small condition. "The deal was that there's been no money exchanged," he said. "I said: 'If I put two tracks on your album, you give me two vocals for my album.' It's easier like that. When you've got to sort out deals before you work, you end up not working."

"He was getting a lot of pressure from his record company, because there was a real buzz about his album, so he was a bit naughty and escaped to Iceland," Björk explained. "We drove around in a four-wheel drive and saw the glaciers and swam in the hot springs."

Their meeting eventually produced *Post*'s two most extreme songs. On the hot side was "Enjoy," a spastic screamer with a crumpled bass line and a trumpet blast supplied by none other than old friend Einar Örn. On the chilly side was album finale "Headphones," a chiming, somnolent dip into Björk's heavy-lidded pre-dream state. Although written with Tricky, the song was actually conceived as an ode to Massey. "I went into my diary and found a complete lyric about receiving a compilation tape in the post from a friend. It's a very personal thing," Björk said. ". . . the lyric is a letter to that person. I had this idea to do a song that is like a worship of headphones. The chorus is 'My headphones saved my life, your tape lulled me to sleep.' All the noises in the song are just-for-headphones stereo tricks. It didn't need a lot of instruments. Tricky feels really strongly about noises and beats, and that is exactly my weakest point."

If she had so desired, Björk could have carved out an entire album solely from the material she'd recorded at Compass Point. But as she wrote new songs and listened to what she'd already recorded, she became convinced that the album wasn't yet complete. Once she returned to London, she started hunting for the missing elements.

"One day she rang up and said 'I want some bagpipes,'" Walker recalls. "I said 'Well, what kind of bagpipes are you thinking of? Gothic bagpipes, Scottish bagpipes, or sort of Irish/Indian pipes?'"

Björk wasn't sure.

"I'd say 'Well, what sort of sounds were the bagpipes?' and she'd make a sound down the phone and I'd think, 'Okay, that's an Uilleann piper. I'll make a judgment on that. Describe me a picture and then go and try and find something that fits. I think from there, pretty much everything changed."

It was a difficult admission to make, but the more she reworked her existing material, the more it became clear that she needed to return to London to regroup. She was nowhere near finished yet. "I was so disappointed," she lamented. "The album was supposed to be delivered the day after we returned, but I delayed and delayed. Everyone was going nuts. In the end, I decided to go and record several songs again, all over London. I went on my own, on a mission, basically taking the songs I'd done in the Bahamas and adding lots of live instruments. I just wanted to bring the album alive."

Björk enlisted the help of a new team of engineers and programmers and spent the next few months tweaking, rearranging, and sometimes completely rerecording her pre-existing tracks. She encouraged risks, pushed for more organic instrumentation, and sought to give her songs a deeper spatial quality. Mixer and sound collagist Markus

Dravs remembers getting the call to mix and refit a few songs, including "Cover Me."

"She was very keen for all the electronic noises to sound a bit like noises from a cave," he laughs. "She was trying to reflect that."

Ultimately, though, it was the inclusion of more "real" instruments that resuscitated *Post* for Björk. They created a proper balance between synthetic and organic that she hadn't quite found yet. "I still find it 10 times more natural for me to deal with live instruments than programmed ones because that's what I've been doing all my life," she said.

The most drastic facelift of them all had been administered to "I Miss You," an old song from the *Debut* era that, thanks to the input of aspiring programmer and Hooper protégé Howie Bernstein, had been transformed from an unassuming castaway into a Latin-tinged rhythmic monster. The song continued its evolution in London, where old standby Talvin Singh was drafted to record additional percussion parts for it. Along with the big band stomper "It's Oh So Quiet," "I Miss You" would be one of *Post*'s few full band moments.

Sometimes, Björk picked her collaborators out from obscurity, other times she plucked them right out of retirement. Brazilian composer Eumir Deodato had been shuttered away for years when Björk came looking for him. After hearing his room-shaking arrangements for a rare Milton Nascimento song called "Travessia," she'd sent her management team on a worldwide hunt to track the legendary Brazilian composer down. "You'll listen to it and go, 'Okay,'" Björk said of "Travessia." "Then after one year, it's your best friend; after two years you can't go a day without hearing it." Björk knew Deodato would be a perfect fit for her work, and wanted him to arrange strings for a few songs on *Post*.

Although his career saw him work with everyone from Frank Sinatra to Sarah Vaughan, Eumir Deodato was probably best known within the dance community for his contributions to Brazilian music. There was also the matter of his compelling funk arrangement of Richard Strauss' "Also Sprach Zarathustra" — the song that has become universally recognized as the theme to Stanley Kubrick's film *2001: A Space Odyssey*. He'd remained largely out of the public eye for a while, but his seeming inaccessibility had only furthered his legendary reputation.

In an effort to locate him, Walker sent phone calls whizzing all over South America. A trail of messages and phone numbers finally led her to his residence in — of all places — New Jersey. "He hadn't really been doing music for quite a long time — he'd been playing the stock markets," she recalls bemusedly. "He'd made some money, but he had not really found anything that inspired him enough [to work].

"He's an extremely charming man," Walker continues. "And I think he was charmed by Björk anyway . . . it was just so lovely to see someone go immediately, 'Yeah, I'd love to do it!' Björk was absolutely over the moon."

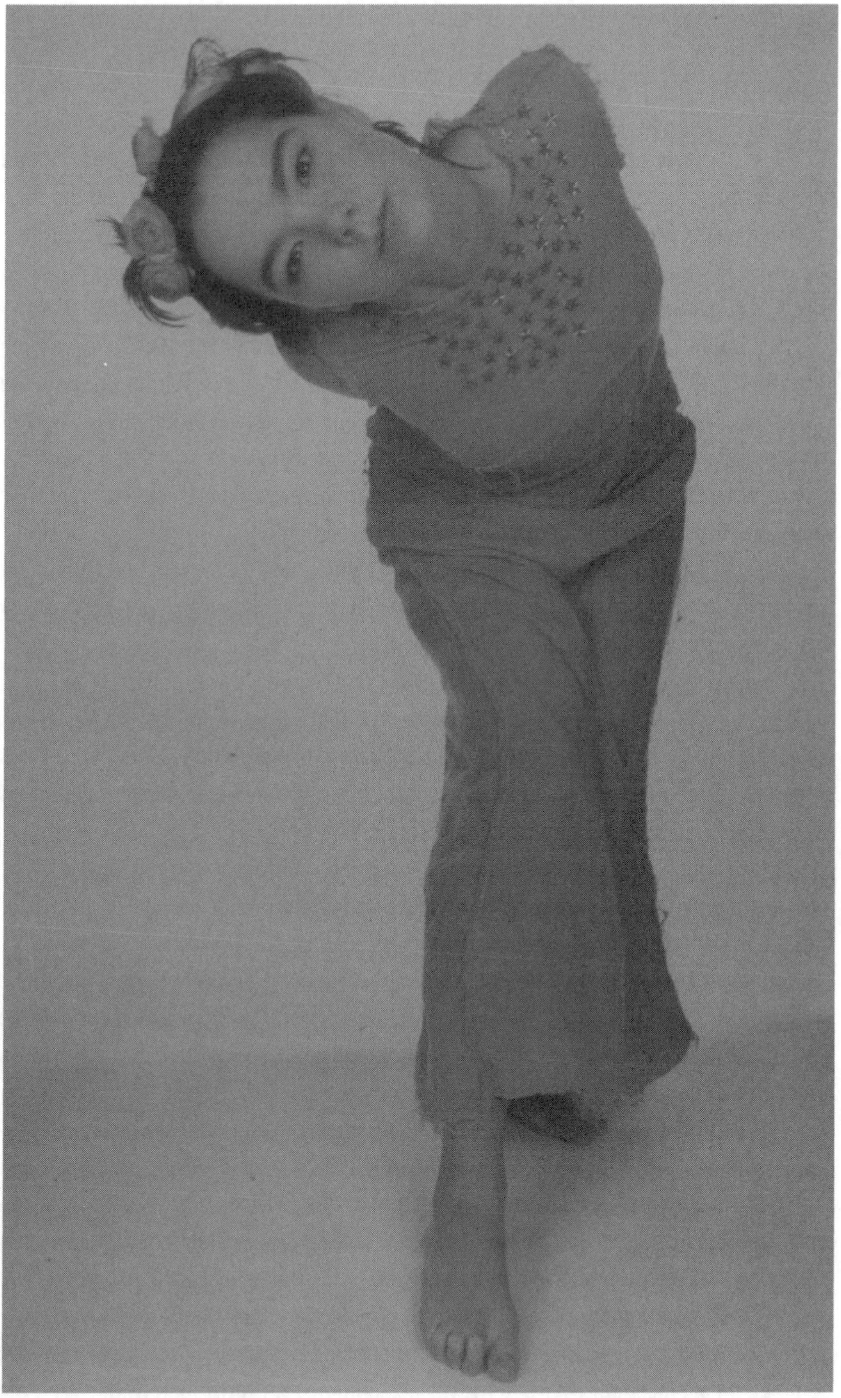

*Preparing to launch Post, late 1994. (Davies & Davies/Corbis Sygma/Magma)*

Deodato's presence as composer and conductor immediately bolstered "Hyper-ballad," "You've Been Flirting Again," and the driving "Isobel." With his input, the latter was transformed into a booming, cinematic fable; it's precisely the sort of arrangement that would serve as Björk's starting-off point for *Homogenic*.

The addition of various strings, brass, and percussion elements had imbued *Post* with the balance that Björk felt her original recordings had lacked. By the time the album was finished in April 1995, the list of co-producers included Björk, Hooper, Bernstein, Massey, and Tricky. First single "Army of Me" was released to radio shortly thereafter.

Björk had worked with a variety of different directors for the five *Debut* videos, and often with diminishing returns. For "Army of Me," she retreated back to the familiar warmth of Michel Gondry, who had begun to establish himself as one of MTV's brightest lights. The consummate surrealist, Gondry didn't disappoint with his new idea; he submitted a video treatment that involved a giant truck with teeth for an engine, a crazed gorilla dentist, an oversized diamond, and an explosive finale.

"When I did the storyboard, I was so sure and proud of myself," he laughs. "It was after a heavy night of drink and I was kind of in this state where you don't really care and you have no inhibitions in the world.

"I did the storyboard and I thought it was really funny. It was maybe eight pages of drawings with little stories — I remember I couldn't draw a proper monkey. I was in a hotel in Los Angeles so I had to fax her the storyboard and I was so sure I had something great that I was scared that somebody would shove a knife in my back on my way down to the office before I could fax it."

Björk adored the idea and instantly approved. As inscrutable as Gondry might have seemed to others, she felt an immediate connection to his ideas. Gondry attributes their successful working relationship to an unspoken mutual understanding: "Because I'm French, sometimes I don't get the meaning of all the lyrics," he says. "I reconstruct stories. If you take a sentence I [might] understand maybe three words, so I rebuild the story in my imagination and reconstruct the gaps, the bridges between those words.

"When people write lyrics, they do the same but the other way around. They don't write all their thoughts, they just take some of their thoughts and put them together. The gaps are what they are really feeling, but it's not written because if you write all your feelings then they become flat. Sometimes if I'm lucky, it matches even closer to what the person was feeling than the lyrics themselves."

By normal standards, there wasn't anything particularly offensive about the final "Army of Me" video, not even its concluding scene, which depicts Björk bombing an art museum where her lover lies comatose. Unfortunately, between the time that it was filmed and ultimately serviced to television stations, America's complexion had changed drastically. Timothy McVeigh's terrorist bombing of the Alfred P. Murrah Building in Oklahoma City had killed 168 civilians and injured over 500 others; right or wrong, national sensitivity to any similar imagery was at an unprecedented high. Out of respect to the issue, MTV pulled "Army of Me" from their playlist before they ever got a chance to air it.

All too used to dealing with the perplexing world of television standards, Walker was suitably nonplussed by the decision. "There's a whole criteria for video on MTV," she says. "No guns or replicating guns, no bombs, and no real overt violence, but it's a shifting thing because it's each individual's perception of what's going on in the video. It's very subjective and some things will slip through . . . but the next video down the line doesn't."

Gondry remembers being miffed by some of the glorious misinterpretations surrounding his seemingly innocuous clip. "Some people said to me it's like we were doing terrorism on modern art," he giggles. "Which never occurred to me, you know? To me, the bombing was one of those contrasting ideas – it's not like she's not with this guy and she has to wake him up so she becomes a terrorist for him. It was *funny* that to wake him up, she has to explode a bomb near his ear because he's so deeply asleep!

"I don't think there was any condescending thought [in it] about terrorism – it was too cartoonish and it had nothing to do with political elements."

The video would eke its way back into MTV's playlist within weeks, but the precedent had already been set; this foreshadowed a string of unlucky events that would further hinder *Post*'s unveiling.

Robin Rimbaud is a U.K.-based sound collagist who has built his entire career on reconstituting various lifted sound elements into his own ambient works. In fact, his alias, Scanner, is derived from his oft-stated penchant for "scanning" public airwaves for sample sources.

For whatever reason, Birkett and One Little Indian had failed to seek permission from Rimbaud for the use of a particularly prominent Scanner sample heard throughout "Possibly Maybe," a track on *Post*. Lifted from his 1994 album *Mass Observation*, the two-second sample in question (the droning, hollow sound of a ringtone connecting) had been looped for a significant portion of the song to form the rhythmic backbone to Björk's nimble lullaby.

In a 1995 *Melody Maker* interview, Rimbaud proclaimed himself a fan of Björk's and stressed that the recently announced threat of a lawsuit had been brought forth by his label New Electronica, and not directly by him. Nonetheless, he appeared to be sympathetic to the complaint. "If she'd contacted me two months ago and said 'Can I sample your track?,' I'm sure I'd have said, 'Yes.' I mean, I'm flattered," he said.

"But they have used rather a lot of my track – about two and a half minutes of it – and the whole rhythm of the track is based around the sample. That's why I can't help thinking that, if they did take it away, they wouldn't have much left!

"I spoke to Derek and I must say that he seemed like a very decent bloke," Rimbaud added. "He said to me, 'Well, what do we do? Do we have to destroy 750,000 albums over the weekend, or do I have to see you in court at dawn?'"

"He also said that they'd cleared 49 samples [for the forthcoming remix album *Telegram*]. I couldn't help thinking, 'Well why didn't you clear 50 then? If you cleared Quincy Jones, LFO, and Black Dog, then why not Scanner?' Really, in my heart of hearts, it's hard not to suspect that they just thought, 'Oh, he's an underground artist, he won't mind.' I really like this track, and I don't want them to have to destroy the records. It would just be nice to be credited for the work I've done, because samples are often credited on albums."

Rimbaud held an impromptu press conference the following week – the day after *Post*'s release – which Birkett also attended. The disagreement was heating up, and both factions appeared to be at an impasse; New Electronica had refused Birkett's compensatory offer of £1,000 (his standard sample clearance rate) and demanded that Rimbaud be awarded a much more lucrative co-songwriter credit instead.

With a standoff on the horizon, Birkett and Björk decided to officially delete and recall the existing version of *Post* upon release. Unfortunately, this move was mere damage control – over 100,000 copies had already been printed and shipped to retailers, who were, quite reasonably, selling them by the bucketload.

The looming cost of remixing, remastering, and reprinting a new version of the album (not to mention the potential losses incurred by destroying the originals) promised to be enormous, but Birkett felt it was the best available option. While he assumed full responsibility for the mix-up ("[Björk] declared the sample to me in December, and it's only because of my negligence that this happened"), he stuck to his principles nonetheless. "Philosophically and morally, I have an enormous problem with paying royalties on samples," Birkett said during the press conference. "In all the adventures I've had in the land of sampling, the general rule of thumb is that you pay what it would have cost you to create that sound in the studio."

"I just wonder what would happen if the situation was reversed – if I sampled somebody like Michael Jackson, Björk, or George Michael," Rimbaud countered. "I'm sure that within 24 hours somebody would be down on me to say, 'This isn't right.' I've spoken to Derek twice, and both time he's been really straightforward. I think both of us were feeling a bit lost in the situation.

"Two weeks ago, we negotiated a remix deal with a very respected Detroit DJ," he added. "What worries me is that people are going to hear that sample and think,

'Isn't that the sound off the Björk album?' So it puts me in a funny situation, because I wouldn't want to be accused of ripping somebody else off. What also upset me was the review of the Björk album in the *Observer*, where it mentioned a 'really interesting use of radio noise and electronics.' I couldn't help thinking, 'Is that one of my sounds?'"

As if that wasn't enough, Björk was due back in London's High Court the following week as a witness in Simon Fisher's lawsuit against her and Hooper, which had finally made it to trial. The strange combination of events had conspired to form the strangest promotional tour anyone could have ever envisioned: in the week since *Post* had been released, Björk had seen her album deleted, her video banned, and two separate lawsuits brought against her.

The added exposure, however unwanted, certainly didn't hurt sales. In spite of all the surrounding confusion, *Post* debuted at #2 on the U.K. charts (behind Michael Jackson's bloated greatest hits compilation *HIStory*) and at a very respectable #32 on America's Billboard charts, almost 30 places higher than *Debut*'s peak position of #61. One Little Indian were also better prepared to promote the album this time around; in support of *Post*, a string of European and American tour dates had been scheduled from the beginning of July into late August.

The reviews were almost uniformly glowing as well. Everyone from the *Mojo* magazine crowd to the rankled college radio scenesters were spinning the record. If there were any rumblings of a sophomore jinx, *Post* had silenced them in one fell blow.

Björk was on tour in Ireland the day she finally got some good news from her lawyer. With a dismissive sneer ("Where there's a hit, there's a writ!") London High Court judge Sir Robin Jacob had cleared Björk and Hooper of all charges in the Simon Fisher lawsuit. Calling Björk a "talented musician," Jacob concluded that Fisher's inconsistent charges (he'd amended his original claim and was now only seeking credit for one song instead of four) rendered him "unreliable, diffuse, and vague." Her considerable court costs notwithstanding, Björk wouldn't have to pay or credit Fisher in any way, shape, or form.

The news came as a tremendous relief, and Björk let off her accumulated stress in fine style. "I've never had a night like it," Walker says. "We were playing in Dublin and she just went mental after the show. The adrenaline of the show and everything else just exploded — she was leaping up and down and screaming at the top of her voice, the ghetto blaster was on full. She was jumping around this bar we were in and climbing up Derek and everyone around her. You just could see it was this spring [inside her] that had been tightening and tightening and squashing smaller and smaller through the period of the court case and suddenly it was like, bang — it had released. Absolutely mental."

More good news was on the way. Somewhere along the line, Rimbaud had undergone an apparent change of heart. He'd never felt entirely comfortable with New Electronica's actions, and in an effort to make amends, he implored the label to honor their original agreement and let Björk use his sample completely free of charge. New Electronica eventually complied, and the threat of a lawsuit was dropped altogether.

"The theme of Scanner's album was that all noises in the world are for free, which I thought was really clever and interesting," Björk later mused. "I [initially] offered them money which they agreed to, but then they signed to a publishing company who thought, 'Oh, Björk has sampled them – let's try to put the Scanner album in the charts by making something of that.' They obviously didn't have a clue what they were talking about – these publishing people are not very into music, they're just trying to get the money."

"[Björk and Scanner] spoke when it was going on and he said, 'We never meant it to be like this,'" Walker recalls. "It was like the machine of the business had got in the way . . . whereas they had had a phone conversation and [had] an understanding between themselves. It was outsiders that had created this situation."

Since stores had yet to run out of stock on their initial run of *Post*, Rimbaud's switch meant that One Little Indian wouldn't have to issue another version of the album after all. For the first time in 14 months, Björk had absolutely no legal problems to worry about. "When people think you're rich, they just try anything," she laughed in disbelief. "If they washed your socks six years ago, they send you a bill for $100,000."

Perhaps the loneliest of all her albums, the relationship-obsessed *Post* had depicted Björk at her most lovelorn. She instinctively veered away from any correspondingly maudlin arrangements, but there was an unavoidable yearning carved into much of the album's lyrical content: for each call to self-sufficiency and independence (the remonstrative slap of "Army of Me"; the celebratory "Isobel"), there was an equally heartfelt lamentation of her own desolation. While couched in upbeat arrangements, songs like "I Miss You" (a forlorn love letter to a future lover) and "It's Oh So Quiet" (on paper, a contemplative resignation to the strange quirks of fate) portrayed Björk as quietly at odds with her singledom, content with independence but rarely satisfied with being alone.

It's not unreasonable to suggest that Björk's ensuing relationship with Tricky was borne partly out of this restlessness. Netty Walker recalls the faint sound of alarm bells going off after first witnessing the couple together. "Björk came up to me in the studio and said, 'What do you think?' and I went, 'Well . . .' She said, 'You don't like him, you don't like him!' I said, 'I didn't *say* I don't like him, but I just don't quite know whether he's the right person.'"

There was something about Tricky that Walker wasn't comfortable with, and her protectionist instincts had kicked in. "Someone with that much irreverence for everything that's happening around him . . ." she trails off. "It's all or nothing; an it's-my-way-or-no-way type attitude. There was also someone else in the background, an ex and a child, and all sorts of complications. I just said to her 'Don't get your fingers burnt, don't get hurt.'

"It was bang passionate, creative, musical, everything, but it was, I think in some ways, Björk rebounding from one thing to the next trying to find someone to care for her. Something personal, something deeper, more long term. No questions, just an understanding that you're together with someone.

"I think she wanted people to approve of him," Walker continues. "She looked at myself and my partner and she wanted that. [Once] in her hotel she said, 'Netty, you have *everything*' because I had the support of someone."

With frequent travel on the horizon, it was probably support that Björk desperately craved. The end of July was poised to see her launch her first proper North American tour as a solo artist. With techno goblin Aphex Twin along as her tour opener, she tore across the continent, working her way east from Los Angeles and pausing to do stops on *Late Light with David Letterman* (where she performed "Hyper-ballad") and *Top of the Pops* (live remotely via satellite) along the way. In the absence of any support from MTV (where airings for both "Army of Me" and "Isobel" had been relegated primarily to the after-hours alt-niche show *120 Minutes*), this North American tour helped maintain *Post*'s momentum and keep Björk in the public eye.

Björk tried gamely to keep her relationship with Tricky afloat, but later admitted that it was never properly defined to begin with. Even at their peak, the duo were only ever sorta-together, with hopes of long-term intimacy made impossible by his notoriously standoffish demeanor. They saw each other infrequently and when they did, they weren't sure where they stood with one another. Their relationship didn't last long, if it ever started.

"I don't think we ever knew if we were going out together or not," Björk said the following year. "I mean, we were going out together and then we weren't. Because, basically, the way our relationship functioned was that we were a support mechanism for each other, and we still have this kind of, like, permission to call each other in the middle of the night, when I'm in fucking Munich and he's in fucking Tokyo. It's a very strange job we've got, and we don't have to explain it: we know. And we know the pressure. So that's more what our relationship is like and still is."

Given the circumstances, the arrival of her third single — the walloping "It's Oh So Quiet" — couldn't have been more timely. A jovial, colorful romp through the rolling emotions accompanying love and lost love, the song was a cover version of

Betty Hutton's 1940s long-forgotten pearl "Blow a Fuse." Björk had first discovered it years earlier while on a nostalgic kick, and subsequently realized that she couldn't live without it.

While in the United States, Björk took a few days off to film the video. This time, there was a new director at the helm. His filmmaking roots planted in the skateboarding industry, Spike Jonze had arrived to the world of music videos in 1993 as a relative upstart; in less than three years, largely on the strength of his iconic clips for both the Beastie Boys ("Sabotage" was a wry sendup of '70s television cop dramas) and Weezer ("Buddy Holly" re-imagined the foursome as a squeaky clean in-house band on the set of TV's *Happy Days*), he had become one of MTV's most bankable commodities. Since "It's Oh So Quiet" had instantly reminded Jonze of a vivacious '60s musical, he wrote a video treatment that involved tons of choreography. When he requested that Björk learn to tap dance before arriving on set, she was suitably thrilled.

Jonze's video proved a perfect encapsulation of the song's rolls of calm and unbridled excitement. Over the course of washing up in the grotty back room of a used tire outlet, rolling out through the revolving doors and into the sunny outside, and meandering down the street, Björk flits between states of not in love (dull colors and churning slo-mo) and most-definitely, positively, unmistakably in love. Punctuated by Björk's endearingly clumsy dancing and Jonze's imaginatively over-the-top flourishes (re-animated mailboxes! twirling umbrellas!), the video very quickly positioned itself at the top of television station playlists. By the end of August, MTV had added it to their "Buzzbin," making it one of the most frequently played videos on the channel.

*Capping off another successful year backstage at the MTV Europe Awards in November 1995. (Cardinale Stephane/Corbis Sygma/Magma)*

*Debut* wasn't fully embraced by the mainstream until its third single; now here were signs that *Post* was traveling on a similar trajectory. Months removed from the album's original release date, it was once again time to regroup and prepare for a whole new onslaught of attention.

After roughly three weeks off from touring (during which Björk presented an award at the MTV Movie Awards and released a companion book of loosely assembled prose and photography called, stubbornly, *Post*), the band reconvened in Italy for the beginning of yet another tour leg. This stint commenced in Milan and wrapped up six weeks later in America, featuring acclaimed drum'n'bass artist Goldie as the opening act. With "It's Oh So Quiet" still resonating on charts and playlists worldwide, Walker remembers the overall mood as being particularly jovial.

"We had a really good reaction from everyone – the press people were great, interviews went smoothly, the concerts seemed to be working right, the lights came together . . ." Walker says. "And Goldie's band was being really nice – it was like family on tour, both bands together. We'd make a point of going around after each show and thanking everybody and Goldie's band were doing the same – that made so much difference.

The tour called for stops in Germany, Norway, Sweden, Denmark, and Holland before winding up with another four weeks in the U.S. The band's final gig came on November 17th, where excitable and devoted fans packed New York's Roseland Theatre. Seven days earlier, "It's Oh So Quiet" had debuted at number nine on the British singles charts, marking the first time in Björk's solo career that she had a single crack the top 10. A week later, the song proved its appeal by rising a single spot to number eight. If there were any doubts that Björk had officially infiltrated pop culture's every crack and crevice, they were eviscerated six weeks later, when the incurably stodgy RIAA acknowledged that even *they* knew who Björk was. *Post* had been nominated for Best Alternative Album at the 1996 Grammy Awards.

It was a nice way to cap off another brilliant and rewarding year. Nineteen ninety-five had yielded a new album, a clearer direction, a firmer sense of purpose, and increasing comfort with her newfound role of pop cultural icon. It had made Björk stronger both as a person and as a personality. Little did she know it, but she would need every ounce of that strength to overcome what the next 12 months had in store.

# seven

With his gold teeth and slightly crazed grin a constant reminder of his mottled past, Goldie's reputation as a barely reformed street urchin had always been his most prominent selling point. Estranged from his parents and his mixed heritage (half-Scottish, half-Jamaican) at an early age, his childhood had entailed being shuttled around various orphanages in the West Maldives. By his teens he had graduated to a life that revolved around a steady diet of breakdancing, graffiti, and petty crime. After stints in New York and Miami (where he reportedly earned his nickname by selling engraved gold teeth), he relocated to London, just in time to be swept under by the city's bustling rave and drug culture. Citing Fabio and Grooverider as influences, he quickly became fascinated with the dark, loping throb of jungle music. He bought a sampler soon after, and some of his first releases rode the wave of jungle's steady but troubled ascent into the dance mainstream.

By the time Goldie's debut album *Timeless* had surfaced in 1995, he was being heartily tipped by eager cognoscenti as drum'n'bass's saving grace. Interestingly, the persona he cultivated over this time wasn't far from Tricky's; both had close ties to Bristol's Wild Bunch, both were regarded as volatile, aggressive, and streetwise, and both had tendencies and attitudes that, when hard-pressed, seemed to verge on nihilistic.

But unlike Tricky, Goldie also appeared to have a lighter, more humanistic side that, in the right light, could make him seem infinitely more sensitive and more reachable. To Björk, he must have appeared downright cuddly — the pair met while touring together at the tail end of 1995 and became involved shortly thereafter.

Walker's impression of Goldie is in line with his public persona: "Absolutely mad as a bloody hatter," she jokes. "A difficult person to come to grips with because he is absolutely in your face and can be quite aggressively so. But courteous as well, in some respects."

By virtue of touring together for weeks on end, the couple became close quite quickly. Björk soon found herself entertaining the notion of settling down, although she had kept fairly quiet about the relationship to the media. Her desire for love had overwhelmed her — she threw herself into this new relationship completely.

Goldie's obligation as Björk's opening act ended when the tour hit North America, and the pair found themselves managing a long-distance relationship. Björk had no time to spare: a string of special shows in England (culminating with a gig at the mammoth Wembley Stadium) spilled over into an extensive tour of Asia, which saw her playing shows in Japan, China, Thailand, and Singapore for the first time in her career. The tour itself was going brilliantly, but Björk, estranged from her lover, was having trouble with the distance. She desperately wanted the opportunity to strengthen her relationship with Goldie, to build towards something, but there was simply no room to move — obligations in Asia, New Zealand, and Australia still loomed.

Still smitten, she bravely did whatever she could to maintain the romance. Knowing that they weren't going to be together on Valentine's Day, she carefully selected a present for Goldie and asked her crew not to send it to him until she had the opportunity to attend to it personally. She wanted to wrap it herself and include her own card, filled with lovelorn messages.

Derek Birkett knew all too well how much Björk missed her boyfriend so he secretly made arrangements to fly Goldie down to Hong Kong. His idea had been for Goldie to surprise Björk onstage by presenting her with the Brit Award for Best International Female. The event, which would be simulcast at the actual Brit Awards ceremony, was intended to be a pleasant surprise, a way to honor Björk's accomplishment while giving her what she'd really wanted; the opportunity to spend time with her deeply missed beau.

Unfortunately, the news of Goldie's imminent arrival had been the tour's most poorly kept secret. Björk had developed mild suspicions that something was up, but nobody in the crew wanted to ruin the surprise by fully coming clean. "I knew that Goldie would be flying out and it was near Valentine's Day and I was having to keep mum and not say anything," Walker laments. "Looking back, that was a big, big mistake for me.

"The crew was in on it and I was in on it, but nobody else knew. Björk didn't know and she was trying to weed it out. She's saying, 'Someone's saying Goldie's coming out!' and I'm saying, 'I don't know.' That means you are lying to someone and that's really hard."

Worse yet, Walker was forced to lie to Björk about the fate of her Valentine's Day present. Björk hadn't had the time to wrap it yet, and when she came looking for it one day, Walker couldn't give it to her for fear that she might send it away herself. "She came running up and she was in tears," Walker says. "I had to say, 'But it's already gone!' knowing that Goldie was on a flight on his way to us."

Although everyone's actions were motivated by the best of intentions, the creeping mistrust around the camp took its toll. Björk's nerves weren't the only ones frazzled that night in Hong Kong — management had to surreptitiously sneak an entire film crew into the venue and Goldie into the sidestage area without ever tipping their hand. In the end, Walker decided it'd be best if Björk had *some* advance notice, however small. "[Goldie] turned up, we snuck him into the venue, and just before I walked out with one of film crews I said to the tour manager, 'You walk down one side with the film crew, I'll walk down the other and then Björk [will] know that this is expected.' I walked out of the office and I said to myself, 'Well, I've either got a job tomorrow or I haven't.'"

Björk was halfway through her last song of the night when she finally spotted Goldie waiting in the wings. When she finished, the video cameras fired up and he strode out onstage, award in hand. Her reaction was one of genuine shock; not thinking, she flung the award away and hid behind him for the duration of the segment, barely able to muster an acceptance speech. To the millions of people watching the feed around the world, Björk's reaction was just more evidence of her peculiarity.

Backstage, Björk and her boyfriend cordoned themselves off in the dressing room while the audience outside roared for an encore. Walker remembers pleading at the door: "I was going, 'Björk, the audience won't go home unless you come out. They're just standing there. And I'm really sorry I've had to lie to you for three weeks. . . .'"

The emotional twists and turns continued: the couple got to enjoy each other's company only for one day before their respective schedules interfered again. With his own album still to promote, Goldie was needed in London while Björk was due in Thailand for her next gig. The following day, disaster struck.

As the quality of Björk's celebrity had changed over the past few years, so had the quality of media she was attracting. In the heyday of the Sugarcubes (and perhaps before *Debut* exploded), she'd only ever been subjected to scrutiny by the music media. Now, as pop caricature, fashion iconoclast, and public curiosity, she'd become fair game for various tabloid outfits as well. For Björk, this new kind of attention was proving much more difficult to handle. "It's a different type of press when you get the mainstream tabloid newspapers and their guys, their paparazzi, outside your house," Walker says. "It's alright when it's music press — yeah, they can build you up and they can knock you down, but at least you might be able to focus on the music. Whereas with the paparazzi and everything else, it's who you're dating, what you're doing, what you're buying, where you're going. You're constantly spied on and you don't get any peace from it."

Of course, the worst thing you can do when you've got a bloodthirsty media nipping at your heels is to give them a story so bizarre and outlandish that they can scarcely believe their luck. On February 21, 1996, a defeated and emotionally depleted Björk did precisely that — in front of an army of journalists and video cameras to boot — when she snapped and physically assaulted television reporter Julie Kaufman at a Bangkok Airport. The incident marked a rare emotional surrender for Björk, who was on edge, frazzled, and exhausted. For the tabloids, it sounded the trumpet for open season.

The venue where Björk had been originally scheduled to perform, Bangkok's MBK Hall, had burnt to the ground only a few days before. Desperate for people to know that Björk's concert had been relocated (rather than canceled outright), the local promoter had pushed for the singer to meet with video crews at the airport immediately upon her arrival. Coming off the heels of two consecutive gigs and a long flight, Walker refused the request. In the end, it hadn't mattered; the promoter called the media anyway.

"We came out into the baggage hall to collect all the baggage," Walker recalls. "We'd done a lot of shopping by then, and there was something like 11 pieces of hand baggage with Björk. I had them piled up on top of this trolley and Sindri was sitting on the top. Björk was pushing and I was walking beside, trying to hold bags on and make sure Sindri was okay.

"The promoter came up and said there were some fans outside so we thought, 'Oh that's okay then.' They were going to lead us through immigration as a group and then out into the main hall. All the crew and everyone were with us, they were walking ahead. As soon as we got through the barrier, there were literally about six or seven film crews with lights, microphones — you name it — all in front of us, walking backwards with their cameras, surrounding Björk and myself. The crew were sort of in there but they were thinking, 'Oh, maybe this is supposed to be happening,' so they started dropping back; I was looking behind them going, 'No, come on, keep them out of the way!'"

This is where the infamous, oft-aired news footage picked up — with a shot of Björk, head down, as she slogged through the maze of cameras and struggled to avoid making eye contact with anyone. As she and her entourage rounded a bend,

Kaufman was to her side, standing amidst a scrum of other reporters. As the news anchor leaned in with her microphone, she was heard to say only, "Welcome to Bangkok" when Björk lunged violently towards her.

"It had been quite a funny flight," touring keyboardist Leila Arab says. "I was wheeling my luggage out and suddenly I just saw her on the floor with someone. What was funny was my instinct, which was, 'Shit, someone's jumped her!' – like some crazy fan. And it's like, 'No, it's a crazy Björk'!"

Consisting of some hair pulling and a few violent throttlings, the attack lasted for about 10 seconds before being broken up by Paul Normandale, Björk's lighting designer. Kaufman, uninjured but still on the floor, was so stupefied that the best she could muster was an enfeebled, "Oh my gosh." Meanwhile, Björk, still enraged, attempted to break the grasp of her handlers while being led onto the tour bus, which was waiting nearby.

Although the entire incident was caught on tape, it's still difficult to know exactly what happened and precisely what it was that sent Björk flying off the handle. From day one, the official party line has been that she was angry at the way Kaufman appeared to be targeting Sindri with her questions, but to be fair, there is absolutely no evidence on tape to support that allegation. Even Walker has no recollection of Kaufman saying anything to Sindri at all. "I can't remember," she says. "It blew up into a huge incident that it never should have been. We thought, 'Oh my God, what have we done – we just walked into someone's country and created an international incident!'

"I was so pissed off with the promoter. I said, 'Why the hell did you arrange this? We told you no and we had good reason for saying that.' He said, 'We didn't ask them,' and I said, 'Rubbish – you set us up. If you expect anything else from us, you are not getting it.'"

The damage, unfortunately, had already been done; it was now up to Björk, Walker, and Birkett to try and minimize it. For her own part, Björk had felt instantly remorseful and quickly took steps to make amends. "As soon as we got to the hotel, she said, 'I need to talk to the woman – I must apologize,'" Walker says. "So we managed to get a phone number and track her down. She spoke to [Julie] and they were fine with each other. She just accepted it – it had been a long, stressful few days."

Although Kaufman declined to press charges of any sort, there was still an unforgiving media to worry about and headlines like the *Daily Mirror*'s "Welcome to Bang-Shock: Newsgirl Is Thumped by Barmy Björk" to avoid. Within hours, the story had been reported in virtually every market, while the damning video footage had been picked up and aired on various North American, European, and Asian television networks. Not surprisingly, Walker's phone was ringing off the hook with press requests.

"As soon as it hit, the [answering] machine started going," she says. "Derek had been talking with Björk's lawyer and he was saying, 'Right, here's a press statement and this is all you are allowed to say because we might get sued.'" A "Welcome to Bangkok" press conference had long been scheduled for the following day, and Björk desperately wanted to use the opportunity to plead her case publicly. She hated the idea of sending out a simple press statement – she felt that it would be too damning and that she'd be better able to defuse the situation by using her own words. In the end, Birkett and Björk's lawyer won out – they were too scared of another lawsuit to risk letting her speak on her own so soon. Björk hated the self-imposed gag order, but adhered to it for as long as was necessary.

When it was safe to talk about the incident, Björk appeared repentant but ultimately justified, content to portray her actions as those of a protective mother. "I completely lost my temper," she admitted shortly afterward. "I'm not proud of it, I'll be ashamed of it for the rest of my life, but I was protecting [Sindri] from my demons, from the silly things that have to do with my job."

Weeks later, in conversation with the British press, she was even joking about it. "The best thing about it is the woman was offered a commercial for a hairspray thing in Asia," she joked to the *NME* in the July 20th edition. "It was going to be, 'I get battered by pop stars all the time but I use this hairspray and it keeps my hair in place!' And she said no! I was gonna call her and say, 'Do it!' I thought that was very funny."

After shows in Bangkok and Singapore, the *Post* tour moved further south for a final three-week stint in New Zealand and Australia. For the first time in months, Björk's relentless itinerary actually worked to her benefit, allowing her to disappear and avoid the crest of negative publicity generated by the airport incident. While she was in Australia, though, new reports began to surface suggesting that she and Goldie were close to marriage. The rumors had been spurred on by recent comments Goldie had made to the *NME*. "I do want to get married one day," he'd said at the beginning of March. "Yeah, settle down and have kids, big house. A big fucking treehouse, man, that'd be the business."

"I'm in love, man," he gushed. "Björk feeds me and I feed her. I guess, musically, we're probably the last two most controversial people in the fucking world, but together we could take on the whole universe. Certain people miss the point with what I'm about but she's fucking hittin' bull's-eyes. It's crazy.

"And, y'know, I think we're a fate thing. I've been down my road, she's been down her road. I'm 30, she's 30, kids, kids, I play music, she plays music, both got histories of music, it's freaky . . . I'm a very complex person and I need someone to work me out, cos not a lot of people can, and she can work me out. She's a step ahead of me. Soul mate."

These very public protestations of love were par for the course where Goldie and Björk were concerned. Over the duration of their short courtship, they'd become increasingly open in the media about their mutual admiration, and often presented themselves as a package. A litany of Björk & Goldie photo shoots and interviews followed, thus cementing their status as the First Couple of Electronic Music. For some reason, Björk's regular rules about keeping relationships private had been tossed out the window.

"I'm not sure why she wanted to be quite so public about that one," Walker muses. "I think in some ways it was because Goldie is the sort of person who courts publicity almost without asking.

"In doing the public bit together I think maybe in some ways, in the back of Björk's mind, she was helping promote him. She knew he used to be a graffiti artist. She had all of these visions of them being together and having this lovely house and things, having his kid there and doing graffiti art and being really creative. That was her vision of what she thought the relationship was. What was going on in his mind, I do not know."

While juggling everything else, the couple were still trying to see each other as often as they could. When Björk completed her Australian tour in mid-March, they retreated to the Maldives for a quick holiday. This didn't end up being the relaxing vacation they'd hoped for. "Björk actually took me along," Walker says. "So it was me, Goldie, and Björk. It was just an experience. Goldie turned allergic to the sea water and had to be taken to the next island for an antihistamine shot which was a bit of a crisis. He panics, because he is actually allergic to shellfish and his throat swells up . . . his skin had reacted, Björk had gone off in a canoe and I was stuck with this guy going mental at me. 'Calm down, calm down, for God's sake!'"

From the Maldives, Goldie accompanied Björk to Bombay, where the couple steeped themselves in Indian culture while doing more press during their downtime. Björk visited some of the Bollywood film studios for a television special commissioned by India's MTV-equivalent Channel V and met legendary Bollywood queen Sridevi in the process. Unfortunately, like their trip to the Maldives only weeks prior, this excursion also ended on a sour note. Both Goldie and Björk fell ill, Björk to a bout of food poisoning so nasty that she collapsed and required a wheelchair just to board the airplane home.

The next few months spelled relative calm and allowed Björk time to unwind and prepare for one final tour leg, which included a number of high-profile European festival stints. She kept a relatively low profile during this point, emerging only occasionally to fulfill a genuinely exciting press obligation, such as one extended by *Dazed and Confused* magazine, who gave her the opportunity to interview her childhood hero, 68-year-old German composer Karlheinz Stockhausen.

"Like all scientific geniuses, Stockhausen seems obsessed with the marriage between mystery and science, although they are opposites," she raved in the article.

"Normal scientists are obsessed with facts: genius scientists are obsessed with mystery. The more Stockhausen finds out about sound, the more he finds out that he doesn't know jack shit; that he's lost.

"Stockhausen told me about the house he built himself in the forest and lived in for 10 years. It's made from hexagonal pieces of glass and no two rooms are the same, so they are all irregular. It's built out of angles that are reflective and it's full of spotlights. The forest becomes mirrored inside the house. He was explaining to me how, even after 10 years, there would still be moments when he didn't know where he was, and he said it with wonder in his eyes. And I said, 'That's brilliant: you can be innocent even in your own home,' and he replied, 'Not only innocent, but curious.' He's such a humorist."

The classical music from Björk's youth was obviously reemerging in her mind, because she also took time out during these months to train her voice in preparation for a performance of another childhood favorite — Arnold Schoenberg's exceedingly difficult (and atonal) 1912 composition "Pierrot Lunaire." At the behest of conductor Kent Nagano, Björk had begun to rehearse different pieces from the opera; Nagano was reportedly so impressed with the results that he invited her to attend Switzerland's Verbier Festival as his special guest. On August 4, 1996, with the Jeunesses Musicales World Orchestra as her backdrop and Nagano as her conductor, Björk performed selected pieces from the composition in *sprechstimme*, a mode of vocalization somewhere between singing and speaking. This would mark the first and only occasion that she would attempt the piece in public.

In the meantime, Tricky's latest record, recorded under the pseudonym Nearly God, had been released largely to mixed reviews. In addition to guest appearances from Damon Albarn, Terry Hall, and Neneh Cherry, the claustrophobic album featured two Björk collaborations. "Yoga" and "Keep Your Mouth Shut" had been hatched as payback for Tricky's two contributions to *Post*, and both were highlighted by critics as standout tracks.

Meanwhile, another of Björk's oft-delayed projects had been postponed further still. Promises of a *Post* remix album called *Telegram* had been circulating since the release of "Army of Me," but with additional songs still to be rehauled and superior remixes to consider, Björk and One Little Indian decided to delay the album until the new year. To compensate, Björk announced the issuance of a string of 12" remixes beginning in June. Limited to only 1,000 copies apiece, the series of vinyl would serve as a taster of what to expect from *Telegram*, and give Björk an opportunity to indulge her underground white-label fetish.

When she wasn't busily writing new songs back in London, Björk indulged herself by house hunting. She and Goldie had postponed talk of marriage, but she was clinging to the dream of a long-term future together. In spite of the growing fear that

she was putting more in than she was getting out, she forged onwards. Netty Walker noticed a change: "Even after two months in Asia — which was fantastic, full of memories, the Goldie issue and the relationship with him was going a bit pear-shaped.

"I think in some ways with Goldie, Björk was going a bit wild," she adds. "At that point I was sort of finding her a bit of a stranger — she wasn't, in some ways, the person I'd known or worked with the rest of the time. There was a different type of dynamic in the relationship and a different dynamic in how she was dealing with things. Whether she was getting very emotional about the fact that it wasn't working out, I don't know, I can't speak for her. But it was very hard, trying to sustain even my involvement with things."

And of course, the sheer magnitude of Björk's stardom meant that there was always something to sustain. With the summer concert season beckoning, Björk once again embarked on tour. Her string of commitments led her from San Francisco (where she performed six songs at the Beastie Boys' Tibetan Freedom Concert) through to various festivals in Reykjavik, Denmark, Norway, Portugal, Belgium, Finland, Switzerland, and the United Kingdom, where she wowed the crowd at the annual Phoenix Festival with a typically fiery performance. With only a few hiccups to speak of (the Lisbon show was temporarily postponed due to laryngitis; the Belgian festival appearance delayed a day when drummer Trevor Morais missed his flight), the summer had gone reasonably well. Perhaps equally impressive was the amount of attention that Björk had been able to generate strictly by changing her hairstyle. Tired of her jet black coif, she'd dyed her hair a tangerine blonde, in the process sending diehard fans and fashion-watchers into paroxysms of anguished debate.

With Warp Records artists Red Snapper along as openers, Björk concluded her summer with a weeklong stint in Israel before returning to London for a homecoming gig at Wembley Stadium. The experience had been bittersweet, the successes tempered the knowledge that her relationship with Goldie was slowly evaporating. Still plagued by the ghost of unresolved emotional issues lingering in his past, Goldie knew that he was in no position to commit to marriage. Although he still felt he loved Björk dearly, he knew he couldn't continue to see her.

"It was weird because it should have been the perfect scenario: this girl wants to marry you, she wants to buy this fucking house, wants you to come and live in this big fucking house," he confessed a year later. "This vision is there, saying, 'Do you want me?' And I said, 'No.' It's like, 'Are you stupid or what?'

"Sometimes . . . you love so much that you can't love anymore, because when it goes, your life is a ruin. Something in me said, 'You're not to be in love, and until you're happy with yourself, this is as far as you can go.' I felt myself being tortured, and Björk was just there with her hands tied behind her back. No one could help me but me. She got a broken heart over it. She was sad.

"It was a fucking wrench," he continued. "But sometimes you can't be taking anyone with you. I couldn't afford to do that. Like, there's three people in a car with you, and you hit on black ice. Fate is at the wheel, and the only thing to do if fate has control over your car is to grab him by the neck, and press the brakes. Now if you have the chance to get those three people out of the car, do you do it? Course you do, because it was my crash."

With Goldie's words came the profound disappointment of another broken heart; Björk had put everything she could muster into seeing the relationship through, and it still hadn't been enough. Emotionally threadbare, hopelessly let down, and terribly exhausted, she had endured more than she could bear; more than ever before, she found herself in dire need of respite from everything and everyone.

That coveted isolation was nowhere in her future — unbeknownst to her, she was mere days away from the single most terrifying and life-altering catastrophe of her career.

Ricardo Lopez spent the early morning hours of his final day on Earth surrendering to the black shapes in his head. Long mired in a suffocating struggle with his own depression, self-loathing, and potent rage, Lopez's knees had finally buckled; on Thursday, September 12, 1996, his pain and misdirected grief overtook him completely and decisively.

Inside his Miami apartment, the 21-year-old pest control worker had gathered all the required implements for one final solitary standoff. Among the items in his possession: an 8mm video camera, blank videocassettes, razor blades, face paint, and a .38 caliber revolver.

The video camera captured every significant detail of his last 12 hours. With the aid of rudimentary schematics that he'd obtained in advance, Lopez hollowed out a paperback book and painstakingly assembled a homemade sulfuric acid bomb inside it. At roughly 3 a.m. that morning, upon completing the project, Lopez wrapped the parcel and addressed it to Björk. Later that day, he made arrangements for the item to be sent directly to her management company, bypassing the regular fan club channels entirely.

A Björk obsessive for the better part of three years, Lopez had reacted to news of her mixed-race relationship with vehement disapproval. "I'm going to have to send her a package," he sputtered on tape. "I'm just going to have to kill her." The next 10 hours marked Lopez's bleak descent into madness. While facing the video camera, Lopez stripped naked and shaved off his coal black hair. With the face paint, he decorated himself — seemingly in the style of Marlon Brando's Colonel Kurtz from *Apocalypse Now* — by painting his nipples blood red, his mouth black and his face a harrowing combination of red and green. Hanging directly behind his head was a large sheet of white bristol board, on which he'd scrawled "The Best of Me" in black marker. Police later assumed that he'd intended to splatter the board with his blood.

At 2:53 p.m. that afternoon, with a Björk video playing silently in the background and her version of "I Remember You" wafting from his stereo, Lopez drew a string of violent, panicked breaths, inserted the revolver into his mouth and pulled the trigger. His suicide was part of a carefully orchestrated string of events that he hoped would culminate with Björk being sent "to Hell" by his hands.

A superfluous irony: Björk and Goldie had already ended their romantic relationship days beforehand. An incredible coincidence: unbeknownst to Lopez, the ex-couple also happened to be in Miami, a mere two blocks away, that very evening.

Four days later, while responding to tenants who'd complained of a foul odor coming from an adjacent apartment, police finally discovered Ricardo Lopez's corpse. He'd left a gruesome scene in his wake, a circus of anguish made all the more harrowing by the reams of Björk memorabilia scattered virtually everywhere.

Dating back to January of that year, the 11 videocassettes discovered by authorities provided a complete chronicle of Lopez's impending psychosis. The final tape, labeled "Ricardo Lopez — Last Day," was the one that tipped them off to the bomb. Miami Police notified Scotland Yard, who successfully intercepted and destroyed the package at a London post office without incident.

Björk's return to the United Kingdom had been roughly simultaneous with that of Lopez's delivery; she was back in London by the time Interpol had alerted Walker. "I rang Derek and said, 'What do I do, do I tell Björk or what? How do we deal with this?'" Walker recalls. "It wasn't going to get to her because all of the fan club stuff and everything else came through the office. The press took it all out of hand, as they usually do — they camped outside her house. She was already very tired." Later that day, with her jacket limply hanging around her shoulders, and a glazed, stony shock on her face, Björk came outside to give a statement to the press. "It's just a very sad thing, obviously, when somebody shoots their face off," she mumbled while camera flashes went off around her. "It's terrible. I'm not sure if I'll dream very properly for a while."

Although she was never in any real danger of being hurt, the incident had a profound effect on Björk's psyche. It brought a direct, sobering message to the fore: that, simply by virtue of being a celebrity, she was indirectly putting herself and her loved ones in constant danger of being hurt. The weight of that realization briefly led her to consider quitting music altogether.

"My only son's life was in danger because I happen to sing through a microphone sometimes," she said during a press conference a few months later. "And that's scary. I can take it myself and the effect it has on my life but the fact that my granny gets calls to make waffles for the *Daily Mirror* and all my friends are asked if I'm going out with so-and-so . . . it's been a test."

"It really fucked up my whole life and the idea of what my home is," she said the following year. "Forty media people were hanging outside my house with a lens on my toilet seat. I didn't feel very welcome at my own home. Of course, I cried for the man and I was very upset over his death. I couldn't sleep . . . for him. But for me, it destroyed my home. I had to rediscover everything. Me and my son, Sindri, talked a lot about it."

Björk also struggled with questions of culpability as a result of Lopez's actions. The extent to which she gave herself to her audience had invited a certain kind of bond, and the sheer size of her fan base meant that there were always going to be a few who overstepped the boundaries. However indirectly or unwilling, she still had agency in fostering such an intensity of fandom, and it was difficult for her to accept.

As the head of Bad Taste mail order in Iceland, Gunnar Hjálmarsson has dealt with his fair share of questionable Björk fans. "Maybe not like dangerous stalkers, more like pathetic stalkers, you know?" he smirks. "One of them came to Iceland, somehow found out where she lived, and went to her house on a Saturday morning. She came to the door, I think with a towel around her head, having been in the shower.

"It's just masturbation fantasies for pathetic losers," he decries. "Maybe she's too personal or gives too much of herself, I don't know."

Whether via mail or by phone, Walker has also been exposed to more than she'd care to remember. "Someone once sent what looked like a rubber dildo in the shape of Björk about a foot high," she marvels.

"You'd open some of the letters in the early days . . . there was one particular one that seemed to recur which was someone who would write a hate letter and a love letter and put it in the same envelope."

Sadly, Lopez wasn't even Björk's lone fan suicide. "About a year before that package arrived, I was getting calls on the office line," Walker says. "I had to work through that Christmas to prep some gigs just straight after the New Year and I'd left my home number on. We were getting calls at home and on my mobile from this weird guy from, I think it was Austria. A complete schizophrenic — no doubt about it. I got this call one night at home and he was saying, 'I want to help Björk. I need to help her. She can't do it on her own.'

"My partner picked up the phone and told him that if he didn't stop phoning on that line, he knew where he lived and then we didn't get them anymore. But the guy committed suicide. I walked in the office one morning and there was this woman's voice, in tears, on the answering machine from Austria or whatever, saying, 'We know it's not Björk's fault, we know it's not your fault, we know it's nothing to do with you, it's just happened.' That freaked Björk out. It was like whatever she was doing was affecting these people, and even though you know you are not responsible for it there is that sort of feeling — 'How do people get like this? How can they be so obsessive?'"

*Besieged by the press, whose blatant disregard for private matters was increasing. (Dina Alfano/Shooting Star)*

"With the bomb, she realized that she was coming up to that stage where she had to begin to think about what she was doing and where she was," says father Guðmundur Gunnarsson. "It took her some time to accept that. I don't think she has yet accepted it in full."

The short term scarcely provided any opportunity to mend, much less time to glean any useful perspective. After arranging to send flowers to Lopez's parents, Björk dutifully plunged right back into work. In addition to a video that needed to be shot for her new single "Possibly Maybe," there were still dates in Norway, South America, and South Africa to worry about. Birkett's request for her additional participation in a Childline Charity Fund showcase only complicated matters further. "Derek needed to do more marketing and the Childline thing was an opportunity," Walker says. "For the record company, it was a showcase and he really wanted it to happen. I looked and said, 'She's tired, she really shouldn't do this. She needs to save herself, get some rest and get ready to go and do South America.'"

Walker's pleas ultimately went unheard, and Björk's inability to let down those who relied on her came back to sting her again. "Derek asked her direct," Walker sighs. "And Björk never says no to Derek."

Not normally an unreliable person, Björk turned up for her Childline obligation an hour late that day. By the time she'd completed her performance, which was also set to be broadcast on *Top of the Pops*, it was clear that she was not at her best. "I walked backstage and Derek was shaking, he was so angry," Walker says. "It was the worst performance I've ever seen her do."

This uncharacteristic collapse carried over to Björk's South American tour, where she let off months of steam by partying a little too excessively. After only two shows into the tour, she was forced to cancel remaining gigs in Argentina, Chile, and South Africa, citing laryngitis as the culprit. "It was the straw that broke the camel's back, her body, and everything, she just couldn't take going out and doing that," Walker says. "It was just too much."

One Little Indian had arranged for Björk to do another round of interviews upon her return to London from the jettisoned tour leg. Walker, meanwhile, had been on vacation and, frustratingly, more wires had gotten crossed; the label had inadvertently given media members the (very) wrong phone number. "I asked people at One Little Indian in the press department to look after the interviews in Europe and they all ended up ringing her at home," Walker sighs. "I got back to Björk telling me it was worst week she'd ever had, why were these people calling her at home?"

It was the last straw for Walker; harried and depleted herself, she resigned as Björk's manager shortly thereafter. "Björk wasn't quite sure what was going to happen," Walker says. "I think she suddenly sort of said to Derek, 'Yeah, I'm destroying Netty's life.'

"The pressure of everyone else getting in the way, getting Björk to make decisions about things and then just watching her sort of flailing about in it all — that was hurting me, because she was destroying herself, she was exhausting herself, and it was like something out of control."

It's hard to imagine that someone so bound to instinct could careen so out of control, but if Björk was capable of crashing, this was as close as she'd come.

# eight

Björk soldiered through her remaining obligations for the year (the *Childline* album, the MTV Europe Music Awards) as if on auto-pilot, comforted by the knowledge that true release waited just around the corner. Of her many needs, the most urgent centered on the new batch of songs she had swimming inside her head. Rest, comfort, family, and perspective could wait; for now, she was starving to write.

Under the assistance of *Post* engineer Markus Dravs, Björk had set up a makeshift recording studio inside her Maida Vale home in North London that August. The opportunity to work on new songs provided some much-needed therapy; whenever she had the energy, she would call Dravs over and the pair would carve out initial treatments together. The German-born engineer recalls a conceptual focus on the geography of her homeland being prevalent from the very start. "Björk would say, 'It should sound like the landscape of Iceland looks,'" he remembers. "'Like rough volcanoes with soft moss growing over it . . . all the beats should be very raw.'" As Björk also knew early on that this would be a comparatively simple record with "only one flavor," she adopted *Homogeneous* as its working title, but eventually changed it to *Homogenic*.

With the album still very much in its infancy, Björk was willing to bestow an incredible amount of creative license on Dravs. "She said, 'Look, just start making noises, sounds, beats, whatever — do what you want!' For someone that you love and respect so much to say, 'Come to my house, do what you want . . .'" he remembers. "She obviously meant within boundaries, but she certainly wasn't looking over my shoulder. She'd given me full access to her house and private life." Acting as a sort of sanctuary from outside events, these Maida Vale sessions had an appropriately calm, casual veneer, with Björk sometimes offering rough guidance before disappearing to fix Dravs a meal. "Then she'd shout down when the next variation of fish pie was ready, or a pizza would turn up," he laughs.

"I take my food very seriously," he adds. "So meeting Björk was worth it just because of all the different dinners I had with her. The fish pies and the Icelandic bread. . . ."

Although she'd given Dravs lots of room to move, Björk had refused to buckle on her basic concepts for the album, which focused on two primary elements: beats and strings. In her eyes, these simple precepts were required for an auditory representation of Iceland's geology. For the sake of simplicity, the inclusion of other elements was to be kept at a bare minimum. "It's really easy to hold the person's attention for 35 minutes if you've got 900 toys," she said. "Doing *Debut* was like, Wooooah! Like a kid in a toy store. It's like, 'I can have anything? Cool!' But I thought the true challenge was to have almost no toys, down to one stick, without a second of boredom. My idea was to have just strings and beats and a voice, the strings on the left and the beats on the right and the voice in the middle. With the balance button on the stereo, people could pick the ambient version or club one, or both."

While the mixing idea (literally) never panned out, the end result would be startlingly close to Björk's initial vision. She respected her peers' abilities immensely, but the only way she would compromise on a sound or an idea was if it was better than the one she already had in her head. Just as important as the customary freedom she'd granted her collaborators was her own right to reject or accept any idea put forth; as such, her most critical function as creator often involved finding ways to articulate precisely what she was after. "She would say, 'The beat should be very aggressive — hard as brick walls or like the Icelandic volcanoes,'" Dravs says. "I just started doing beats and she'd go 'Yeah, that one is kind of getting there, that one is totally off the mark, oh, I *totally* like that one. . . .'"

One of the first songs tackled during these sessions was the emboldened "5 Years," for which Dravs birthed a crunched, skittering beat. Björk gravitated towards this beat immediately, and it paved a route for the rhythmic tones of the album that LFO's Mark Bell would later retrace in Spain. "I wanted *Homogenic* to reflect where I'm from, what I'm about," Björk explained. "I wanted the beats to be almost distorted; imagine if there was Icelandic techno! Iceland is one of the youngest countries geographically — it's still in the making, so the sounds would be still in the making."

These Maida Vale sessions continued on, whenever Björk found herself at home, right up to the week before Lopez's suicide. After that incident, however (with a small media circus camped out on her lawn), it became obvious that London wasn't the place to continue writing. Björk began to seek solace elsewhere.

While holed up inside her home during that frenetic week, she dealt with the turmoil by imagining herself as the protagonist in an overwrought Spanish television soap opera. This recurring image, in turn, inspired a boomy, melodramatic song called "So Broken." She'd sing this song at the top of her lungs while flailing about her kitchen, stopping only to punctuate it with an over-the-top "Ole!" Somewhere over the course of her dramatics, she decided that the song demanded flamenco guitars.

Fortuitously, her *Debut/Post* tour drummer Trevor Morais just happened to own a studio in Spain, which he'd offered to Björk recently for temporary respite. Needing desperately to get out of London, she decided to kill two birds with one stone. She arranged to meet with famous flamenco guitarist Raimundo Amador and set out for Malaga, Spain, that November.

Björk had only planned on staying in Spain briefly — perhaps just long enough to record the guitar parts for "So Broken" — but she quickly became transfixed by her surroundings. Spiked with trails, the nearby Moroccan mountain ranges proved too alluring to abandon; after only a few days, she decided to record the whole of *Homogenic* there. Before she could return, though, there was a holiday ritual to tend to.

Since she moved to London, Björk had made a habit of returning home to Iceland every Christmas; but that December, Reykjavik seemed to take on a different resonance for her. After the incessant flux of the last four years, spent largely on tour and traveling, the familiar terrain of home provided some much needed constancy. It was here that Björk realized the true motives behind her actions: if *Homogenic* was shaping up as a tribute to Iceland, it was because Iceland was a tribute to her. In the act of restaking her ground as a human being, she'd ended up home, in every sense of the word.

"I went away from Iceland four years ago and started this completely frantic, very exciting lifestyle," she said. "I went around the world and visited all these places, lots of clubs, lots of exciting people. . . .

"So when I did this album I was like, 'What am I made of?' And I'm from Iceland, I'm born '65. Iceland is full of fucking ruptures, very raw lava. I'd wake up in the morning and have a walk by the ocean and scream and sing. There's snow blizzards and people might die because the weather's terrible — all these kinds of things. I wanted to get closer to what that is. . . ."

While home, Björk reacquainted herself with the country's glacial landscape. Her father had rented her a cottage in the south, not far from Geysir; Björk shut off her cellphone and retreated there for some time alone. The isolation ultimately

*Puckering up between photo shoots. (Davies & Davies/Corbis Sygma/Magma)*

proved fruitful. Her long exploratory hikes (much like the ones she'd taken as a child) yielded a clearer head and a batch of new songs, which included "Joga," a sweeping tribute to her best friend and tour masseuse of the same name.

The isolation was not only welcome, it was needed. Reykjavik had once provided reprieve from the rigors of celebrity, but recent events meant that even the locals could no longer conceal their curiosity. Things had changed in her absence; now, even Iceland's normally subdued and respectful populace seemed a little awestruck by her presence. Father Guðmundur Gunnarsson remembers his appalled daughter returning from the cottage and relaying a frustrating tale. "A car drove by her, suddenly stopped and backed up," he says. "The mother pointed at [Björk] through the window frame, the kids in the backseat pointed through the glass. Björk was furious about that. She said, 'Why didn't they come out of the car and say, "Hello Björk, how are you doing?" instead?'"

Nonetheless, December had been a welcome homecoming on the whole. The opportunity to be surrounded by friends and family allowed Björk to reclaim an important piece of herself, and gave her the chance to reconnect with the stability and tradition of home. "It's always the same thing," she enthused. "On the 24th, we eat dinner at six. Actually, I can almost taste the rice pudding with raisins and cinnamon. And after all the presents are open, we sit by the fireplace. New Year's Eve was brilliant as well because I invited most of my mates over, like the people I had been working with in London. There were 40 of them, and with my family there were, like, one hundred of us. And we rented a ski hut in the mountains, and we had fireworks. And all these people playing and doing magical tricks. It was very special. People snowboarding left, right, and center."

Before she could return to Spain to record, Björk was sidetracked by a two-week worldwide press tour in promotion of the recently released *Telegram*, which had been lukewarmly received by critics. While many had been quick to laud her for releasing such a brazenly challenging collection, others had dismissed the album as a cash-in, a contractual in-betweener. Worse yet, some critics, perhaps crushed by the weight of Björk's overexposure, questioned the concept of a remix album altogether.

For Björk, who had in some ways considered *Telegram* to be just as vital to her overall aesthetic as *Debut* or *Post*, the mixed reaction had been disappointing. Nonetheless, she justified herself admirably. "For me, *Telegram* is really *Post* as well but all the elements of the songs are just exaggerated," she explained. "It's like the core of *Post*. That's why it's funny to call it a remix album, it's like the opposite. The cover of *Post*: me [smiling] in pink and orange and a big ribbon — it's like a pressie for you. But *Telegram* is more stark, naked. Not trying to make it pretty or peaceable for the ear. Just a record I would buy myself."

"A lot of people still think the word 'remix' means 'recycle' as in 'trash,' like it's just a way for a record company to make a song more radio-friendly," she said to *Melody Maker*. "But I think they're just being snobs. In music there's always been a tradition of having many versions of a song. Like when Bach did his organ fugues. . . .

"I'd like to point out here that I'm not comparing myself to Bach," she continued. "I may be mad, but I'm not that mad . . . [but] when Bach did that he didn't write all the notes down, and every time an organ player played it, it was different. Same with jazz standards like 'Round Midnight' or 'My Funny Valentine.' There's 500 versions of those tunes and none of them is correct."

There were also issues of context to surmount. Many of the tracks on *Telegram* had meandered off into distinctly uncommercial territory without Björk's pop-leaning ear to guide them. With contributions from a stable of decidedly unpopulist electronic artists (junglist Dillinja, or Mika Vainio — one half of Finnish techno duo Sahko), the album's lineup was also unyieldingly obscure. Positioned alongside the simultaneous world-beating success of Prodigy's "Firestarter" and the Chemical Brothers' "Setting Sun" (singles which, for better or worse, had redefined "electronic music" to the mainstream), *Telegram* must have seemed positively out of step.

Björk's North American press tour (which included stops in New York, Chicago, and Toronto) was mercifully brief, and like any impassioned music geek, she bemoaned the sorry state of populist America upon her return. "I went to New York last January and did some interviews and they were all like, 'Electronica is the next big thing,' and I'm like, '*Please*,'" she complained. "And they put it under the same thing as Prodigy, Kraftwerk, Massive Attack – the whole lot. To them it's this thing that was born half a year ago."

"The Chemical Brothers are hard rock!" she wailed in another interview. "Americans are so dumb! The one band they pick as electronic, and it's a rock band. It's like MTV did a show with Wu-Tang Clan and called it a rockumentary. It's rap! If it's not four white guys holding a beer, then they don't know what to do with it!"

Due partly to mainstream disinterest and partly to its slight promotional schedule, *Telegram* left album charts rather unbothered. Although claims of it being a record label toss-off were easy to refute (Björk went to the trouble of recording entirely new vocal tracks for many of the remixes), its appeal was relegated mainly to the hardcore fans, many of whom had already become ingratiated to the sounds of 808 State, Eumir Deodato, and Tricky by association.

Björk's return to Spain later that January allowed the focus to shift to *Homogenic* once and for all. As with *Post*, she entered into this album with a solid set of pre-established criteria. One thing was definitely certain: Nellee Hooper would not be back in any capacity. "It came to an end because he and I stopped surprising each other," she said. "It was quite magical when we met, and it exploded with the same intensity, but we're really good friends now. I like to think that I can survive on my own."

Emboldened by the positive artistic gains from *Post*, Björk once again planned to produce *Homogenic* entirely by herself. In a concerted effort to maintain a uniformity of whole, she pared her collaborators down to a core cast that included Dravs, Howie Bernstein, Guy Sigsworth, and LFO's Mark Bell.

Incredibly, the Wu-Tang Clan came within a hair of actually contributing; had scheduling difficulties not arisen, *Homogenic* might have been a very different album. "I can't remember if RZA contacted me first, but it seemed to be a very mutual sort of thing," she said. "He said he wanted to come to Spain, but the Wu-Tang album took longer than they thought."

The meeting ultimately did happen, but not in time for *Homogenic*. At the end of 1997, Björk flew to New York to collaborate with the entire Clan. Afterwards, a bemused RZA likened Björk to Las Vegas. "We brought in some of the New York Philharmonic Orchestra, mixed up hip-hop and saxophone," he said of the sessions. "You can rock it inside a techno club or on the radio. Just like Las Vegas! A lot of people, they scared to be around us sometimes, but Björk just runs around goin', 'Ark ark ark!' It's like we from the same motherfuckin' cusp. She's unorthodox."

Sadly, the RZA's soundbite would be the best thing to emerge from these sessions; although the union was reportedly fruitful enough to fill an entire EP, their original material has yet to surface anywhere and is assumed abandoned.

Implicit in the album titles *Debut*, *Post*, and *Telegram* was a trajectory with a built-in finish line, a chronology of travel that Björk had tacitly charted and conquered. She may not have been cognizant of it while in its midst, but, as evidenced by her naming convention, Björk had been quietly preparing for regeneration all along. If those earlier records were the sound of her learning to crawl, walk, and finally run, then *Homogenic* was destined to be the sound of her standing still.

It was a testament to the poetry of her intuition, then, that this creative watermark so beautifully coincided with the most turbulent time in her life. In 1997, she spoke of how the bomb incident indirectly triggered a period of self-evaluation that seemed a long time in the making. "It felt like it – apart from the drama of it – it was symbolic for what was happening in my own life, in a professional and in an emotional way," she said. "Also, I was once obsessed. By something completely different, especially by new and exciting challenges, but still. Suddenly I saw how such a thing could escalate. So yes, I did learn a lot from this incident. It was as if I had returned to reality with one blow and that I had been acting like a child during the last four years in my quest for 'kicks.' It sobered me up."

"Last September everything exploded," she said in another interview. "My unconscious had asked for that. A lot of things ended in my life. I went to Spain in the same week and crashed. I'd been holding my breath in London for four years. Emotionally, this album is about hitting rock bottom and earning your way up. So it's the darkest album I've done emotionally, but it's got a lot of hope. 'Okay, I'm on the bottom but I'm fucking going there.' It's the darkest, but the bravest."

This turbulent period in her life, not coincidentally, all occurred alongside the realization that the London chapter of her life had concluded. "It's been great," she opined, "but I'm gonna move."

Björk's creative rebirth invited her to reassess the way she'd handled herself in the wake of such fame. She'd allowed elements of her personal life to be submerged by her celebrity; now, she was coming back to her friends and family and realizing the importance of home. For someone who'd spent the past four years perpetually undone by travel and tour, these concepts of home and belonging resonated strongly. Accompanying her new perspective was a sense of ownership for the turmoil she'd been through. "The most outrageous, mental year of my life," she said. "I sent out messages and I got answers: Please put me on the edge of a cliff and will someone please kick me off."

As it became increasingly evident that the steady pull of *Homogenic* was about

Björk embracing her homeland (or more widely, about her reclamation of *self* as home), the songs began to fall into place. Most of them came the same way: with Björk penning the melodies in her head, working out the accompanying string arrangements on a small Casio keyboard, and then bringing them to her programmers, who'd start on the long and difficult process of establishing a suitable rhythm part.

Although Bernstein and Sigsworth both contributed at various helms, *Homogenic* owes its greatest debt, sonically, to the talents of Mark Bell. As one half of Sheffield electronic luminaries LFO, Bell had long been at the forefront of the IDM movement, cutting and splicing some of the genre's tautest, cleanest techno. He and Björk soon discovered that they shared many of the same musical tastes, so their reference points in the studio came readily. But that wasn't enough to stop her from lapsing into Björkspeak from time to time. "She'll go, 'Can you make the bass line more furry?'" Bell recounted. "It's always poetic, which is good, because if she tells you exactly what to do, you're more like an engineer. This way, you get to create atmospheres too."

"I'd been watching [Mark] since 1990, when he was doing LFO, because I like the pioneers who have stayed faithful to techno," Björk said. "He did several remixes for me — for example, the first remix on *Telegram*. He played with my voice, adding effects. That's another thing I'd never done, which I'd love to try more. That's one reason why Mark and I work so much together; I trust and respect what he does for me. If I were to say who influenced me most, I would say people like Stockhausen, Kraftwerk, Brian Eno, and Mark Bell, because the work Mark did when he was 19 proved to our generation that pop music is what we understand. We walk around with all these telephones and car alarms, and we hear all these noises. We can keep saying, 'No, it's soulless, it's cold,' but it's part of our lives."

Their free-flowing rapport also made it easy to improvise ideas on the fly. The iron-clad squelch of *Homogenic*'s most savage song, "Pluto," came directly as a result of one of their makeshift jam sessions. "That was me and Mark having a laugh in Spain," Björk recalled. "It was a [hot] day like this. We got a little amp outside and a keyboard and I just did all these really punk things, just really thinking heavy metal. Most of the tracks I wrote before Mark started on them, so they're more like song-songs, and then Mark would work on beats and arrangements with me afterwards."

From the shimmering beats and reversed accordion in album opener "Hunter" to the chugging, gently propulsive bass line in "Joga" to the glowing rhythmic backbone in "Alarm Call," Bell's influence is stamped all over *Homogenic*. He was eventually credited with co-production credits for the majority of the album's 10 songs.

The gorgeous seclusion of Morais' El Cortijo Studios had fostered a tight-knit feeling of family that facilitated an easy flow of ideas. As such, Björk abandoned any intentions of producing the album herself and shared production credits, variously,

*Björk previewed Homogenic for a select group of press members at Truman Brewery in Brick Lane, London in July 1997. (Photo by Björg Sveinsdóttir)*

with Bell, Bernstein, and Sigsworth. "When you work with Björk, you are one of her closest relatives," Dravs explains. "When you're part of the team, then yeah, you are almost like her brother."

Programming chops or musical virtuosity weren't always a prerequisite for being included in the family, either. Björk prized enthusiasm as a virtue on par with technical aptitude. Upon noticing that her long-time babysitter, Rebecca Storey, had begun to show interest in the equipment that Dravs had set up in her Maida Vale home, she encouraged her to get involved. Although she had no prior experience, Storey joined the team in Spain, with Björk's blessing, as a full-fledged recording assistant.

"I think [Björk] appreciates people who are interested in things rather than those who are just doing their job and who are bored by it," Dravs offers. "She's got a lot of compassion for people who are interested in things, whatever they may be."

Much like the Compass Point sessions in the Bahamas, Björk was intent on harvesting her picturesque surroundings to full reward. "I remember she wanted to record a lot outside on the balcony," Dravs says. "She was quite inspired in terms of experimenting with recording in different locations. On *Post*, it was caves. On *Homogenic*, it was a balcony looking out towards Morocco in the Spanish mountains."

All of Spain had been this loose, this easy. With those mountains behind them and Marbellan beaches in front, El Cortijo's was a pacifying atmosphere, one that these close-knit people were only too happy to share with each other. Björk and the crew had fallen into a happy state of ritual there; they'd share breakfast together in the morning, record all day, and retreat to a nearby flamenco bar in nearby Puerto Banus to get joyously drunk at night. For four months, El Cortijo was Björk's very own beautiful place in the country.

Although a vital component of the record, the string parts were actually among the last things to be recorded for *Homogenic*. To facilitate the sessions, Björk turned to old friend Eumir Deodato who joined them in Spain long enough to conduct, transcribe, and compose original treatments for the few songs that Björk hadn't already arranged herself.

In keeping with the album's theme, Björk commissioned the services of an Icelandic string octet. Although they'd all been stationed with various symphonies in different parts of the world, the eight-piece brought a uniquely Icelandic sensibility to the album once they converged upon Spain. "Some string players would come from New York, some from Berlin, some from Australia, but obviously they were all Icelandic," Dravs laughs. "To see them talk, and also to see them party, you would think that they were all raving lunatics. They'd go out on the town and then sort of crawl into the studio the next day after doing aerobics in a Spanish flamenco bar or whatever."

Since the crew spent the majority of their time in Spain faithfully preparing Björk's compositions in deference to the vision she'd had in her head, these string sessions were their first opportunity to get a clear sense of her abiding vision. "It wasn't until the strings [were added] where I thought, 'Oh my God, this is *amazing*,'" Dravs says. "When you actually hear a really good eight-piece string session play over some of those beats, with her sometimes singing at the same time . . . it was very special."

Ever the armchair anthropologist, Björk later developed a roughly hewn theory to support her beats-and-strings motif, one which correlated nicely with the abiding beats-as-lava, strings-as-snowfall precept. "Scientists haven't discovered it yet," she enthused, "but the human nerve system — which is basically our soul — is very similar to a violin string, cause when you hear strings it's like you get all mushy. It's not a coincidence it has the same effect on everybody.

"When I was in Spain, I never liked lace. I thought it was kind of cheap. But then I started thinking, 'There's lace everywhere! Why is it everyone around the world wears this same pattern and thinks it's sexy?' It doesn't matter if it's a millionaire's wife in Dallas or a whore in Honolulu. Maybe our blood cells choreograph themselves into a state of passion. The beats are like the blood and the strings are the heart!"



Of course, a Björk album wouldn't be a Björk album without a last-minute delay, and *Homogenic* was no exception. In May, after realizing that she was horribly behind schedule, Björk was forced to cancel a handful of American radio festival obligations. The only contract she didn't break was the one she'd made with the Beastie Boys to play at the 1997 Tibetan Freedom Concert in New York, which she kept out of moral obligation.

The album's final months were marked by harried indecision. By June, with the dependable Mark "Spike" Stent presiding over the mix, Björk was still unsure about a number of critical elements, including the final tracklisting. A few songs, like the patently atypical strum of "So Broken" and the storming "Sod Off," were on the bubble, and remained so until the eleventh hour.

Elsewhere, a mounting list of delays conspired to detain the album further still. There were problems on the design end (photographer Nick Knight required a reshoot of the cover photo) as well as with the final product – ever self-critical, Björk was still not completely satisfied with a few of the album's vocal takes.

Near the end of August, One Little Indian made the difficult decision to delay the album by another month. This meant that Björk's scheduled jaunt across Europe at the beginning of September would now precede *Homogenic*'s release, and that she'd be testing her new material on largely unanointed crowds. With a backing band that consisted entirely of Mark Bell, she made stops in Germany, the Netherlands, France, Belgium, Spain, and England, juggling a string of brief, half-hour live shows (that consisted exclusively of new material) with standard press duties at every post.

Björk's approach to her promotional obligations now seemed to be balanced by a healthy caution, something that had certainly been absent in the past. She was managing herself differently as a public figure; now, she seemed willing to exchange a degree of lesser commercial success for some semblance of privacy. It took a while, and a lot to get her there, but she had finally learned to say no.

This slightly guarded approach was evident in many of her artistic decisions. The video for lead single "Joga" had been shot in Iceland that summer, with Michel Gondry once again at the helm, and is an elegant, computer-aided tour of the country's varied landscapes. Simpler and more direct than its predecessors, this promo succinctly captures the spirit of Björk's new, uncluttered headspace. With its long, sweeping shots of the Icelandic geology and absolutely none of Björk (save for a computer-generated version that briefly appears in the end), it is also a patently uncommercial offering, one perhaps more easily mistaken for a documentary on plate tectonics rather than an MTV-friendly music video.

*Another occupational hazard: learning to decipher the meanings of questions posed by foreign journalists. (Yoram Kahana/Shooting Star)*

Designer Alexander McQueen's final concept for the *Homogenic* cover toyed with Björk's visage in a similarly subversive way. Although originally based on photos, the end result was drastically retouched and exaggerated so as to simultaneously imply Björk's presence and also to negate it. There — draped in a motley assortment of traditional garb that borrowed liberally from Ethiopia to Japan — was not Björk, but rather someone we understood to be her.

Arguably more than any artist of her generation, Björk's face had been her brand. In choosing to conflate the presentation of that brand, she was drawing clear new boundaries between her private and public personas. Whether computer-generated or artificially retooled, this was, for the time being, as much of herself as she was willing to give. It was simultaneously a riff on her status as pop creature exotica and an excuse to escape entirely.

Ironically, *Homogenic* would soon be praised by critics and fans as Björk's most personal album yet.

Although the surface of *Homogenic* was all jagged rock formations and scraggy volcanoes, there was a gush of bright blue water bubbling at its core. Where *Debut* and *Post* had both dealt with love in a more overarching, universal fashion, *Homogenic* had the scars of personal experience bravely braided into its seams. With the loping, heart-rending "Unravel" as its benchmark, this album was the sound of a lovelorn soul letting go of the wheel and resigning her path to the hands of fate.

"I used to have all these opinions about love because I'm fierce, a helpless romantic," Björk said. "What happened is my expectations about romance were there but what was really happening was here. The elastic stretched so much it cracked. And now I'm more realistic about things. I love so many people. Your mate doesn't have to replace everything. I don't know and I'm not going to pretend I do.

"It's back to basics, being self-sufficient. Now I'm back to how I was as a kid when I used to spend most of my time alone. So I'm spending time by myself and enjoying it very much. It sounds sad, but when I was a kid I didn't really have friends. The most magical moments I had in my life I had alone. Like climbing mountains or swimming or singing or listening to music."

Happily, Björk found new love the moment she stopped looking. And, unlike the way she'd handled some of her prior romances, she was doing everything in her power to keep this relationship private. She'd done a good job: she'd secretly been dating Howie Bernstein for months before anyone in the media caught on.

"I've known him for seven years and he engineered a lot of *Debut* and most of *Post* and he's just one of my best mates, you know, and I'm just so pleased," she confessed at the end of that year. "Sometimes you really, really try to organize things and make them happen? It can work for a lot of areas of your life but for your love life, it doesn't work. You don't go out and get it. I'm not even going to pretend I know, 'cause I don't. But I recommend going out with your best mate 'cause you're already great mates. Things can't really go wrong."

"Joga" would be Björk's third consecutive lead single to fail to garner significant support from radio or television, but that wouldn't matter much to fans. In spite of this or any real supporting tour, *Homogenic* debuted admirably upon its release in late September, opening at #28 on the Billboard album chart and at #4 on the British album chart. This kind of success – especially on the back of what was widely being touted as such an uncommercial album – only cemented Björk's status as one of music's few populist experimentalists.

Also gratifying was the influx of positive critical response that greeted the album, a nice turnaround from the lukewarm reception to *Telegram* and solid proof that there was no tangible Björk backlash to speak of. *Spin* and *NME* led a massive charge of critics proclaiming the album as her finest work yet; the general consensus across the board was that she had hit a career benchmark.

And yet, with only a few notable exceptions (an appearance on *Saturday Night Live*; the filming of the video for second single, "Bachelorette," again with Gondry), Björk kept a relatively low profile throughout it all. When she finally did announce details of a European tour, it was on a comparatively smaller scale. Beginning in late October and promising stops in Italy, Switzerland, France, England, Scotland, Germany, Ireland, and Denmark, this brief jaunt was scheduled to last less than four weeks. A two-week North American stint followed in December; after that, there was absolutely nothing on her itinerary.

Of course, nothing could be that easy. In late November, after complaining of a high temperature, Björk was admitted to a Reykjavik hospital and diagnosed with a routine kidney infection. The prognosis was healthy — there was absolutely no danger in view — but, as she'd been advised to rest for three weeks, she was forced to cancel any remaining obligations for the year. Her entire American promotional tour (consisting of various radio concerts, a few high-profile shows, some video channel interviews, and a performance on *Late Night with David Letterman*) had to be postponed. In good spirits, but disappointed nonetheless, Björk retired to her home in Iceland for another Christmas break. It had been a bittersweet end to an otherwise satisfying year; she looked forward to the time ahead, knowing full well that, for once, she had time on her side.

Nineteen ninety-seven had been about a figurative return to home; 1998 was going to be about a literal return to home. The intense media scrutiny and urban squall of London had taken its toll. Newly enamored with Reykjavik and calmed by the change of pace it afforded, Björk and Sindri (now 12 years old) relocated back to their homeland.

Björk's resettlement to a more serene climate set the tone for her entire year; although by no means eventless, the next 12 months would be comparatively quiet, bestowing her with some much needed calm and tranquility. In her absence, *Homogenic* was still performing admirably. Gondry's mind-boggling concept for "Bachelorette" had resulted in one of his best videos yet, and had thrust Björk back onto television channel playlists.

Björk's original idea for the video had been neatly in sync with her own experience over the past few months; she saw "Bachelorette" as the continuation of a character established in the songs "Human Behaviour" and "Isobel." "When she called me for Bachelorette, she said to me . . . now this character is leaving the forest and she decides to go to the city to have a normal life," Gondry says. "She tries her best and it doesn't work out and she comes back to the forest and she is happier there."

For the time being, Björk was also very content to be living back in her forest. She'd appear at various award shows to accept plaudits for *Homogenic* (she accepted Best International Female at the Brit Awards with a simple speech: "I am grateful grapefruit"), but other than that, she stayed far out of the spotlight.

Plans to co-headline a North American tour with Radiohead were announced and subsequently jettisoned when it became evident that both artists' elaborate stage requirements made it impossible to orchestrate the transition from one to the other with any degree of effectiveness. Björk made up her canceled dates with a relatively low-key tour that summer which took her across Europe for a few months. She concluded by finally coming through on some oft-postponed stints in Chile, Brazil, and Argentina; by the end of August, she was home in Iceland again.

The same mistakes were not to be repeated.

# nine

Much like his status as a brilliant conceptualist, Danish-born filmmaker Lars Von Trier's reputation as independent film's resident *enfant terrible* had been hard-fought and well-earned. As one of the founding members of the infamous Dogme 95 movement (whose manifesto demanded that the truth of a film never be compromised by standard Hollywood crutches such as mounted cameras, pre-built sets, or music that wasn't actually part of a scene), Von Trier had taken a rabble-rousing approach to his craft early on. His Dogme 95 film *The Idiots* and his most recent film – the 1996 Cannes Grand Prize winner *Breaking the Waves* – had both been critical successes, positioning him among independent film's most lauded directors.

For his next project, Von Trier set out to turn the American musical on its ear. His screenplay, provisionally titled *Taps*, focuses on a tatty immigrant named Selma who has been transposed from her native Czechoslovakia to a low-paying industrial job in '60s backwoods America. On the verge of losing her eyesight, Selma's single motive in life is to raise enough money to fund an operation that will save her nine-year-old son from a similar fate. Her vivid imagination and reverence for '50s style musicals would be the film's driving force, paving the road for its lavish but strangely untraditional bursts of digitally filmed, unconventionally edited song-and-dance.

Von Trier's perverse compulsion for tragedy also meant that the screenplay could not emerge from his hands a mere musical; as a series of events in the second half of the film sends Selma through excruciating horror, the accompanying songs become more wrenching, the film more tormenting. By the time he'd completed it, *Dancer in the Dark* revealed itself as a grueling psychological drama merely masquerading in a musical's skin.

The amount of emotion and sheer musical awe written into Selma had suggested someone of Björk's character for the part. Even though she had little experience as an actress in feature film, there were many in Von Trier's community who had enough faith in Björk's natural ability to start mentioning her name. "When you see her in her video clips, you see she can be so charming," offers *Dancer in the Dark* co-producer and *Rokk I Reykjavik* director Friðrik Þór Friðriksson. "It's like the camera is in love with her, so there's always something visual going on onscreen."

While Von Trier insists that his inspiration for casting Björk came after seeing her performance in the video for "It's Oh So Quiet," there are others who openly suggest that Von Trier wrote the entire screenplay with Björk in mind. "He didn't write that film and think, 'Oh, should I get her or Lisa Stansfield?'" Leila Arab jokes. "It's her — it *had* to be her.

"It's no joke writing a film for someone," she continues. "You don't do that out of fucking boredom. So obviously, it was loaded. Yeah, she wanted to believe it could be more gracious, and yeah he was utterly totally respectful of her, but then it's hard. . . ."

One thing is for certain: if he hadn't written it as a tribute to her, it wasn't long before Von Trier became intent on procuring Björk to play the part. His Danish-based film company Zentropa Productions had long enjoyed a relationship with various members of the neighboring Icelandic film industry, and through those connections, he began floating the suggestion around. Longtime Zentropa affiliate Hilmar Örn Hilmarsson was the last person he contacted.

"I am responsible in the sense that I got Björk in touch with Lars Von Trier," Hilmarsson sighs. "I had been working a lot for Lars' company and I've known Lars for a number of years. To my eternal shame, I actually talked Björk into it."

In an effort to win her favor, Von Trier sent Björk a copy of *Breaking the Waves*, which she in turn adored. Her original instinct, however, had been to contribute strictly in a musical sense, to leave the film work to someone else. The idea of acting didn't seem natural to her — not in the same way that music did — and it took serious coercion from numerous parties before she would even consider it.

Hilmarsson was one of those who encouraged the collaboration. While he now regrets it, he insists that his original reasons for doing so were noble — as strong creative entities, both Von Trier and Björk stood to learn a great deal from the experience of working with one another. "I actually thought it would be good for Lars to work with Björk because he's intent on molding people, breaking them down and building them up in his own image," Hilmarsson says. "I thought it would be an interesting experience for him."

The Zentropa camp regarded Björk with similar intrigue. Producer Vibeke Windeløv says, "From what I'd read about her, she was the Lars Von Trier of the music business. I saw her as the same kind of unique artist, [one] who would use the normal media but still maintain her own unique way of doing things, completely uncompromising in the sense that she wouldn't go for something that would sell, she would do something she thought was right."

Friðrik Þór Friðriksson, whose sometimes tumultuous relationship with Zentropa had gone back 10 years and spanned over 20 films, gave Björk slightly different advice: "I didn't tell her they were bad guys because they're not," he laughs. "But they are just like kids. They're *Danish*, right? They are naughty guys — there's a strange kind of sense of humor, sometimes it's okay but sometimes it's way, way over the line and it's very childish."

Indeed, Von Trier's reputation for psychological manipulation was something that he had made no effort to conceal. In *De Ydmygede* (translation: "The Humiliated"), Jesper Jargil's documentary on the making of *The Idiots*, he's shown ruthlessly cutting lead actress Louise Hassing down to size. By the end of his relentless tirade, she is broken, reduced to tears, defeated. It is enough to suggest that what Von Trier really means when he suggests collaboration is total ownership by him and surrender to him.

Björk knew all about this, even the extent of it, but chose to regard Von Trier's prickly reputation as a challenge rather than a deterrent. So surefooted was she in the realm of collaboration that she felt like she could handle whatever he leveled at her. "I think to a certain degree, because I had worked with so many people, and it had gone so well, that I was maybe just a little overconfident," she said. "Maybe that was one of the reasons why I agreed to do the film. Because here was a person who was notorious for being impossible to work with — so, you know, if I could work with him, it would unite everything."

Even so, intellectually she knew in advance that this project would end in turmoil. "My instinct is 50 times more wise than my head," she said. "From the start my instinct was saying, 'Go go go' and my head was going, 'This is the most ridiculous thing you could do in your life.' I had to follow my instinct."

Björk's instinct was to cede to the doubt and embrace the opportunity. In doing so, she insists she made it clear to Von Trier that her commitment to the project hinged on some very critical guidelines. As the resident musician, she wanted control over all of the film's musical elements, including having final and definitive say over every aspect of the songs, ranging from the production and arrangements right down to the lyrics. "I wrote out a manifesto saying: I want to mix my own music, I want to be there if they change it and take part in the decision-making on my songs, I want to finalize my own CD when it's in the shop, I want to decide what picture goes on the cover of the CD," she recalled.

Speaking on behalf of Zentropa, Windeløv suggests that this was not the case; she states that there was nothing in Björk's initial contract that dealt with the issue of creative control. If Björk had an agreement with Von Trier, it was a verbal one. "This was something that was actually said a lot of times: she would write the music and once she had done the music, she would put herself in the hands of Lars and he would continue from then on," Windeløv claims. "Considering how hands-on Lars normally is with composers and things like that . . . she took the freedom, but I wouldn't say it was given to her."

By October, Björk began to prepare in earnest for the project. While still living in Reykjavik, she attended tap dancing lessons three times a week and had started the long process of writing songs for the album. Composing these pieces with Selma in mind allowed her to get an emotional head start on the acting process and to form a close relationship with her character six months before filming. It was an intuitive and sometimes wrenching process. "I read the script and my immediate reaction was very emotional," she said. "So I would start writing the songs from a very emotional point of view. More like a form of love for Selma rather than anything else. For me to react in an intellectual way. . . . I couldn't even though I tried, it's not what I'm about."

With the assistance of Bell (who'd flown out to Reykjavik), Guy Sigsworth, local luminary Valgeir Sigurdsson, and erstwhile lyricist Sjon Sigurdsson, the music of *Selmasongs* began to take shape. In addition to the seven songs that would ultimately comprise the whole of the album, these sessions also yielded "Amphibian," a stark and intimate track that foreshadowed the minimalist direction in which her more autonomous songs had been heading. If *Homogenic* had been about finding strength through resiliency, then these new songs were revealing themselves to be about the beauty of fragility.

Even though he remained in Denmark, Von Trier did his best to assert his presence during the course of these writing sessions. Friðriksson remembers getting frantic calls from the embattled director, who'd call his number looking for Björk or Sjon. It was obvious, even this early on, that the two sides were having trouble agreeing on the nature of the music. "I told Sjon to never give in on the music side because these guys are Hitlers when it comes to music," Friðriksson says. "They have absolutely no taste for music. They don't know what they are dealing with when they are dealing with Björk."

"It was very much that she really left Lars out," Windeløv counters. "She had promised to send things to Lars and they weren't coming. The frustration was very big." 

One of the first issues of contention involved the preliminary lyrics that Von Trier had provided. Björk disliked some of them; she felt they weren't in keeping with Selma's character. Windeløv recalls the words to "I've Seen It All" as being particularly problematic. "That was really Lars' lyric," she says. "Björk's manager was ridiculing Lars about how it was impossible for Björk to sing and how ridiculous it was and how could she ever sing something that was so . . . they found whatever Lars wrote extremely bland and not sophisticated. But Lars wanted it to be like that because he thought that was how Selma was. He didn't want it to be sophisticated, he wanted it to be extremely plain."

The mounting problems and lack of communication between both sides allegedly escalated to a point where Von Trier and Windeløv decided to sever ties with Björk early on. "At one point Lars called me at five o'clock in the morning," Windeløv recalls. "I was in Cologne and he said, 'Vibeke, this can't go on. How can we co-operate in this movie? It doesn't seem as if she is really interested in doing this with me.' And I said, 'Judging from the messages I get through her managers, you're right. If you want to, you can tell her that maybe we should stop.' Lars said he thought we should do that, and so we told her.

"She got very upset," Windeløv continues. "I went to London to talk to some other music people [about the project], but it was completely half-hearted in the sense that even though I thought it was difficult [with Björk], I had no doubt that she was what I thought [Selma] should be. To have Lars put together with some rock/pop big shot made no sense. For me, the whole uniqueness of the project was that it was Björk and Lars put together. It would just be a normal film with a great soundtrack if we put some other person on it.

"Then Lars wrote me a letter. Or maybe it was a copy of something he sent to Sjon. He said that maybe we can find somebody else to be Selma, but in our hearts, we'll always know that Selma is Björk. When he wrote that, I was in London, and I was like, 'I have to make this work.' So I called Björk one morning when I came out of a meeting and we talked for a couple of hours about Lars and about her relationship with Lars and what she wanted to do and so on. And it was actually a really good conversation. I called Lars and I said, 'We have to try. It *has* to work.'"

While her obligations to *Dancer in the Dark* precluded her from going ahead with her solo career, Björk quietly chose her spots where she could. Partly in an effort to quell inaccurate rumors of her desire to retire from touring, she performed a handful of live dates across Britain. This sparse and intimate mini-tour culminated with a secret gig in a Bristol church that featured the Brodsky Quartet as her backing orchestration. The conditions for this show would provide another clue to Björk's quieter, more contemplative headspace; in an unprecedented move, she performed the entire concert acoustically, her voice reverberating round the tiny church walls without the aid of any microphones.

Impressively, *Homogenic* was still kicking around; a new video for the album's fourth single "Alarm Call" (the original version of which had been shot earlier that year and promptly jettisoned) had been filmed with fashion designer and first-time director Alexander McQueen at the helm. Björk's relative absence hadn't diminished her critical appeal; "Alarm Call" was rated *NME*'s Single of the Week in November before quietly disappearing.

But her most impressive visual coup was just around the corner. Having once worked as an assistant to Stanley Kubrick on the project that eventually became Steven Spielberg's *A.I.: Artificial Intelligence*, British director Chris Cunningham had earned a name for himself in art circles as an up-and-coming director of unparalleled talent. Like anyone fortunate enough to actually see them, Björk had been impressed by Cunningham's eye-popping (and often disturbing) video clips for leading electronic luminaries such as Autechre, Squarepusher, and Aphex Twin. Cunningham's clear lines, sci-fi leanings, and jarring imagery had Björk raving about his work. "Most video directors have one trick that they use all the time," she gushed. "Then there are people who build a whole world around them. Chris is like that. We have only seen the tip of the iceberg with Chris. He is only just coming into his own."

Björk's track record as talent scout was, once again, about to bear her out. Nineteen ninety-nine would see Cunningham unveil his two most brilliant works — the dystopic, gleeful headfuck of Aphex Twin's Cali-bashing, porn-soaked "Windowlicker" and the goosebump-inducing shudder of Björk's "All Is Full of Love."

Cunningham's stunning treatment for the video hinged on a simple concept: two androids with technoid appendages and fluid faces modeled after Björk's likeness are assembled piecemeal by sterile machinery before meeting in a sensual embrace. Their final kiss, erotic and gentle, is accompanied by a carefully constructed flow of imagery. Gears chug, tongues tickle, metallic tendrils extend, a milky liquid surges, the kiss fruition.

The considerable achievements of videos like "Human Behaviour," "It's Oh So Quiet," and "Bachelorette" notwithstanding, "All Is Full of Love" marked an unquestionable creative apex for Björk's visual work, a perfect synthesis of form and content. Having favored Mark Stent's superior original treatment of the song over Howie Bernstein's flaccid, torpid remix (which regrettably, was ultimately the one that found its way onto *Homogenic*), the stunning clip eventually propelled the single to a very respectable #24 placement on the U.K. singles chart. Considering that it was her fifth single from the album, that the previous single "Alarm Call" had peaked at #33, and that the video had been banned on many television stations due to its robo-erotic content, this marked a considerable achievement and a fitting send-off to the unqualified artistic benchmark of *Homogenic*.

The basic outlines of the tracks on *Selmasongs* needed to be written and recorded before shooting began the following summer, so Björk gathered a small team of collaborators at Iceland's Greenhouse Studios to begin tracking that January. The opportunity to work on such a grand scale – with a full orchestra for each song – had been a lifelong dream realized. It also put her childhood skills to better use: "I was in a classical music school when I was younger and this was the first time my academic side could be expressed," she said. "It was a personal victory for me. I learned craftsmanship and discipline."

With the filming process officially scheduled to begin in May, Björk packed her bags and relocated to Trollhättan, Sweden. The relocation would signal Björk's permanent departure not only from Iceland, but from Bernstein. After roughly a year together, the couple parted ways as quietly as they'd begun.

Trollhättan may have seemed an odd choice for a film location, but there weren't many other options available. Von Trier's well-documented fear of flying meant that the cast and crew were inevitably landlocked and unable to shoot on location in the U.S. If the film's questionable depiction of industrialized northwest '60s America seemed overtly European in nature, it's because Von Trier had never seen the real thing firsthand. Like any willful contrarian, the Dogme 95 founder later professed to take a perverse pleasure in the inauthenticity of his settings. "We shot in Sweden and places that could look like America," he said. "And that may be more interesting than actually going to America. I'm always reminded of Kafka's *Amerika*. He had never been there and in the first pages of the novel, when he sails into the harbor of New York, he describes the Statue of Liberty carrying a big sword . . . I always thought that was quite poetic."

With a cast rounded out by veteran actors Catherine Deneuve, American David Morse, and Sweden's Peter Stormare, Björk had good reason to feel somewhat out of their league as an actress. The lack of experience that she struggled with in less demanding roles like *The Juniper Tree* was about to catch up with her.

Unlike her peers, Björk lacked the ability to move in and out of her character with any fluidity. She'd already become attached to Selma over the course of the songwriting process; now, peering out from behind her Coke-bottle glasses, slouching underneath her tatty dresses and mumbling her fragmented words, there was truly no escape. In lieu of technique, Björk donned Selma's skin. "When Lars convinced me to act the [part], he asked me not to act," Björk said. "Acting was bad; that's what professionals do. I had to become the girl. That was fine with me, because I'm not interested in being technical."

It started smoothly, with Von Trier and Björk developing a comfortable rapport. "I remember the first couple of weeks in Sweden as being good," Windeløv agrees. "Björk worked really hard, and Lars was very respectful of what she was doing. Maybe I'm painting it a little too rosy right now, but I was listening in on a lot of the shooting while I was sitting and watching what was going on. Lars was extremely responsive, and she was very, very good."

But by the time shooting moved to Denmark in June, that feel-good vibe had dissolved, and tensions between Björk and Von Trier had formed. According to Björk, the director's manipulative working methodology stretched far beyond was she was prepared for. "Lars doesn't consider it his responsibility to make sure people are psychologically stable after he's worked with them in such an intense way," she said. "As far as he's concerned, they can be ruined emotionally, but that's just not his responsibility."

Windeløv counters on behalf of Von Trier by suggesting that Björk had difficulties adjusting to the protocol of a film set. "I think part of what was really tough for Björk was that she had been used to a life where she can decide everything," she said. "At one point she said to me, 'Vibeke, I'm usually the Queen Bee. I'm the one who makes all the decisions, I'm the one who sets the time, the speed, everything. And this is really tough for me.' The first day she was handed a call sheet . . . in a way I sometimes feel that it wasn't until she was standing with that call sheet in her hand that she realized that she had given up her time completely."

Whether her time or her peace of mind, it was obvious to the most seasoned actors around her that although she was doing a brilliant job, Björk's methods were, at very best, unsustainable. One of the film's most pivotal moments called for Selma to murder a close friend; after filming her scene, Björk collapsed into tears off-set. According to actor David Morse, part of this pain came from "the way she had to experience things. For instance, I don't think she's ever picked up a gun in her life. So to bring herself to do these things that were deeply, genuinely repulsive to her — she couldn't pretend to do them. But I think she truly has the instincts of an actress."

"Going through what Selma was going through was very painful," Björk said. "It was painful just to wake up in the morning. [Acting is like] going to the Vietnam War. I believed I might die. Acting is like jumping from a cliff without a parachute."

"Björk is not an actor — which was a surprise for me because she seemed so professional, and she really isn't," Von Trier said. "And that what's so good about the whole thing. She's not *acting* anything in this film; she's *feeling* everything, which is incredible. She was really feeling the core of this person and the fate of this person, which made it extremely hard for her. And extremely hard on everybody. It's like being with a dying person all the time."

"She would defend certain things about Selma where she thought Lars was

*Lars Von Trier and a very nervous Björk greet media and onlookers at the Cannes Film Festival as they debut Dancer in the Dark. (Eric Robert/Corbis Sygma/Magma)*

wrong," Windeløv agrees. "Selma would feel like *this*, and she knew because she *was* Selma."

It would be one of many debates between the two. At the heart of Von Trier and Björk's communicative tangle lay a whirlwind of complicated issues. Their relationship was founded on an imbalance of power, maintained by mutual respect, derailed by each other's ability to hurt one another, confused by similarity, compromised by betrayal. This tension seemed to fluctuate constantly: on any given day, it would be impossible to know what to expect from their frazzled dynamic. Some scenes came easily, others painfully, but nothing with any consistency. "That's what these relationships are," Arab explains. "It's everything from the most banal to the most profound. So I think it's really a little too basic, you know, these creative, trusting . . . it is like little marriages. They are little love affairs. But my argument with her was look at the state of his other film, the geezer is obviously a fucking fuck-up. Like, hello, goodbye." Björk knew one thing with certainty: she was deeply unhappy in the process.

"You can see if Björk is going through a dilemma or problem when she has called in some of her old friends to be with her, like the first month after the bombing incident," father Guðmundur Gunnarsson says. "When she was out in Denmark, she was living with two or three of her girlfriends."

The presence of close friends Andrea and Joga wasn't enough. Exhausted by the acting process and frustrated by the roadblocks that she was constantly encountering on the musical end, Björk was nearing her wit's end. "I had done one and a half years of work with an 80-piece orchestra, and then I'm working on the set as an actress," she said. "I'd come home in the evening and they'd say, 'Oh, they cut a minute out of the middle of something,' and I would say, 'No, you can't do that; I'm ready to co-operate but you just can't do that. . . .'"

This is where stories begin to differ. Windeløv claims that Björk started making unreasonable demands at this point. "There was that horrible morning where [Björk's manager] Scott Rodger had set a meeting and said if she didn't have final cut of all the music then she was going to walk out, and that by the way, she was not coming in that day," she says. "Which is, to me, completely outrageous. And that's the first time I realized that we weren't dealing with an actress. We were dealing with a rock star who did not understand, and who really had no respect for the people she was working with."

But for Björk, the issue had *everything* to do with respect; from her vantage point, there was no collaboration happening — she was simply being pushed around, emotions extracted and then discarded. If she tried to assert herself, Zentropa spun the story by playing the spoiled rock star card. If she rolled over for dead, her vision for Selma would be trampled. It was a lose-lose situation.

Nevertheless, she stood her ground. The confusion between both sides resulted in a panicked renegotiation of terms. Derek Birkett flew over from London to attend a meeting with Björk, Von Trier, and Windeløv and brokered a deal that officially gave Björk some creative control. The renegotiation was against the co-producer's wishes, but she was afraid of losing her star in mid-production, so Windeløv made the requisite contractual obligations and gave the contract back to Birkett. "We finally end up with an amendment to the contract saying there will be mutual agreement on the music scenes," she recalls.

Not by a longshot would that be an end to the on-set turmoil. Windeløv maintains that when Björk finally returned to the set later that week on a Friday night, she was uncommonly distant and unresponsive, present but not. "Lars cannot reach her at all — she is completely out of his range," she recounts. "Joga, her assistant, says she hasn't been able to be in touch with her either and that Björk is just completely closed off. What happens is that Lars gets completely desperate. At one point, I can see her standing in the hallway, I know Lars is standing in a room next door and he somehow has eye contact with her but still there's no communication of any kind. He gets so completely frustrated and he doesn't know how to get in touch with her. Finally, he takes a chair and throws it into a video monitor and runs off. Björk runs after him, they have a discussion out somewhere in the field, and she comes back with him. And we do a fantastic scene, which is the scene where she's carried out by the people into the police car."

The weekend off didn't make things any easier. Depressed, Von Trier called Windeløv the following Monday and told her he didn't want to come to work. "I think it was his frustration that I had given up what he should have — final cut of his movie — and that it was so tough with her," Windeløv says. "I think he felt that she was completely running the set by being so impossible."

Arab counters with a different scenario: Von Trier's mounting frustration was borne out of the realization that he couldn't break Björk down in the same way that he'd done with previous actors. "Any other actress he worked with will say, 'Fuck me, he's difficult!' but not like that, because he would have changed anyone else," Arab says. "With this one, he couldn't. There was no one else in the world to do this with him.

"I think it's really fundamentally important to understand that there was an enormous and profound respect there on behalf of both of them. She's fucking cultured and educated, she watches stuff, she wants to learn, she respected him as a film director. So there was a huge profound respect, but as I've said, it's a testimony to how very flawed the human character is, especially the artist's character. That it can all go so desperately to shit when the instinct is so good."

Björk wasn't handling things any better — despite small victories, she constantly appeared on the verge of breaking down. Friðriksson had been shooting a film nearby in Denmark when a very downtrodden Björk paid him an unexpected visit. "She came to the set when I was shooting *Angels of the Universe*," he says. "She told me horror stories. She said it was an awful experience that she would never go through again."

Von Trier, Windeløv, and the rest of the crew could see the same panic and resignation in Björk's eyes. They claim they spent the second half of that summer terrified that she would abandon the project entirely. "It was really scary, because I think we all felt from then on that we couldn't trust her," Windeløv says. "That she would do whatever she felt like, that she would sacrifice the film, anything. From then on, we completely changed the schedule in order to do all the important scenes first and the least important at the end. So, in case she walked out again, we would be more or less able to finish the movie."

Von Trier's elaborate plans for *Dancer in the Dark*, which included shooting certain scenes with no fewer than 100 cameras simultaneously, required an unprecedented $15 million budget, making it by far Zentropa's most expensive project. Windeløv says they were forced to acquiesce to Björk's demands because the company simply couldn't afford to abandon the film. "If she had walked out, Zentropa would have been finished," she says. "It turned out that the contract we had with her was very good, and we probably would have been covered by whatever insurance we had and we could have sued her and all these things, but we also all knew that I would have spent the next two years in court and there would've been no film."

Hilmarsson, who happened to be living in Denmark at the time, had frequent discussions with Björk that summer. He acknowledges that she was flustered, but doesn't believe that she ever considered abandoning the film outright. "She had some really bad moments, and we talked about it," he says. "But there were also some really nice people working with them that she genuinely liked. I think Björk is a happy trooper. She does things and she is responsible for people — she doesn't really run out on a project."

A major source of acrimony between Björk and her film company centered primarily on the way that Zentropa's public relations department spun certain stories in the press. One particularly damning tale alleged that Björk had bitten her dress to shreds after a heated row with Von Trier. Friðriksson, Jónsson, Hilmarsson, and numerous others finger Zentropa as being complicit in perpetuating these fabrications. They insist that Zentropa helped circulate these stories with the intent of exploiting Björk's public image to generate advance word of mouth. Windeløv disagrees, steadfastly claiming that these incidents actually happened and were somehow leaked to the media.

"I was there, I was a part of it," she says. "By coincidence, I was in her private room to talk to her about something. She comes in and suddenly she sees, on the bed, the clothes that she's going to wear after lunch. One of them she doesn't like because, I don't know, she thought it made her look big or something. There was a reason. So she says that Manon [Rasmussen, costume designer] has promised her that she would never wear it again. Manon says, 'No, I have promised you that you will never wear it again without something on top of it, because what you don't like is that it gets all big around you. If you have a cardigan over it, it's not a problem. I haven't promised you that because there's continuity. There's no way you can not have it on.'

"And so Björk starts to scream. She takes the blouse and runs down the stairs and I run after her outside onto this big football field. As she's running, she's biting the blouse and throwing pieces of the blouse on the ground and I'm walking behind on her and picking them up. It's a huge football field, and we're walking the diagonal and I'm behind her trying to get all of the blouse. And she's really fast, really furious — biting and throwing, biting and throwing. . . ."

"Then we get to a fence and she crawls up it — it's two or three meters tall. She goes over it, throws the blouse to me, jumps down on the other side, and that's it. There I'm standing, really far away from anywhere where there's phones or anything I can do.

"I got worried about her — she was so completely freaked out. We look for her everywhere and we don't find her. She shows up at her house, I think five or seven hours later. Somebody had seen her walking in the streets; the dress she had on was quite long and she didn't like that either, so she had somehow managed to tear off the lowest 20 centimeters of it, and I think she lost her shoes too. Wardrobe spent the entire weekend sewing the small pieces back on her shirt and having a special painter come in (the skirt was green and secondhand) to paint the lower 20 centimeters of the skirt and attach it to the dress."

A Zentropa-endorsed documentary on the making of *Dancer in the Dark* was alleged by their publicity department to depict this sordid incident in full detail. Titled *Von Trier's 100 Eyes*, Katia Forbert Petersen's plodding film did nothing of the sort. Because Björk chose not to participate, the documentary's account of the episode relied on shots of a few recovered blouse segments and vaguely disconcerted looks from cast members.

As for where the story began: "I tried to keep it away from the press," Windeløv insists. "But there's always informants somewhere who tell the story, and that was why it was in the newspapers.

"Lots had happened, but in a way I think [Zentropa] used it to strengthen that image," Hilmarsson says. "[Björk] was really hurt by the way Zentropa's publicity department handled the whole thing because they decided to go for this 'Björk is mad' type of publicity. I actually phoned my friends there and said this is ridiculous and they apologized but they kept on using it. It got a lot of attention and probably sold lots of tickets, but . . ."

"There definitely were some conflicts, even though she was not eating her clothes as the press in Denmark would say," Jónsson sighs. "I think one of the chapters in her bad experience with press was how the PR people of the film were actually using gossip to promote this film. That was really, really ugly.

"The promotion was too negative in many ways. It affected the general public to go and experience this film in the right way," he adds. "For people over here, it was over the limit. This theory of all promotion being good or whatever it is — I disagree with that. I think if you are living out of a negative headspace it strikes back at you in a negative way as well."

Not surprisingly, Arab's take on the situation is markedly different from Zentropa's. Based on discussions she had with Björk at the time, she asserts that Von Trier's treatment of Björk had extended way beyond the acceptable boundaries of a director-actress relationship. Björk, meanwhile, was buckling under the stress of wanting to escape the conditions and wanting to see Selma through to the end.

"She was punishing herself," Arab says. "I wasn't surprised because everything I had seen, read, heard by or about him is fucked. That's the nature of his work.

"I think there's an element with her where she wants to believe in the good faith of this and the good will of that, especially at that point in her life. I really think it was just all those things, it was just like she believes in trying very hard and she believes in believing very much. And once she believes, everything becomes a lot with her. She's a very extreme character and I think at that point, she was probably quite kind of messed up from it all. From all the touring, all the everything, so it didn't surprise that she got into what was in effect quite a violent relationship.

"You can tell from what anyone said about the film, it's a violent experience to even watch it. My friend saw it and said she's never felt so much like throwing something at the screen, just to fucking making it stop. She cried all the way through it at the injustice of it all. So when I use the word 'violence' I don't mean literal violence."

A muted sigh of collective relief accompanied the film's wrap that August. Zentropa were stunned that the neverending soap opera had actually yielded a film, and Björk was thrilled to be able to escape back into something more familiar — music. The experience permanently scarred both parties. "The last three weeks were hell," Windeløv says. "For me at least. I can't see the movie. It was the worst experience of my life."

Meanwhile, Björk — on the verge of uniformly rave reviews and some major acting awards — denounced film altogether. "I knew when I said yes that not only would that be my first role but also my last one," she said. "And I'm very happy that this experience would be the one.

"I have to do music now. I have lost a lot of time. I have only 50 years left. . . ."

Björk may have escaped acting when she left Copenhagen in the summer of 1999, but she was a long way off from leaving *Dancer in the Dark* behind. Constant discussions between her and Zentropa about the content of the music combined with her own indecision meant that she was frequently in the studio retouching or remixing work that she had already done. In the end, the album was fully mixed on two entirely separate occasions, once before premiering at the Cannes Festival in May 2000 and once again afterwards, at Björk's behest.

The ideological debate at the heart of her dispute with Zentropa centered on a fundamental disagreement over the final concept for *Selmasongs*. Zentropa wanted it to be a faithful representation of the music in the film, complete with the other cast members' occasionally flat, certainly unlearned vocal contributions. Björk had other designs: "I see the album not as the soundtrack to the film but rather as the realization of Selma's dream," she said. "I want this record to be my gift to Selma." In the end, this ongoing dispute between Björk and certain factions at Zentropa trumped her tumultuous actress-director relationship with Von Trier.

"I had been working 16 hours a day, every day, [and they] were changing the songs," she explained once the film and soundtrack were complete. "They would chop a minute out of the song — which I don't mind; I actually prefer my songs to be four minutes long," she said. "But it would have to be the minute chopped out that I agreed with. I'm really a collaborator; I sit and talk about it, not just they take over and I go home. I can't do that. After 20 years in music I can't do that."

Zentropa wanted actor Peter Stormare's lifeless vocal on the duet "I've Seen It All" to remain on the soundtrack, a suggestion which Björk vehemently rejected. She had other plans for the song; she wanted Radiohead's Thom Yorke to come down to the studio to record Stormare's part for the final album version.

"We were always just about to do something together, and we were just waiting for the right situation," she said of Yorke. "I was really excited about this song. I thought that I finally had a song that deserved his voice, 'cause he's definitely my favorite male singer in the world. I asked him, and he being the kind of guy he is, full of integrity — there's not a grain of artificial, show-business behavior in him — he kind of insisted that he would turn up in the studio and be there for quite a while, so the communication in the song, the recording, was real and genuine. It wasn't just a turn-it-on, you know, 'I recorded my bit in Las Vegas and he recorded his . . .' — you know, we never met or something. It was the opposite, and that actually came from him, 'cause I was all just kind of being in work mode, 'Yeah, we have to get it done,' and he was all, 'No, no, no.'"

The pair met in the studio in March 2000 and spent the better part of a week working on their parts together. With Yorke's undeniably gorgeous vocals as a counterpoint to Björk's voice, the end result was a markedly different song, one miles away from the more ramshackle version that appeared in the film. "I think the way I sang that song was pretty explosive, and for him, it's a very different approach," Björk said. "He made me sing it differently. It's kind of more sensitive and more in touch, you know. I was very flattered by his effort."

In the end, Björk won more of the battles surrounding *Selmasongs* than she lost. In a way, she'd been anticipating them from day one. "She always said when she came into [Von Trier's] office and saw some of his records then she knew this guy didn't know anything about music," laughs father Gunnarsson.

"I always pointed out that punk came so late to Denmark," Friðriksson adds. "Like, in '86, when I was making my first picture there, the streets were crowded with punks and the music was terrible. They are something like 10 years behind us in music and I believe they are still."

"At the end of the day," Arab says. "She argued her rights fucking well. She got to do her music as she wanted."

*Dancer in the Dark* premiered at the Cannes Film Festival on May 17, 2000, to widespread audience and critical approval. As word spread of its rapturous reception (most audiences responded with standing ovations), Von Trier's film emerged as a viable contender for the festival's most prestigious prize.

The attendant groundswell of hype seemed to be building around her, but Björk maintained a cautiously low profile throughout the week. She declined to appear at the festival's inaugural photo call and seemed uncomfortable amidst the paparazzi at the movie's red carpet screening, preferring to remain hiding coyly in Catherine Deneuve's shadow throughout it all. In spite of her relative absence from the press junket and Cannes socialite circle, she was widely tipped as a favorite to win Best Actress plaudits by week's end.

The history of Cannes' judicious prize selection tendencies suggested that it would be unlikely for any single film to scoop nods for Best Overall Film as well as Best Actor or Actress. Four days later, *Dancer in the Dark* confounded expectations by doing precisely that. Von Trier took home the Festival's coveted Grand Jury Palm D'Or for Best Overall Film. Meanwhile, Björk capped off her sparse acting career in fine style by receiving a Palm D'Or for Best Leading Actress.

She was gracious in accepting the prize, but Björk couldn't help but feel slightly put off by the overall reaction to her work as Selma. In her eyes, her primary contribution to the film had come from a musical standpoint, so she felt slightly awkward to be accepting an award for Best Leading Actress. Not soon after, as a show of

*Playing a game of hide and seek with members of the paparazzi at Cannes. (Eric Robert/Corbis Sygma/Magma)*

thanks for support, she gave her award to a friend. "What was going on on the set was nothing compared to the work that went into the music," she mused afterwards. "And nobody said one word about that."

"I immediately thought [the award] was for the music," she added. "And when they told me it was for the acting, my feeling was, 'I don't want to sound ungrateful, but it's not where my heart is.' My heart definitely belongs to sound."

With the announcement of the 2001 Academy Award nominations months later, Björk would finally be honored for her musical contribution to the film. Although overlooked in the Best Leading Actress category, her work on *Selmasongs* received its due recognition — "I've Seen It All" was one of five songs nominated for Best Original Song.

This, of course, not only meant that Björk was (rather unbelievably) going to the Oscars, but also that she was going to be a vital component of the show. As was customary, all Best Original Song nominees were invited to perform their song during the Academy Awards ceremony. It was just another pearl in an increasingly unlikely string of events that followed her participation in *Dancer in the Dark* — on the strength of music she'd written for a decidedly un-Hollywood venture, she now found herself faced with the prospect of performing in front of an audience of a *billion*.

For a brief moment, it appeared as if she wouldn't be the only one crashing the party. She asked Yorke to sing the song with her onstage and, to the delight of everyone bored silly by the Oscars' typically dull performances, he accepted. It's a surreal pop cultural moment that never happened; hamstrung by the Academy's decision to pare down the allotted time for live song segments, Björk was forced to excise Yorke from the performance. She eventually delivered a criminally shortened version of the song — voice quivering — by herself.

But her Oscar night performance wasn't what resonated most with audiences the morning after. In spite of the fact that "I've Seen It All" failed to win in its category (Bob Dylan's "Things Have Changed" won instead), Björk still emerged from the proceedings as the Oscars' most talked about entity. The reason? Her dress.

*That* dress.

It is an image which probably resonates deepest with America's middlebrow fashion commandants. One of Björk standing on the red carpet, sheepish but proud, clad in a prim white dress fashioned unmistakably in the shape of a perished swan, its limp neck slung around her shoulder and feathered bottom hanging around her knees.

The perceived gaudiness of her outfit sent America's self-appointed doom patrol of fashion-watchers into breathless convulsions; where Björk was concerned, Oscar night's most oft-repeated question ("Who are you wearing?") had morphed into a derisive "*What* are you wearing?"

In her earnestness, Björk didn't seem to mind the sniggering. To her, the dress

*The infamous swan dress, with the newly 'laid' egg pictured just out of shot. Meanwhile, son Sindri shows his disdain, top right. (Paul Fenton, Moonglow Photos)*

was a symbol of fertility, an idea she brazenly riffed on by innocently dropping eggs in her trail along the red carpet. The ensuing media dissent didn't faze her much either; she seized on the attention as an opportunity to lambaste the mainstream fashion industry for being so insular and closed-minded. "A lot of fashion is about control, all these big companies telling you, 'If you don't spend that much money, you're not fashionable,'" she said. "And that seems to be about the worst crime anyone can commit. I like it when people are individuals."

"She's not one of those stars you can accuse of telling people what to think and how to dress," Arab said. "That's why she's so fucking out there and wears things that no one would bloody even dream of wearing. It's so funny, she came to see my mom in the hospital and she was wearing shoes with little fucking cowbells on them! I'm surprised the sheep off the heath weren't following her, like it'd bloody matter. . . ."

Over the next year, the swan dress would be tirelessly referenced by celebrities and comedians in search of an easy laugh. David Letterman took nightly jabs in his Top Ten Lists; host Ellen DeGeneres opened the 2001 Emmy Awards by clumsily emerging onstage in a swan dress facsimile; and fashion critic Mr. Blackwell denounced Björk's sensibilities by including her on his infamous Worst Dressed Celebrities list, in the process dubbing her "Alice In Blunderland."

The mainstream's snorts of derision weren't enough to dissuade Björk from abandoning the image outright. In blissful contempt of public sway, she stubbornly appropriated the swan into *Vespertine*'s visual aesthetic by donning it for her album art cover photo and for the first half of each live *Vespertine* show. "I don't really know why I'm obsessed with swans but as I said, everything about my new album is about winter and they're a white, sort of winter bird," she said. "And obviously very romantic, being monogamous. It's one of those things that maybe I'm too much in the middle of to describe. When you're obsessed with something, you can explain it five years later, but in the moment, you don't know exactly why. Right now, swans seem to sort of stand for a lot of things. . . ."

# ten

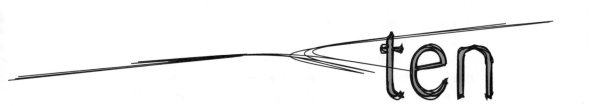

Provisionally titled *Domestika*, Björk's fourth solo album was shaping up to be a product of two major forces: the love she'd forged with New York-based artist Matthew Barney and the tension she'd accumulated while under duress as an actress for *Dancer in the Dark*.

Indeed, the residual effects of playing Selma had remained with Björk long after filming was over. In addition to the myriad professional and collaborative differences, she'd found the process of being on set for *Dancer in the Dark* counterintuitive to the way she normally worked. The very social process of filmmaking, with its huge cast and crew, had demanded her to be extroverted for the entire process, leaving scarcely any room for herself. The absence of this much-needed solitude profoundly affected the music she was making; whenever she escaped to write or record, the resulting material was introverted, tranquil, and hushed.

"All the songs I did then were like silk scarfs [sic]," she said. "Almost like the opium of the film. All my vocals were whispers, and it was like the most peaceful lullaby calmed down, sort of stroking the wounds."

In an effort to keep herself grounded in music while shooting the film, Björk commissioned Valgier Sigurdsson to relocate some of his studio equipment from Iceland to her temporary residence in Denmark. The makeshift recording hub allowed her to come back from the set and unwind by testing out new song ideas. "While Björk was on the film set during the day, I would be in the studio working on beats, creating sounds," Sigurdsson said. "Often she would come in the evening and work on her vocals or a new idea she got that day while filming. Sometimes she was inspired to sing on top of a beat and some amazing songs just turned up."

One of Björk's favorite records while in Copenhagen that summer was by an obscure electronic artist named Opiate. Opiate's album, named *Ideal Objects for Broken Homes*, had barely sold 3,000 copies worldwide, but Björk had discovered it while digging in London and thought enough of it to bring it along to Denmark. One afternoon, upon realizing that Opiate (a.k.a. Thomas Knak) was probably stationed somewhere in Denmark himself, she left a message with his label.

Knak, who was convinced that absolutely nobody outside of Denmark had heard his record, was stupefied by the gesture. Nervously, he called her back and made plans to meet up for the first time. "I invited her to my house because I thought it might be a bad thing to meet up for the first time in a café or somewhere public," he says. "We really had a fun time, just talking about music and life in general."

Knak's first impressions of Björk echoed the sentiments of many electronic musicians before him. From her knowledge, Björk could have been a hermetic vinyl collector just as easily as a million-selling pop star. "We talked about everything from the early composers from the '20s up till now. It was a pretty wide range," he says. "I don't really know how she finds the time to consume all this, but then again, she is eight years older than me, so she's a few years ahead. I think it becomes quite natural if you're interested in music and you feel that it's more than just something you have to listen to. If you live music, then it kind of absorbs through the system. Just as I remember all the titles and catalog numbers but I don't remember to buy my groceries.

"She's got the ability and the money to work with so many people and to buy all this stuff and to meet all these people. She really absorbs things from the people that she's working with; she takes what they know and puts it into her bank, her memory. It was just like meeting a person you've never really met before but you kind of figured must be somewhere out there listening to music and feeling the same way about music. That was the basic start to our relationship.

"She fulfilled my ideas about how she was," he adds. "I knew she could be quite outspoken and an extrovert, but I know her more from the introvert side. She was exhausted after a couple of days shooting the film, and she was really relaxed, which was nice."

The pair struck up a casual friendship during those first meetings, but it wouldn't be until much later that Björk would suggest collaborating. "Even though I had my sampler here, we didn't try to make anything," Knak says. "It was more like having some of my other friends around and just talking about music instead of making it. That was really nice — there wasn't really any tension or anything and there wasn't any obligation for me inviting her around. I just thought it could be fun to meet her because I really admire her work."

San Francisco–based duo Matmos hadn't owned a single Björk record between them when they got the call to lend remixes to "Alarm Call" earlier that year. Nonetheless, the found-sound obsessives (comprised of Drew Daniel and Martin Schmidt) soon charmed Björk with their attentive treatment of her request. "At first I started writing out the lyrics to her song, putting every single word on its own slip of cardboard and then rearranged the words like Scrabble tiles," Daniel recalled. "And then I thought why stop at words and started dividing into the phonemes, thinking about the lyrics as a cut-up text along Burroughs lines. When I told her about it she was cautious, and wanted us to let the vocals go 'from A to Z' on one version, but we wound up using that technique to generate a new kind of 'chorus' at the end. She was very trusting, and requested two mixes, one with vocals intact and one where we could do anything — that took some of the pressure off."

Where many of Björk's prior collaborators had very certainly been part of an attendant scene (be it trip-hop, IDM, or whatever), Matmos had gone to great pains to separate themselves from any palpable movement. In the context of IDM's digitally-mulched, math-obsessed aesthetic, Matmos were odd ducks, zealots who preferred to soundtrack porn films, pluck away at rat cages, and trace grooves out of field recordings instead. Their latest album, 2000's *A Chance to Cut Is a Chance to Cure*, had consisted almost entirely of samples obtained on site during various cosmetic and reconstructive surgeries. With a bit of ingenuity, they'd recontextualized the scrapes of scalpels and warm suckles of liposuction into something practically danceable. It was a marvelous achievement.

Björk appreciated their fresh approach to sampling, and made an effort to stay in contact over the ensuing months. "It kind of snowballed from a remix to a friendship, and we stayed in touch and she came to some shows," Daniel explained. "And she sent us some files of sounds she was playing while she was working on the film."

The threesome even cut some demos at Matmos' studio in San Francisco; Martin recalls the comical difference in ideology that became evident at the time. "We were like, 'just make weird noises' and she was like 'ah . . .' and then comes out with this beautiful song," he laughed. "And we're like, 'No . . . *no* beautiful song!'"

Like Knak, Matmos were consistently amazed by Björk's enthusiasm for music. "She once rang me up from Iceland to play me a Hans Reichel daxophone piece over the phone," Daniel said. "We were hanging out with her in L.A. in her hotel room and she started to DJ for us on her little stereo, playing us Cylob, Tomita, Opiate, Ensemble, Arovane, and Mortiis one after the other, very excitedly. However glamorous she might be, she's also a big music geek, for sure."

Fellow music geek (and Rephlex recording artist) Bogdan Raczynski first met Björk at a Warp Records Lighthouse party where he was DJing. Backstage, the pair exchanged pleasantries and admitted a mutual admiration for each other's work. Raczynski, who is usually rather shy, remembers feeling immediately at ease in her presence. "I think there are a few distinct people types on this planet," he says. "There are those who are ignorant to energy from other people. Not to say that Björk doesn't have her own distinct reactions aside from what people around her are emanating, but the times I've met her I felt that she picked up on my nervousness or my excitement or others' happiness to see her, and she collects this energy, positive, negative, fearful, and sometimes it came out in the same way she picked it up. Either that or she's just skilled at listening to what people aren't saying when they speak and accommodates.

"There's always been too much noise and movement when I've been with her; she's always surrounded and seemingly mentally busy, so many things to do, so many people wanting her attention. But she's always been warm. I can only imagine it's even more so when she's alone or just with one other person."

Not surprisingly, their relationship blossomed into a collaborative one. "I contacted her a bit later about swapping tasty fish recipes," he adds. "She not only swapped, she sent me five tracks from her upcoming album, giving me free reign to do as I pleased. That's when we decided to work on a totally fresh track ["Who Is It"]. It was very warm initially, the foundation. There've been so many permutations of that tale called 'Who Is It,' with the variables all being really human and as open as the sky."

With new friendships being formed on many different fronts, Björk had begun to involve others in her work. While in Denmark, she swapped ideas long-distance with Matmos, sometimes with varying degrees of effectiveness. "We started to make some songs out of that, but they didn't gel, because we don't really understand verses and choruses and sort of proper pop song structure," Daniels said. "And that's still important to her, the carriage of a song, and fair enough — she's got to sing. She is not going to do a microtonal freak-out for 10 seconds."

Björk's subtly changing taste in collaborators reflected the new headspace that her departure from London had facilitated. Far removed from her clubbing days and generally more subdued after living in Iceland for a few years, she found herself drawn to music and film that rewarded patience and calm. As she interacted with things differently, she began to write differently. "A lot of it's to do with the sort of things I was interested in at the time, too, the sort of books I was reading and films I was enjoying," she said. "Books that don't scream for attention, that are very private and personal. Stuff like Tarkovsky. Three years before, you'd put me in front of it and I'd be, 'Fucking hell, c'mon, sort it out! What happens next! C'mon, car chase!'

But I'd watch on my own and rewind and watch the same scene over and over until I grasped it, really devour it."

The decidedly more subdued crackle of the album that would come to be named *Vespertine* was a manifestation of these changing tastes, which were suddenly miles away from the clang and clatter that she had been reveling in circa *Post*. Her appetite for thumping techno had been, temporarily at least, subsumed by a desire for stark melodies and minimalist production. "I was bored with big beats," she said. "I'd listened to a lot of it, to drill'n'bass, a lot of Rephlex stuff, the most mental cut-up shit that you could find. This is more electronic folk music, music for the home. It's corny to make a soundtrack for making a sandwich, but I quite like it. For so long, I wanted to whisper."

"The idea of making a record in a kind of 'a domestic mood' soon surfaced and I know that she had been carrying the idea with her for some time," Valgier Sigurdsson said. ". . . so it was all about making music as you would prepare food and enjoy a glass of wine. Everyday moods and everyday noises translating into melodies and beats."

Crucially, Björk had also began to use her laptop as a compositional tool. Its tinny speakers weren't made to blare club beats, but the molecular clicks and pops that she was laying out as rhythms sounded wonderful on it. "On a musical level, I was obsessed with my laptop," she said. "I was getting really into it, the last three years, doing beats and recording my vocals straight on it, which is revolutionary for me. So I was really obsessed, obviously downloading stuff from the Net and emailing back and forth and getting occupied with that element of laptops. It's all a secret. There's no oxygen in that world. It operates like your mind. Your thought process is very similar."

The small world of music that she forged on her laptop was manifest in *Vespertine*'s oft-repeated idea of cocooning. "I used micro-beats, a lot of whispery vocals, which I think sound amazing when they're downloading because of the secrecy of the medium," she added. "The only acoustic instruments I would use would be those that sound good after they've been downloaded, so the harp, the music box, celeste, and clavichord. They're plucky sounds. . . . And the strings – it took me ages to work out if I should use strings or not. Obviously they shouldn't be a quartet or an octet where they're very narrative and in your face. They ended up being more panoramic textures in the background. It's about being in a little house, on your own. You're creating paradise with your laptop, or underneath your kitchen table where nobody knows about it. It's survival in that sense. The strings would be like white mountains outside."

*Homogenic* was a record made for scaling mountains; *Vespertine* was made for peeking out at them through the warmth of your bedroom window. Whether this change of pace was purely circumstantial or a direct product of her age seemed not to matter; either way, the 33-year-old Björk embraced suggestions that she'd tapped into a new maturity, an admission that probably would have made the Björk of old scowl with stubborn disapproval. "When people tell me this album's mature, I go 'WHOO-HOO!'" she said. "It's my favorite word. Everybody else goes, 'Whoops, reminds me of cheese.'

"I'm more interested by things people do at the age of 50," she continued. "A novelist writes anarchistic poems about killing the government when he's 19, but maybe he writes his best book when he's 50."

Björk was writing about love differently, too. Where, lyrically, past works had favored grandiose extractions and generalizations over specifics, the lyrics that she'd composed for *Vespertine* were so detailed, so intimate, and so revealing that simply listening to them felt oddly invasive. Since Björk had historically admonished herself for revealing too much in her lyrics, the poetry to *Vespertine* marked a stunning about face. Particularly intimate was the album's emotional centerpiece, "Cocoon."

"It took me a while to work on that one, but the emotional heart of the record was still not there," she said. "I had kept away from that personal stuff for a reason. I just didn't want anybody to know. I wanted it for myself. The lyric to 'Cocoon' was a whole diary, then I had to edit 90 percent of it out. It's very hard to explain, but when I read it and the other person it's about reads it, we don't feel abused or anything. I think there's songs where I've been more . . . scruffy about what I'm expressing. I have a problem with music that's too self-indulgent. It's like, 'Keep your own dirty laundry, please.'

"I guess a part of me wanted to be truthful about what it is that really drives me," she added. "And maybe give back to the place that was nourishing me."

The nature of the album's changing shape was implicit in the eventual title change from *Domestika* to *Vespertine*. Where the former signified a focus on extracting magic from the platitudes of everyday life, the latter (evoked to describe that which is blossoming in the evening) suggested a creation of magic through much more powerful forces.

In fine style, Björk had set out to write an album about making sandwiches. She'd ended up with an album about making love.

Recorded in Spain, Iceland, and New York in 2000, *Vespertine* arguably relied more heavily on collaboration than any of Björk's prior outings. Each of the album's 12 songs seemed to have a drastically different point of origin. "Harm of Will" was hatched by a lyrical collaboration between Björk and dewy-eyed screenwriter Harmony Korine (*Kids*), whom she'd met in Denmark; first single "Hidden Place" featured programming input from no fewer than five entities; and "Heirloom" was

*A changed woman; taken just months before the release of Vespertine. (Richard Phibbs/Corbis Outline/Magma)*

actually an existing song by German electronic artist Console with Björk's vocals added overtop.

"She called me one day at the beginning of the year 2000 and told me that she got my record *Rocket in the Pocket* and that she liked it a lot," recalls Martin Gretschmann, a.k.a. Console. "She said there was one song that she really loved and she always had this melody in her head that she sings along to the song. She asked me if I wouldn't mind her singing on this track.

"I went to London with all the tracks; I was actually there while she sang over them," Gretschmann adds. "We talked about Radiohead actually — it was around the time when *Kid A* was released. We also talked a bit about the last Madonna record. I'm really a fan of it, but Björk said 'Oh, I think she's playing safe. . . .'"

With the production already finished, "Heirloom" had taken less than a day to complete. The ornate "Undo," meanwhile, was sparked by an intense two-week writing session between Björk and Knak that January in Reykjavik. "'Undo' began as a sketch I already had," Knak recalls. "I had my sampler with me and I played it for her and she immediately hooked onto it, saying, 'I want to work with this one.' So it began half an hour after I arrived . . . I think we recorded it the last night I was there."

Knak left the song in Iceland with a spare rhythmic backbone and sparse melodic accompaniments. By the time he heard it again four months later, Björk had transformed it from microscopic to epic by adding a full choir and a string section. "It was kind of a weird experience but very, very nice when I got used to it," he says. "My music is very minimal with not too many layers and normally there are no vocals or strings or anything. So for me it was taking it from the most basic to the most extreme and all the way to heaven somehow. I was just sitting here and listening to it and she asked me if I had any changes or thought it was too much.

"She wanted me to feel relaxed, and she let me know that if I had any changes not to hesitate," he says. "I know that if I had any changes I could definitely make them."

Ultimately, the song that Björk was working on with Raczynski would prove too frenetic for the record's gentle feel. Since they worked on it diligently, the pair promised to resurrect it at a later time. "'Who Is It' is a bit too much in the wrong direction for *Vespertine*," Raczynski says. "It's a good 120bpm fishy flappin' faster than anything on that album and the energy was far more rough like asteroids and shooting stars, and not cushy sweet orange-fruit soft. She originally started the track in Brazil or somewhere I can't remember, and then we worked on it a touch in New York, Toronto, London, and the chinese noodles and cherry dessert. As sure as weather it may never be heard by more than a handful of ears, some things are better left secret like dreams you have when you're five years old."

"Cocoon" was one of the last songs to be written for the album, and its melody had come to Björk one evening in a sudden rush. Charged by the inspiration, she made a long-distance, late-night phone call to Knak in Denmark, waking him up in the process. "I didn't have any track of time so she didn't really know that I was asleep," he smiles. "She was explaining that she had this melody in her head and maybe, if I had the time, she would still have two or three weeks to decide if this track could be worked on. I said I would really love to do that because then maybe there was a chance of doing a more minimal, more Opiate-ish track. I really liked the idea of having two songs on there, so immediately after I put down the phone, I just started working. That was basically 'Cocoon.'"

This final song was hatched with relative speed. Save for a few adjustments, Knak's original treatment of "Cocoon" appeared relatively intact on the final version. "She had two changes: one for one semitone up and another for I think about 20bpm slower or something," he says. "I don't really make vocal music so I'm not really used to thinking could the singer really sing in a tempo.

"From there she started working on the lyrics and one more melody for the vocal. We met up in January 2001 in London; I got the same sampler there as I'm working on here because that's the only instrument I know. It's an Ensoniq ASR-10 and it's from 1990 or something. . . . I went into the studio and there were all these technicians and programmers — I came with just three tracks for this mix! They had just been mixing Oasis or something and probably had been using a hundred.

"She was really protecting the idea of this whole 'Cocoon' thing and said, 'This is how we want it to be.' We added maybe two changes to it and then we spent the rest of the day recording the vocals. I think the track is very intimate and personal because of the way the vocals were recorded. We wanted to have one take that really worked so that we didn't have to edit different takes. I think we ended up with 20 takes and we used the fifth or the sixth. That really worked, even though there are places where normally a very trained singer in a very big pop production would say, 'No, this has to be changed.' It's kind of rough in the way that it's all recorded. It's also very close to the mic; all these things that you wouldn't normally keep. In that sense, it is very kind of, almost naked. In the structure and in the feeling because of the lyrics."

By the time *Vespertine* was completed, it had graduated from being a resolutely minimalist album to an album that merged minimalist structures with determinedly more grandiose arrangements. Featuring glassy, static-tickled rhythms locked in embrace with warm strings, oily choir sections, rolling harps, chiming clavichords, gently plucked celestes, and brittle music boxes, *Vespertine* had crystallized into a wintry, labyrinthine charm.

When Björk first met him, Matthew Barney was a married man but his relationship with fellow artist Mary Farley ended shortly thereafter.

A filmmaker and visual artist, Barney had established his reputation with the *Cremaster Cycle*, an ongoing series of arty, surrealistic films that he'd gradually been assembling out of order. Thanks to his art and films, he'd enjoyed tremendous cachet within the world's most discerning art circles. This attention culminated in 2002, when his *Cremaster* works were the focus of an exhibit at New York's prestigious Guggenheim Museum.

Like Björk, Barney had a predilection for taking risks with his art. This drew her closer to him. "The first time I saw it, I thought Matthew's work was the closest I'd ever come to seeing my dreams," Björk said. "It's incredibly similar to the inside of myself, the things that I can't put into words, maybe a side of me that's hidden. And you can't really talk about those things with people if they have a different interior from yours. You know? To me, Matthew's work feels very natural, organic, and healthy. I guess he proved to me that you can go to the most decadent, deepest places, far, far, far into the subconscious, without being destructive. That's important to me, especially after the film."

By mid-2000, Björk left Reykjavik to move into Barney's Manhattan apartment. She acknowledged in the process that her love for Iceland was temperamental. "No disrespect, but it's the same village I was born in," she offered. "I love it, and I know it'll be there when I'm 40 and when I'm 60 and when I'm 80 . . ."

"I think my nature is more to be in Iceland but as soon as I get too comfortable I get a hunger to surprise myself," she said in another interview. "Going abroad for the adventure element, the shock treatment of the cities."

Leaving Reykjavik meant parting ways with Sindri, who had no desire to relocate again. At 15 years old, Björk's son opted to stay in Iceland instead. "He's having an excellent time," she said. "He's living with his father in Iceland – they're bonding and shaving and talking about girls, which I think is excellent."

With *Vespertine* near-finished, Björk gathered in Manhattan with Matmos to put the finishing touches on the record. She had fallen in love with her new home, and enjoyed creating music there. "It was a good exercise, I think, to make such completely secretive songs in a place like Manhattan," Björk said. "You know, there could have been 50 gangs murdering 29 people outside my house, but I was still able to make peaceful songs in my fantasy-land bubble."

"When she actually asked us to work on the album, it was eight-tenths completed," Schmidt said. "I mean, we were sent recordings with a full orchestra and a full choir. Like, 'Add things to these!' I mean, what are we going to add to this?! So it's like, good luck. So it does sound a little bit piled up on top of a big pile."

Although slightly overwhelmed by Björk's lofty production standards, Daniel and Schmidt quickly caught on; by the time the album was finished, Björk had tapped them to join her on tour. "When she asked us to be in her band for this tour and to take on this role of working on a day-to-day basis on how to convey her songs live, I said, 'Oh, I don't think we're really professional enough to do this,'" Daniel said. "She's not going to put her whole live show at risk by trusting us with more than we can handle. But she's always wanted a certain element of anarchy in her live shows. I think Björk's always willing to walk up to the cliff, and that's really unique for someone in her position. . . ."

With fond memories of her 1999 acoustic concerts still in her mind, Björk seized upon the *Vespertine* tour as an opportunity to do something special, grandiose. Tired of playing in venues with poor acoustics, she decided to limit her engagements strictly to theaters, churches, and opera houses. Knowing that it might be her only opportunity to indulge in such an extravagance, she justified the decision by bringing a 54-piece orchestra on tour with her.

For most, the opportunity to perform with a full orchestra would have been sufficient, but Björk was insistent that *Vespertine*'s full scope be realized for this tour. With Matmos and harpist Zeena Parkins as the newly formed core of her touring band, she'd struck upon a fairy-tale mix of crackles and strums. To send her songs into the stratosphere, she required one final component, which came in the form of a 14-person Inuit choir from Greenland, complete with a Canadian throat singer named Tanya Tagaq.

The sudden scale of the tour took Matmos — a couple of self-described bedroom hobbyists — by surprise. As she had done with Arab in the past, Björk encouraged the pair to embrace the overwhelming risks involved. "This orchestra has about 60 lifelong trained classical musicians in it, and man, I barely know how to play guitar — barely," Schmidt joked. "It's kind of a thing where I'm going to wake up in my underwear with 60,000 people staring at me, pointing and laughing."

Starting in Harlem's Riverside Church on September 5, 2001, Björk embarked on a four-month tour that would see her play some of the world's most prestigious venues. With Matmos, Parkins, the Inuit choir, and the orchestra backing her up, the Björk realized *Vespertine* tour was becoming the unequivocal highlight of her live career, as delicate and whispery as it was rousing and huge.

"In the past I've done completely cathartic and confrontational shows that were all brittle," she said. "But this time I didn't want to run around the stage going, 'Waaah!' I guess I wanted to create the kind of show I was in the mood to see myself."

The tour's true brilliance came from the way that Björk and company managed to successfully articulate *Vespertine*'s most miniscule sounds in the midst of their expansive surroundings. Much of this was owed to Matmos, whose delicate and innovative modes of sound extraction added to the show's overall spectacle. Special things happened in their corner of the stage: micro-beats emerged from shuffled cards and scrambled rock salt. Every night, during "Cocoon," Schmidt would generate static by sensuously rubbing a small microphone along Daniel's neck and head. The sight of the two of them, lovers as well as bandmates, generating delicate sounds from such tender interplay, stood up as the tour's most resonant image.

It was, in one fell swoop, everything that *Vespertine* was about.

If there were any doubts about Björk's waning interest in celebrity after her decision to tour such exclusive venues, then the accompanying videos for *Vespertine*'s three singles ("Hidden Place," "Pagan Poetry," and "Cocoon") erased them completely. Although helmed by three separate directors, the videos shared similarly minimalist qualities and themes. Austere, daring, and completely unsuitable for mainstream television, they were indicative of Björk's newly uncompromising headspace.

"Hidden Place" (directed by Inez Van Lamsweerde and Vinoodh Matadin of the M/M design company) consisted solely of a close-up on Björk's face as computer-generated fluids darted between her eyes, nostrils, and mouth. "Cocoon" (directed by designer Eiko Ishioka) portrayed a seemingly naked, porcelain Björk (complete with bleached eyebrows) being enveloped by red ribbons emanating from her breasts. However, with its stark nudity and sexual imagery, Nick Knight's "Pagan Poetry" may have been the most daring clip of them all. Its recurrent images — pearl chains and nipple piercings — came at Björk's behest. "She approached me with the idea," Knight said. "Her original idea in Iceland was to sew pearls into her nipples. She wanted to show her sexuality.

"I wanted to strip her down. She's actually quite raw, womanly, and sexy. There's a different side to her that doesn't come across normally in her videos. That's what I asked her to do and that's what she did. Her dress stops just below her breasts and she's sewn pearls into her skin." Nudity, bodily fluids, penetration, strings of pearls, red ribbons – the images from this set of videos echoed *Vespertine*'s eroticism with startling effectiveness.

With an emphasis on quality over quantity, the tour made just over thirty stops across Europe, North America, and Japan before concluding with two very special shows in Iceland that December. By the beginning of 2002, Björk had declined to tour any further, fulfilling a very select number of promotional engagements before returning home to Barney in Manhattan. A month later, she became pregnant with her second child.

Over the course of her solo career, she'd pushed boundaries, courted success, challenged herself, tasted stardom, rejected it, endured tragedy, defied convention, and won respect from all sides. Now, at 36 years old and preparing for motherhood again, Björk had come full circle, back to where she began – as a new mother, in love with a man, and still very much in love with music.

"Her life is changing very rapidly, over the last year or two," Björk's father says. "She's never been so happy as she is now. She's certain about herself. She's very happy, busy, relaxed, in love."

On October 5, 2002, while vacationing in Paris, a happy, busy, relaxed, and very much in love Björk gave birth to a baby girl, Isadora, with Barney by her side. Soon after, the couple returned to Manhattan to share the beginnings of their secret new life together.

The release of a *Greatest Hits* compilation followed in November. With a tracklist selected by fans via her official Web site, the record offered a roughly-hewn sketch of past musical accomplishments and signaled a definitive demarcation point in Björk's creative landscape. She acknowledged this signpost by simultaneously releasing a six-CD box set featuring material hand-picked straight from her vault. Containing separate discs that related to various components of her past (Roots, Beats, Strings), *Family Tree* gave Björk an opportunity to reflect on the past. "I started off feeling a little guilty because I was so eager to just move ahead," she said. "I couldn't handle the past. I would just tell them, 'The recordings are up in the attic.' And then they would just pile up there and become bigger and bigger and bigger, so it was time to start going through them. . . . It's something that I wanted to do. It's all the different songs I did before *Debut*. It's like the story of how I got there. We ended up asking the fans on the Internet to choose the *Greatest Hits* songs, but I've been listening to old stuff of myself for months now and I never do that. It's like the last thing I would ever do. It's sort of been awkward. Part of it has been great. It's been very emotional. But I'm getting very, very eager to move on and do new stuff and forget that all this ever happened. It was a stronger feeling than I expected it to be. It's quite liberating."

Lyrically, the lone new song ("It's In Our Hands") was a burning reminder of the empowerment that she'd always preached. Musically, it was a joyous mess of expertly arranged crackles, bell tones, micro-clips and – most poetically – hand claps.

As her show-stopping performance of the song during the *Vespertine* tour had affirmed, it was definitive proof that Björk had not lost her childly wonder. Every night, to close the show, she'd scamper around the stage, joyously clapping her hands in double time to Matmos' skipping beats.

And if she had been wearing shoes, one of her laces would have surely been untied . . .

# Songbook

What follows are song-by-song accounts of every track officially released by Björk over the course of her solo career, along with a few noteworthy offerings that never saw the light of day. For obvious reasons, this songbook only covers original versions of songs; for information on various official remixes, please consult the Singles Guide (page 199).

**5 YEARS > From *Homogenic***

"5 Years" first appeared on *Post* tour setlists as early as 1995, under its original title, "I Dare You." Punctuated by splashes of static and a dissonant assortment of scattered noises, these initial live renderings were poorly arranged at best. The only original elements to survive Björk's disassembly of the track for *Homogenic* were her lyrics and vocal line, which she ultimately performed with decidedly less fire. Everything else on the album version, from the sputtering beats to the quivering strings, was brand new.

Lyrically, "5 Years" revolves primarily around Björk's impassioned taunt to a hesitant lover. Although she claims that many of her songs aren't aimed at specific people, "5 Years" debuted live within weeks of her perplexing split with Tricky, leaving some to speculate on a link between the two.

**107 STEPS > From *Selmasongs***

Originally titled "141 Steps," this ceremonial march needed to be re-edited to fit Lars Von Trier's last minute adjustments to *Dancer in the Dark*. The original version of the film (which premiered at the Cannes Film Festival) included an extended final sequence that showed Selma taking a total of 141 steps to the electric chair. After the Cannes screening, Von Trier decided to excise a portion from that final scene, reducing Selma's walk to 107 steps and forcing Björk to re-edit her song accordingly.

The voice heard counting up in the background is that of actress Siobhan Fallon, who co-stars in the film as Björk's cellmate. Although Björk stops singing at 100, Fallon's counting continues all the way up to 141.

**AEROPLANE > From *Debut***

One of *Debut*'s earliest songs, "Aeroplane" first appeared on a three-track demo tape that Björk recorded in Iceland with the hopes of launching her solo career. Her newly-formed relationship with British DJ Dominic Thrupp also spilled into this song, their distance from one another spawning the lovelorn lyric. It was evident that leaving Reykjavik was weighing heavily on her mind.

The off-kilter arrangements contributed by World Saxophone Quartet leader Oliver Lake contorted this into one of *Debut*'s most challenging songs. With a variety of different time structures and seemingly incongruous scales, "Aeroplane" ranks among one of the album's most musically complicated pieces.

**ALARM CALL > From *Homogenic***

With it originally pegged as *Homogenic*'s third single, Björk and Me Company designer Paul White converged in Los Angeles in May 1998 to film the "Alarm Call" video. The resulting clip was reportedly so subpar that it was deemed unfit for release. With "Hunter" being tapped for inclusion on the forthcoming *X-Files* soundtrack, One Little Indian postponed any immediate designs for an "Alarm Call" release and went with "Hunter" next instead.

Boasting a new video helmed by fashion designer (and first-time director) Alexander McQueen, "Alarm Call" was eventually released as the album's fourth single in late 1998. In case you're wondering: the version of the song that features in McQueen's clip is not the album version, but rather the vastly superior "Mark Bell Radio Remix."

**ALL IS FULL OF LOVE > From *Homogenic***

While the best-known version of "All Is Full of Love" is not the one found on *Homogenic*, it is the version most preferred by fans and by Björk herself. Known variously as the "Video Mix" or the "Mark Stent Mix," this highly superior take was slated for the album before being superceded at the last minute by Howie Bernstein's comparatively lifeless version. As Stent's version was later used in Chris Cunningham's video as well as on 2002's *Greatest Hits* and *Family Tree* retrospectives, the last-second substitution is something that Björk evidently came to regret.

"The song, in essence, is actually about believing in love," Björk later reflected. "Love isn't just about two persons, it's everywhere around you. Even if you're not getting love from Person A, it doesn't mean that there's not love there. Obviously, it's taking the piss too — it's the most sugary song ever."

**ALL NEON LIKE > From *Homogenic***

The first snippets of the lyric from "All Neon Like" were revealed in the form of a poem called "Techno Prayer," which Björk published in the July 1996 edition of *Details* magazine. Images of cocooning and thread-weaving weighed heavily in that original poem, proving that these thematic ideas had obviously been with Björk for some time before she explored them in greater detail on *Vespertine*.

The wavering bell tones that enter this song at roughly the 0:29 mark come courtesy of Alasdair Malloy's glass harmonica. Although not frequently used in pop music, the basic principle of the glass harmonica is familiar to anyone who's ever run a wet finger around the rim of a wine glass. These hollow, sustained chimes form the bedrock of much of this track, especially the verses.

Finally, "All Neon Like" also showcases Björk's tendency to take liberties with the English language for added effect. Here, she memorably furnishes the song's most emphatic word ("luminous") with an extra syllable: "lou-min-NEE-ous!"

**AMPHIBIAN > From *Being John Malkovich* OST, *Cocoon* CDS 2/2**

With its heavily layered vocals, microscopic beats and ambient surges, 1999's "Amphibian" could be considered a reasonable precursor to the gentle gush of *Vespertine*. Interestingly, it has no verifiable lyrics – Björk's vocals on this track are a Dadaist stream of indecipherable sounds and noises that are not in any particular language.

Co-written with LFO's Mark Bell and Icelandic musician/programmer Valgeir Sigurdsson, "Amphibian" was recorded primarily for use in Spike Jonze's feature film debut, *Being John Malkovich*. Of the two versions that appear on the film's official soundtrack, the one labelled "Film Mix" is commonly regarded as the original version of the song. The "Mark Bell Mix" is more intimate yet, with sparse layers of pianos and vocals gently intercutting the rhythms.

In addition to featuring on the aforementioned soundtrack, this song was one of the first to be made widely available for download through various official partner sites on the Internet. Its availability during that time has surely contributed to its status as a fan favorite.

**THE ANCHOR SONG > From *Debut***

Written during a freefalling summer in 1990 that saw Björk traipse across Iceland's farmland, "The Anchor Song" was one of three tracks to appear on her very first demo cassette later that year.

Although she originally composed it on a church organ, Björk envisioned the song as being better served by a horn section; for *Debut*, she cycled through various potential treatments before happily surrendering the track to Oliver Lake, jazz saxophonist for the vaunted Art Ensemble of Chicago.

With his melodies in frequently unsustained conflict, Lake's arrangement replicated the ebb and tide of an ocean's peaking tops, an image reinforced by Björk's fiercely patriotic lyric.

**AN ECHO, A STAIN > From *Vespertine***

The fact that this is one of *Vespertine*'s most maligned tracks may be linked to the fact that it is also among Björk's broodiest compositions. Underpinned by a creeping choir line and Matmos' nibbling clicks, there's an unresolved, ominous tension to "An Echo, A Stain" that is not typical of Björk's writing style.

That may be because "An Echo, A Stain" pulls its dramatic lift almost wholesale from a 1998 play written by troubled British playwright Sarah Kane. Most of the lyrics in the song speak so directly to incidents in Kane's play that it was named after it (*Crave*) right until the last minute. Comprised of a series of monologues that deal with the destructive powers of love, *Crave* would be the last of her own plays that Kane would see performed. After a long battle with depression, she hanged herself in 1999.

**ARMY OF ME > From *Post***

Written and demoed with Graham Massey during a 1993 recording session in Manchester, "Army of Me" was saved for 1995's *Post*, where it became the album's first single. Containing a drum sample from Led Zeppelin's "When The Levee Breaks," "Army of Me"'s driving, insistent bass line served notice that Björk was capable of even more than she'd let on with the varicolored *Debut*.

"It's actually written to a relative of mine who had been a bit out of order for a while, " Björk said. "I'm not sure why I wrote it. Maybe I felt that *Debut* had been such a polite, shy album — there was a side of me that was so shy and such a beginner. I was very flattered when everybody loved *Debut* but also a bit confused because it wasn't really me. Maybe 'Army of Me' was an attempt to balance it out."

The video clip for "Army of Me" depicted Björk driving an oversized recreational vehicle, a sight that brought back old memories for friend Kormákur Geirhardsson, who recalls her driving "skills" as a teenager with mock horror. "She was *so* bad," he says. "It was horrible, and people were scared to death after five minutes in the car with her. If she doesn't have her feet on the ground, you shouldn't be around her . . . don't let her drive anything, whatever it is."

Another point of trivia: Michel Gondry's video for "Army of Me" was the first to utilize stop film motion techniques to achieve a rotational transition between two points of focus, a technique later popularized by *The Matrix*.

**ATLANTIC > From various live bootlegs**

A sparse studio version of this song — sung in Icelandic and featuring nothing but vocals and a flute arrangement — first appeared as a b-side to the "Human Behaviour" cassette single, and then later as a bonus track on the Japanese version of *Debut*.

Conceived and executed as a lonely, oceans-apart missive in the spirit of "The Anchor Song," "Atlantic" was later resurrected for *Debut*'s live shows, where Björk and her band gave it a churning, multicultural vibe. Although this more fully realized version (sung variously in Icelandic and English) was never recorded in a studio, it is still widely available on various bootlegs, as well as Björk's official 1994 live video, *Vessel*.

**AURORA > From *Vespertine***

The harp and music box arrangement for "Aurora" began in the form of an extended instrumental named "Avignon," which Björk wrote as backing for a joint art installation between friends Alexander McQueen and Nick Knight. Knight and McQueen's elaborate exhibit housed thousands of living maggots, color-dyed and compartmentalized in such a way as to resemble a woman's face from a distance. The installation, to be shown in Avignon, France, as part of a city-wide festival named "La Beauté," was terminated prematurely when the accompanying refrigeration system failed. Without the required cooling, the maggots in the exhibit began to metamorphose into giant flies, ruining the intended effect.

Matmos' wanton try-anything influence is quite literally stamped all over the studio version of "Aurora." Listen closely at the very beginning as the closing chimes of "Frosti" fade and you'll be able to make out a warm, faintly crunchy sound. Those are Matmos' samples of Björk's footprints in the freshly fallen snow, magnificently reappropriated as the song's subtly shifting beat.

**BACHELORETTE > From *Homogenic***

When Italian filmmaker Bernardo Bertolucci commissioned Björk to write original music for his film *Stealing Beauty*, she responded by composing a rough sketch of the song that would eventually become "Bachelorette." At some point early on in the writing process – either because the song was too personal, too good, or both – Björk faxed Bertolucci and informed him that she'd regretfully be hanging onto the song for her own album.

With working titles of "Bertolucci" and "Shape Shifter," "Bachelorette" sounded the conclusion to the three-part story set up by "Human Behaviour" and "Isobel."

"Isobel decides to return to the city and to take a train, like in the '30s, in South America somewhere," Björk explained. "She decides to confront love with love and confronts the cowards that don't have the guts to fall in love with love. So you see, it's like Isobel has returned."

"Because I wanted the lyrics to be so epic, I got my friend Sjon – who's a poet in Iceland – to write them," she said elsewhere. "We sat together at the kitchen table and drank a lot of red wine and I told him the whole story for hours and days and he wrote the words from that story."

**BATABID > From *Pagan Poetry* CDS 2/2**

This warm, gushy instrumental (done with Mark Bell) surfaced early on during the *Vespertine* sessions under the working title "Bati." Although never considered for inclusion on the album, it's a beautiful, fleeting piece — instantly reminiscent of some of the more tuneful interludes on Aphex Twin's seminal *Selected Ambient Works Volume 2*.

**BIG TIME SENSUALITY > From *Debut***

Emboldened by the creative spark between her and Nellee Hooper, Björk wrote "Big Time Sensuality" as a tribute to the producer and his courage. "I think it's quite rare, when you're obsessed with your job as I am, when you meet someone who's your other half jobwise and enables you to do what you completely want," she raved in an interview.

The third single from *Debut*, "Big Time Sensuality" was the first Björk song to be accepted and playlisted by mainstream television and radio stations alike. Opting for the Fluke remix over the album version, the single solidified Björk's burgeoning dance-floor credibility. The video for the song, directed in New York by soon-to-be beau Stephane Sednaoui, would yield the first of Björk's many run-ins with television censorship boards. "[It] was almost pulled from play — they had to do three edits on it," recalls then-manager Netty Walker. "The BBC and MTV didn't like the head shaking because they thought it was a bit frightening."

**CHARLENE > From *Isobel* 1/2 CDS**

The complete story behind this fan-favorite b-side is still shrouded in relative secrecy. Because of its sexually suggestive content and ambiguous narrative, "Charlene" has been the cause of much conjecture over the years.

The most information that Björk has given regarding the inspiration for the mysterious song came from an online chat in 1999, where she said it was inspired by "Kadamba." This was a reference to burgeoning model and actress Kadamba Simmons, who lived with Nellee Hooper from 1993 to 1995 before the two parted ways. Simmons (who also dated Oasis' Liam Gallagher for half a year) and Björk became good friends during that time, maintaining a friendship even when neither had links to Hooper any longer — she's even thanked in the liner notes to 1997's *Homogenic*.

Tragically, Simmons was murdered by her jealous boyfriend Yaniv Malka in June

1998. When she was on the verge of ending their relationship, he strangled her; she was only 24 years old.

**COCOON > From *Vespertine***

The starkest song on the deeply intimate *Vespertine* was actually one of the last tracks to be written for the album. It was sparked by a collaboration between Björk and Thomas Knak (a.k.a. Opiate) who traded ideas by airmail for a few weeks before taking it into the studio together.

In retrospect, the inclusion of this incredibly private piece gave the album its much-needed focal point. "She showed me the lyrics and said, 'I know this is very personal so don't blush,'" Knak smiles. "I thought they were very honest. As long as something is honest, humble and not afraid, then I can recognize something in there."

The video for "Cocoon" was directed by 62-year-old Japanese artist Eiko Ishioka, whose résumé includes film costume design (*Bram Stoker's Dracula, The Cell*) and Grammy Award-winning album artwork (Miles Davis' *Tutu*). That she'd never done a music video before "Cocoon" was one of the things that attracted Björk most, her questing thirst for risk still intact.

**COME TO ME > From *Debut***

"Come to Me" marked the first of Björk's many collaborations with London-born percussionist/musician Talvin Singh, who was still years away from finding solo success at the time. Dreamily plucked piano bits and rolling synth pads aside, the song's musical highlights came directly from Singh's contributions. Recorded in Bombay's Beats Studio and arranged by Sureh Sathe, Singh's lush strings reinforced Björk's melody line with deceiving ease. Meanwhile, his assured tabla playing appears at around the four minute mark, sending the song out in fractal patterns of gorgeous rolls and waves.

**COVER ME > From *Post***

While the vocals for this song were famously recorded in a cave off the beach near the Bahamas studio where Björk and company were recording *Post*, many of the ambient or spatial sounds on the album version were later added in London, presumably in an attempt to simulate a specific type of physical space.

A stark song lyrically, "Cover Me" was written after Nellee Hooper offered to cover for Björk should she falter in the producer's chair for *Post*. This would be the first of two songs (see "Hunter") where Björk would liken her creative process to the art of hunting and gathering.

**CRYING > From *Debut***

In addition to having the dubious distinction of being Björk's first litigated song, "Crying" was one of the oldest tracks to appear on *Debut*. Written while Björk was still living in Iceland and burning to move away, it's rife with the telltale isolation of someone suffering from intense log cabin fever.

Featuring an accelerated tempo and a wild emphasis on percussion, this song eventually mutated into a live stomper, and proved to be a highlight during Björk's *Debut* tours.

**CVALDA > From *Selmasongs***

"Cvalda" is Selma's term of affection for her best friend Kathy — played by Catherine Deneuve, who also lends vocal duties to this track. Since it marks the first musical moment in *Dancer in the Dark*, it is our introduction to Selma's life of daydreams. The way that the clattering rhythms of Selma's industrial landscape are incorporated into this song vaguely echoes the spirit of the American percussive troupe Stomp.

**DOMESTICA > From *Pagan Poetry* CDS 2/2**

Björk's original concept for her fourth record was to make an album called *Domestika* that celebrated the banalities of everyday life at home. As that initial idea gradually became superceded by the love call of *Vespertine*, some of the existing material that Björk had written in the earlier vein was either altered or squeezed off the album entirely.

Originally titled "Lost Keys," "Domestica" is a gentle, humorous snapshot of a scatterbrained Björk rummaging around her home in search of her misplaced keys. One of the airiest, most light-hearted songs from the *Vespertine* sessions.

**ENJOY > From *Post***

*Post*'s most abrasive track came as the result of a fruitful writing session between Björk and then-boyfriend Tricky, who flew up to Reykjavik to escape the circus surrounding his own record, the frazzled *Maxinquaye*. With a small army of portable synths and samplers at their command (including a Yamaha QY-20, which Björk used quite often during this period), the duo wrote and sequenced most of "Enjoy."

Björk frequently describes herself as being a person of utter extremes. As such, "Enjoy" is a resolute expression of her hedonistic tendencies, the way she'll often go out on missions to immerse herself in sheer happiness. With its military drums and squalls of noise, that sense of purpose is embedded firmly into "Enjoy."

One other small piece of trivia: the caterwauling trumpet blasts that occur in the song's outro are courtesy of none other than ex-Sugarcubes foil, Einar Örn Benediktsson.

**FOOT SOLDIER** > **From *Hidden Place* CDS 2/2**

In seeking out collaborators such as Matmos and Opiate, Björk had demonstrated a preference for the more human, sequenced, and organic spectrum of the electronic music circuit. On "Foot Soldier," she hints at her awareness of computer-synth advocates such as Kid 606 and DNTel by toying with more overtly digital working methods.

Although heavily DSPed, this mid-tempo b-side bears the distinction of being the only song from the *Vespertine* sessions to feature the adventurous Björk on harp. Her impressive performance is obscured by the track's bleeding edge arrangements – few pieces from the *Vespertine* era so willingly and completely hand over the reins to a computer.

**FROSTI** > **From *Vespertine***

Although barely two minutes long, the fragile "Frosti" is *Vespertine*'s glacial centerpiece, a chiming, swirling piece that Björk arranged and then had adapted for replication on a specially commissioned music box. "In the beginning, the music box company weren't very excited," she said. "They'd made wooden boxes for eons and I wanted see-through plexiglass. They couldn't get their head round it – they were like, 'Why?' They wanted to make the plonky sound softer with wood but I wanted it hard as possible, like it was frozen. In the end, they said it was the best thing they'd ever done."

While probably not intentional, it's a nice stroke of synchronicity that the song turns on a melodic phrase that instantly echoes the notes sung to the phrase "All Is Full of Love" (see 0:25 mark).

A final note of origin: "Frosti" is not just an apt descriptor for this chilly instrumental; it's also the name of Joga's son.

**GENEROUS PALMSTROKE** > **From *Hidden Place* CDS 1/2**

This gentle lullaby depicts Björk in hymnal mode, basking in resignation to the joy of a newfound love. Decorated with overdubbed backing vocals, Zeena Parkins' harp twinges, and Matmos' reversed cuts and switches, Björk's circular melody repeats to fruition; these four minutes see her transcend her individual self and arrive at the gracious, universal state of love.

The shift in perspective in the song's second half is the song's major lift; a symbol of something celestial at work. Possibly one of Björk's most overtly spiritual tunes.

**GLOOMY SUNDAY** > **From *Stormy Weather*** (AT&T promotional CD)

Björk's one and only performance of this dreary elegy came during an April 1998 concert at Los Angeles' Wiltern Theatre. Organized and spearheaded by Don Henley, the Walden Woods benefit show saw her join the likes of Gwen Stefani, Natalie Cole,

Stevie Nicks, Joni Mitchell, and others to deliver covers of old standards to an audience who reportedly paid upwards of $1,000 U.S. each for the privilege. The highlights from the evening were later released on an AT&T promotional CD called *Stormy Weather*. Although Björk actually sang four songs that evening, her version of "Gloomy Sunday" was the only one to appear on the 10-track album.

Covered by artists such as Billie Holiday, Serge Gainsbourg, Elvis Costello, and Sinéad O'Connor over the years, "Gloomy Sunday" has a very bleak history. The first version of the song was composed and released in 1933 by Hungarian Rezsô Seress; over time, it gradually became linked to an alarming number of local suicides. Its minor-key shifts and dark imagery struck a chord with disaffected listeners, many of whom referenced the song's lyrics in their suicide notes. By the time it was translated to English, "Gloomy Sunday" had been given an extra, more optimistic final verse; unfortunately, these revisions weren't enough to rid it of its dubious nickname — "The Suicide Song." By the mid '40s, many major radio stations, including the BBC, had banned the song outright — a move that has not surprisingly helped it maintain its notoriety over the years.

While never commercially available, *Stormy Weather* was issued as a complementary gift to AT&T customers and is still easily obtained through most online auction sites.

**GLORA > From *Big Time Sensuality* CDS 1/2**

So named after the farm Björk worked at for two summers as a teenager, "Glora" is a holdover from her days with Kukl and the Elgar Sisters. An instrumental, this two-minute song contains subtle variations and harmonies on a plaintive, recurrent flute melody. As it was the first instrument she learned to play, all three flute parts in this song are performed by Björk.

**HARM OF WILL > From *Vespertine***

The lyric to "Harm of Will" was composed by New York–based filmmaker and poet Harmony Korine (*Kids*, *Gummo*), whom Björk befriended years before he became a high-profile part of the next wave of Dogme 95 directors. "I met him at some celebrity party in New York," Björk said. "I was about to leave and he came out of nowhere and told me stories for two hours. I didn't have a clue who he was. I was pissing myself laughing.

"When I was doing *Dancer in the Dark*, he was directing *Julien Donkey-Boy* with the same production company in Denmark. It was good for me to call up someone who understood the problems of a film shoot, when you've had it up to here. It was a great phone relationship. And he wrote these words. I got them and the next day I sang them. It wasn't planned. I like things when they happen like that; they grow like natural plants. His lyrics are similar to his films. They have this force of nature. There is a spontaneity, an impulsiveness, of letting things run loose. Harmony is not inhibited."



**HEADPHONES > From *Post***

The second *Post* song to be co-authored with Tricky was inspired by the mixed tapes that Björk used to get in the post from friend Graham Massey. With lyrics extracted from her personal diary and a final mix purposely backloaded with stereo pans and sleep-inducing headphone tricks, "Headphones" was more broadly about the power of music to offer solace after a terrible day.

"You're pissed off with things generally," Björk said. "You save it until the evening, and after you've had your bath and brushed your teeth, you go to bed and take your Walkman and put your headphones on and you fall asleep. . . ."

**HEIRLOOM > From *Vespertine***

The music to "Heirloom" was lifted wholesale from Console's 2000 album *Rocket in the Pocket*, where it originally appeared as an instrumental called "Crabcraft." In exchange for his co-songwriter credit on *Vespertine*, German Martin Gretschmann (a.k.a. Console) barely needed to lift a finger. He spent a day with Björk in the studio as she recorded vocals for the song, and didn't see her again until September 11, 2001, at a concert she gave in Munich, Germany. Because of events in New York City earlier that day, the show almost didn't happen. "It was really strange because everybody was completely knocked out, including the band and the musicians," Gretschmann recalls. "But it was a really good thing that she did play. . . ."

**HIDDEN PLACE > From *Vespertine***

Containing programming insight from five separate sources (among them Matthew Herbert and Matmos), "Hidden Place" marked the ultimate in cut-and-paste collaboration. "People would pop in during the mixing process, the last month," Björk said. "Matthew Herbert just came to the studio for a visit. He wasn't going to work. And then I needed a beat and he ran into the studio and came back with a DAT a few hours later and it was perfect."

Björk micro-managed the micro-cuts; according to lore, the section Herbert provided accounted for a miniscule 32 beats in the song's middle eighth. Matmos' ingenuity was also on full display – they created the granular, barely audible beat (heard in the song's first seconds) by sampling the shuffling of a tightly-packed deck of cards.

As *Vespertine*'s first single, "Hidden Place" delivered characteristically small returns; part of that was owing to its slightly offputting video. Directed by Dutch couple Inez Van Lamsweerde and Vinoodh Matadin, the "Hidden Place" clip consists entirely of a close-cropped shot of Björk's face. As she sings, computer-generated globules travel between various points on her face (out from her nostrils into the corner of her mouth, out from her crow's feet onto her outstretched tongue), circulating like tiny vessels on a self-sustained transit system. The squeamish no doubt saw it, thought "spit and snot," and promptly changed the channel.

**HUMAN BEHAVIOUR > From *Debut***

Björk presented a crude version of "Human Behaviour" to the Sugarcubes in 1991, when it was still a loosely formed sketch with a working title of "Murder for Two." At a loss as to how to support the song's bizarre lead melody, the band ultimately shelved her suggestion; for Björk, this was nothing new. "A lot of the melodies on *Debut* I wrote as a teenager and put aside because I was in punk bands and they weren't punk," she said.

The song's recurrent motif fell by the wayside until 1993, when Hooper rescued it for *Debut*. With a sample of the Ray Brown Orchestra's "Go Down Dying" serving as their starting point, Hooper and Björk promptly re-imagined "Human Behaviour" as a boomy, tribal stomp.

With its gutsy pastiche of atonal elements and its lack of any immediately perceptible refrain, "Human Behaviour" may have initially seemed an unwise choice for Björk's first solo single. It left the U.K. Top 40 charts relatively unbothered upon release (it opened at the #33 position), but its clandestine impact on Björk's public perception was inarguably substantial. More than a single, "Human Behaviour" was an effective preventative strike, an opening salvo that instantaneously positioned Björk as an experimentalist while keeping other doors propped open enough to facilitate later excursions into more overtly poppy or dance floor terrain.

By virtue of the fact that it heralded Björk's arrival as a solo artist by sounding like absolutely nothing else (a rare thrill in the realm of pop), "Human Behaviour" may still arguably be her landmark single.

**HUNTER > From *Vespertine***

Björk's increased success and ballooning public profile circa *Post* required a supporting cast of a decidedly larger scale. With that expansion came a growing awareness as to how her work ethic and creative output directly affected the livelihoods of those around her. During the mid-'90s, Björk tested her own limits rather than risk disappointing those around her, touring incessantly and exhibiting a creative burst.

With its savage lyrical conceits and suppressed twinges of doubt, "Hunter" speaks to the inherent pressure involved in having the fate of a small workforce hinge on your every action. That these realizations surfaced on Björk's most sparsely promoted album was no coincidence.

As with the majority of *Homogenic*, Mark Bell proved a crucial conduit between Björk's vision and the final outcome; his programming on "Hunter" echoed a suitably militaristic mode, in turn enhancing the song's sense of mission.

"I think that beat is very much a Mark Bell beat interpretation of her," offers engineer Markus Dravs. "The idea of it being a Boleric beat was hers, but we tried different versions and I think it was Mark in the end who came up with the idea of just doing it on a 909. Then we all had a go on the filtering and played around with the decay of each individual drum."

**HYPER-BALLAD > From *Post***

Containing what is arguably some of Björk's most resonant lyrical imagery, "Hyper-ballad" is, on the surface, a stylized fairy tale about the need to maintain emotional balance and re-awaken life's pleasant danger in the context of a long-term relationship.

"For some terrible reason, which I'm actually a bit pissed off with, when you fall in love with a person you start to separate into two sides and you're only sweet with them," Björk said. "So basically, 'Hyper-ballad' is about having this kind of bag going on and three years have passed and you're not high anymore. You have to make an effort consciously and nature's not helping you anymore. So you wake up early in the morning and you sneak outside and you do something horrible and destructive, break whatever you can find, watch a horrible film, read a bit of William Burroughs, something really gross and come home and be like, 'Hi honey, how are you?'"

The song's seemingly morbid lyrics actually revealed Björk's simmering *joie de vivre*. Embedded in the gesture of picturing her own death is an irrefutable reality – for now, in this total moment, she is very much alive.

**I GO HUMBLE > From *Isobel* CDS 1/2**

Before *Post* came out, Mark Bell had sent Björk a cassette full of new LFO demos and told her that she was welcome to use whatever she liked. Björk seized upon this track – an up-tempo jaunt built around a squelching synth line and fluttering drums – and built a simple, direct melody around it. Its ambiguous lyric – which is about being overwhelmed by another person – is open-ended enough to apply to virtually anyone.

Björk's adaptation of this song didn't preclude Bell from using it in his work; an instrumental version of "I Go Humble" appeared on LFO's 1996 album *Advance* under the title "Shove Piggy Shove."

**I MISS YOU > From *Post***

A loose version of this song dates all the way back to the *Debut* era, where it allegedly had a working title of "Gail Biffen." Comprised almost entirely of scatted lyrics and meaningless phrases, this frustrating early sketch (glimpsed briefly during one of the backstage interludes in *Vessel*) was eventually left on the studio's cutting room floor. It wouldn't undergo its radical transformation until a few years later, when Björk resurrected it for *Post*.

"I Miss You" was reborn as a Latin-inflected stomper, with redrawn lyrics and Howie Bernstein's fresh insight breathing new life into it. Replete with a braying horn section and Talvin Singh's electric percussion, it became *Post*'s most robust track. As the album's last single, it was also the benefactor of a colorful video, courtesy of original *Ren & Stimpy* creator John Kricfalusi.

Björk had long been a fan of early episodes of *Ren & Stimpy*, and approached Kricfalusi near the beginning of 1996 with the request to work together. The ensuing four-minute clip for "I Miss You" — done in a *Ren & Stimpy* animation style — took nearly a year to complete, and was promptly censored by MTV for cartoon nudity and cartoon violence. Said the irreverent Kricfalusi of his video subject: "Most bands try to imitate others. But Björk is as original as Elvis — and she's got a cuter groin thrust."

**IMMATURE > From *Homogenic***

Built around a looped ascending melody, "Immature" finds Björk admonishing herself for mistakes made in past relationships. Less self-pitying (more like a slap on the forehead) she nonetheless wrings every drop of drama out of the song's lyrics.

"Immature" made its first appearance shortly after the end of Björk's relationship with Goldie, and is obviously a by-product of her post-breakup autopsy. With only one real musical motif, it's certainly one of the least interesting songs on *Homogenic*, but its contemplative subject matter is in simpatico with the rest of the album.

**IN THE MUSICALS > From *Selmasongs***

Two distinct versions of "In the Musicals" appear in *Dancer in the Dark* — the *Selmasongs* soundtrack includes both, spliced together, with the switchover happening at roughly the 1:42 mark.

There are, however, still discrepancies to be found between the album and film takes. The film version features the vocals of actor/dancer Joel Grey, who portrays the fictitious silver screen legend, Oldritch Novy, but Grey's vocals have been excised from *Selmasongs*.

Another possible point of interest: additional footage on the North American version of the *Dancer in the Dark* DVD depicts Björk rehearsing the entire courtroom dance scene . . . with her shoelace untied.

**ISOBEL** > **From *Post***

Conceived as the second part in a roughly hewn trilogy that began with "Human Behaviour" and concluded with "Bachelorette," "Isobel" follows the trajectory of one central character as she matures, moves out of the forest, and ventures into the city.

"She's not a real person, she's more like a myth — like Atlas represents strength and Neptune is the god of the ocean, she represents intuition," Björk said of the title character. "So she clashes all the time with people all around her who function with their heads and are quite clever — she gets into a lot of trouble, because she doesn't understand morality. She falls in with the wrong people and things go really badly, until she decides to isolate herself. So she withdraws, but she still decides that she was right, that people should function more with intuition that with their brain.

"So she collects all these moths and sends them outside her window, and they fly all over the world, and they go inside the houses of all the people who are pretending or trying to be clever and they stop them from being clever . . . by flying straight in their faces and going, 'Na-na! Na-na, na-na, na-na, naaa!'"

With parallels that mirror the arc of her own personal experience from *Debut* through to *Homogenic*, the semi-autobiographical element of *Isobel* is difficult to deny. Fittingly, after giving birth to a daughter in 2002, Björk christened her Isadora, a variation that implied equal parts extension and individuality.

**IT'S IN OUR HANDS** > **From *Greatest Hits***

Although it was recorded early in the *Vespertine* sessions and appeared frequently on the ensuing tour, "It's in Our Hands" wouldn't get a proper studio release until two years later, as the lone new track from Björk's *Greatest Hits* compilation. In its live incarnation, the song had encouraged frenzied communal hand claps; the studio version recasts those sampled, digitally spliced claps as finely processed rhythms.

With its typically empowering lyrics and warm, forward-thinking arrangements (again, courtesy of Matmos), "It's in Our Hands" served as an appropriate rejoinder to *Vespertine*'s chilly façade. "It was nice to do a full-blooded song after doing a whole album that didn't have any blood in it, though that was the point of *Vespertine*, that it was see-through like a crystal," Björk said. "When we played it live, we were all looking forward to rocking out."

**IT'S NOT UP TO YOU** > **From *Vespertine***

"It's Not Up to You" was initially conceived in November 1999 as a joint single between Björk and fellow Icelandic group Gus Gus to protest the construction of an environmentally harmful power plant named Fljótsdalsvirkjun. In an effort to raise funds and awareness for their cause (which also had support from filmmaker Friðrik Þór Friðriksson and Björk's father Gudmunder Gunnarsson), their goal had been to sell the protest single online. Unfortunately, Gus Gus' subsequent personnel problems made the collaboration nearly impossible to facilitate; by late 2000, Björk had claimed the song's title for herself and re-envisioned it as a meditation on the perils of steering fate.

Arguably *Vespertine*'s finest pop song, "It's Not Up to You" contains a gently rolling refrain, a gorgeous choral outro, and some of Björk's most resonant imagery.

The Fljótsdalsvirkjun power plant was never built, but another was touted for the same location (just north of Vatnajokull — Iceland's largest glacier) in 2002. The most vehement public opposition to this proposal — named the Kárahnjúkar Hydropower Project — came from Björk's mother, who embarked on a much-publicized three-week hunger strike in protest.

**IT'S OH SO QUIET > From *Post***

Buoyed by Spike Jonze's theatrical, MTV-friendly video, "It's Oh So Quiet" soon became Björk's most successful single of all time. However, its ensuant ubiquity and significant novelty factor conspired to backfire on her; as her career wore on, Björk grew to resent the fact that a tossed-off cover from the '40s had become her most identifiable song. "When you go blindfolded into the unknown and you've been on a mission that the world needs new music and you've experimented with all sorts of people and have this excellent adventure," she said, "Doing that for 10 years and sitting down with the record company people and they say, 'Oh, forget about everything you've ever done. The only thing that's worth anything is 'It's Oh So Quiet.' You just go, 'What?!' I didn't work like a lunatic and wave the flag and the trumpet, with this fierce belief for all this time, to have that song be the only result."

Björk's hardcore followers seemed to concur with that assessment; to her delight, 2002's fan-programmed *Greatest Hits* compilation left "It's Oh So Quiet" off the final tracklisting. "I was so pleased when the fans voted and there were like 15 other songs that they thought were better," she said.

**I'VE SEEN IT ALL > From *Selmasongs***

Beginning with their shared billing on Adam Yauch's inaugural Tibetan Freedom Concert in 1997 through to their eventually jettisoned plans to co-headline a North American tour together in 1998, Björk and Radiohead lead singer Thom Yorke had been in frequent contact with each other. As they discovered shared tastes and mutual artistic philosophies, the pair developed a friendship that eventually led to discussions regarding a possible collaboration.

Dissatisfied with actor Peter Stormare's vocal performance in the film version of this duet, Björk had desired a replacement partner for *Selmasongs*. Not surprisingly, Yorke's was the first name that came to mind. Recorded over a four-day span in March 2000, "I've Seen It All" would be *Selmasongs*' first and only single. This dream collaboration would also earn Björk her first Academy Award nomination for Best Original Song.

**JOGA > From *Vespertine***

Written by Björk while roaming around Iceland's destitute landscape in solitude, "Joga" is both a tribute to her best friend and an attempt to voice Iceland's spirit and geography in song. "With this song, I really had a sort of Icelandic national anthem in mind," she said. "Not the national anthem but certain classic Icelandic songs — very romantic, very proud, very patriotic. Mountains, glaciers, that kind of thing."

Director Michel Gondry spent days shooting aerial footage from a helicopter for the video, no small feat given his crippling fear of heights. That footage was taken to an animator, who recreated the landscape in CGI and fluidly morphed the scenes together. Because the technique they were employing to do so was relatively unproven, there was a great deal of worry involved; Gondry had no idea how the video would look when it was finished. "Every time we tried a technique like this one, it had never been done before," he says. "Then as others come with similar concepts, the technique gets more perfected. If you put those videos together, maybe my video would look less achieved, but I have to say, in my defense, we were going there but we didn't even know if it would work!"

**KARVEL > From *I Miss You* CDS 1/2**

Not to be confused with "Jóhannes Kjarvel" (the 11-year-old Björk's self-penned tribute to Icelandic painter Jóhannes Kjarvel), "Karvel" was hatched with Graham Massey in 1994. In spite of being relegated to b-side status, it still enjoys standing among acolytes as one of Björk's better dance tracks.

Even though its mid-'90s production values are easily identified, "Karvel" has dated better than some of Björk's other overtly dance-leaning excursions from this period. Massey's fast and frequent variations to the track's simmering breakbeat are the key; this b-side is noteworthy for its rhythm section alone.

**KEEP YOUR MOUTH SHUT > From *Nearly God*** (Tricky)

At Tricky's request, Björk reprised the melody and lyrics from *Post*'s "You've Been Flirting Again" for "Keep Your Mouth Shut," which he then recast as one-half of a hazy call-and-response segment between the two. With his bilious sentiments acting in bitter opposition to her pleas of comfort, "Keep Your Mouth Shut" is about the push/pull of a doomed relationship, or better yet, the strain of an anti-courtship ritual specific only to the hopeless romantic and hopeless misanthrope.

**LIKE SOMEONE IN LOVE > From *Debut***

Björk and Corky Hale recorded the vocals and harp track for this song during a 1993 pre-*Debut* demo session in London, England. At the time, Björk had no designs of including this song, a cover, on her first album, but some in-studio tinkering by Nellee Hooper gave it a feel and a sense of place that worked well in the context of the record.

Sequenced on the heels of the thumping "There's More to Life than This," the moonstruck "Like Someone in Love" conjured an image of a lovesick Björk escaping a club at 3 a.m. to go trawling along the beach. To create that effect, Hooper augmented Björk and Hale's original demo with some outdoor field recordings.

Hale hadn't had a chance to hear the final album version before it was released. She stumbled into a copy of *Debut* at a record shop and was shocked by what she heard. "I must say, I was not happy that they overdubbed," she says. "We listened to it and my husband said, 'My God, do we have a bad record?'"

**LILITH > From *Not For Threes*** (Plaid)

The permanent dissolution of Black Dog in 1995 gave members Ed Handley and Andy Turner cause to return to their original project – Plaid. Released in 1998, the duo's splendid full-length debut as Plaid (*Not For Threes*) saw them draw on Black Dog's moody ambience as the basis for a much more melodic, almost cartoonish sound. With its thumping hip-hop loop and winsome, descending piano line, "Lilith" is one of the album's many thrills – a swoony nighttime melody which is wonderfully served by Björk's mischievous delivery.

Although something of an enigma lyrically, the song's central ideas are well-communicated: the end notion is of protagonist as Earth mother and self-righteous independent, perhaps in exile but never in need. The most crucial clue to unlocking this riddle may lie in the song's title – in mythological terms, Lilith is generally acknowledged to be Adam's true first wife. Created not from rib but earth, Lilith refused to cede to Adam's requests and was subsequently exiled from Eden. Many orthodox readings detail how Lilith then disappeared to the Red Sea, where she mothered thousands of demons with stolen seed – the various interpretations and legends mean that Lilith is presently identified with everything from feminism and equality to infidelity and impurity.

**THE MODERN THINGS > From *Post***

"The Modern Things," written and demoed with Graham Massey in 1992, features lyrics hinged on a fantastic slice of conceptual doublethink. Evoked in response to doomsayers who regard technology as a regressive, soul-crushing threat, it posited the comical notion wherein all modern things were actually forebears to nature.

As precocious as ever, Björk obviously took great delight in imagining a world where toasters and cellular phones roamed with sacrimony and entitlement. "They've just been waiting in a mountain for the right moment, and have been listening to the irritating noises — dinosaurs and people outside — and now it's their turn to come out and multiply," she explained. "I thought it was really funny. I don't know — I might be the only one laughing."

**MOTHER HEROIC** > **From *Hidden Place* CDS 2/2**

One of two songs from the *Vespertine* era to reference the work of E.E. Cummings, this track's opening line ("Oh thou that bowest thy ecstatic face") is borrowed from Cummings' poem "Belgium." No doubt taking her cue from that uncharacteristically ostentatious lead, Björk's lyrics for "Mother Heroic" rank as some of the loftiest she's written; they also reveal the teenaged fangirl lurking inside her. With accompanying lines written to fit Cummings' cadences, the prevailing sense is of a wide-eyed pupil dutifully emulating her admired.

Even for a b-side, such an experiment is a bit of a risk, but Björk carries herself nicely here. Featuring a sparse chime accompaniment from Guy Sigsworth, "Mother Heroic" is a Spartan, moon-dipped lullaby that ranks as one of her finer interludes.

**MY SPINE** > **From *Telegram*; *It's Oh So Quiet* CDS 2/2**

Co-written with deaf percussionist Evelyn Glennie, whom Björk met through her *MTV Unplugged* performance, "My Spine" is a completely spontaneous, mostly improvised piece. Like five other tracks (four of which were never released), it was completed during a one-day writing and recording session at Glennie's home in 1994, which by all accounts was completely informal, experimental, and friendly.

"The important thing was finding out that we both had a soft spot for chocolate and from there on we knew we get on like a house on fire," Glennie says. "We did not want agents or record companies as part of this initial collaboration, but [rather] to do things without any expectations.

"We ended up at a local Indian restaurant," she adds. "[Björk] wore a jumper that had a huge turtle neck that covered a good part of her lower face, which meant a messy encounter when trying to eat anything. I hasten to add that the sleeves and lower part of the jumper were mighty short. . . ."

**NATURE IS ANCIENT** (a.k.a. "My Snare") > **From *Bachelorette* CDS 1/3; *Family Tree***

A longtime source of confusion among fans, this 1997 b-side actually has two separate titles. It first appeared with the name "Nature Is Ancient" as one of five bonus tracks on the Japanese *Homogenic*; two months later, the exact same recording would be recycled on the "Bachelorette" single, this time renamed "My Snare." Compounding the confusion, it re-appeared on 2002's *Family Tree* box set, once again titled "Nature In Ancient," leaving one to deduce that Björk was not fond of her last-minute decision to rename the song in the first place.

With a facile lyric and an unexciting Bell-Björk arrangement that merely conjures memories of vastly superior *Homogenic*-era songs, "Nature Is Ancient" is probably one of Björk's most forgettable b-sides. Nonetheless, while promoting *Family Tree*, she seized upon the five-year-old song as a benchmark, even issuing a video for it.

**NEW WORLD > From *Selmasongs***

In the months following the release of *Dancer in the Dark*, Björk began to speak more publicly about her ideological disagreements with Von Trier as they pertained to the film's resolution. In that time, she made it clear that she regarded its outcome as a manipulative conceit designed to rouse emotion and contended that Selma's bitter destiny reflected Von Trier's rampant fatalism more than it did any overarching truth about humanity.

As the film's concluding song (and by extension, Selma's last gasp), "New World" sees Björk attempt to repeal the negativity with her own exhortations of hope. Even if the abiding message is that this cruddy world is no place for someone of Selma's purity, at least the song's lyrics imply some sort of vaguely useful resolution: deliverance.

Musically, "New World" marries the leitmotif established in "Overture" and "Next to Last Song" (it's not on the soundtrack, but in the film nonetheless) with a boomy, loping beat reminiscent of mid-period Massive Attack. As finales go, it's pretty unimpeachable — the horns trill and the strings swell at all the right moments, further exaggerating the intended divide between this acinematic film and its unswervingly cinematic soundtrack.

**NU FLYVER ANTON > From the film *Anton***

Danish director Aage Reis' low-budget 1995 film *Anton* told the story of a 10-year-old boy fascinated with airplanes. Hilmar Örn Hilmarsson had been commissioned to oversee the soundtrack because of his frequent association with the Danish film industry. When it came time to record the title song, he immediately thought of Björk.

Written and recorded over a weekend in Denmark in mid-1995, "Nu Flyver Anton" (translation: "Anton flies now") afforded Björk the opportunity to put her Icelandic education to good use.

"One thing that Icelanders have in common is that we hate Danish because we were all forced to learn in it school, so I thought it was a nice joke to have her sing something in Danish," explains Hilmarsson. "She came over to Denmark with Sindri and he went to Tivoli Gardens, which is this fun park in Copenhagen. We went into the studio with a bottle of champagne and a bottle of cognac, butchered the Danish language and had fun doing it."

Since no commercial soundtrack for *Anton* was ever released, this track is only officially available via the difficult-to-procure *Anton* radio samplers. Thankfully, with its dated, out-of-the-box arrangements and grating chorus, "Nu Flyver Anton" remains inessential.

**ONE DAY > From *Debut***

Although, contrary to popular belief, the baby gurgles heard at the beginning of this song are not samples of Sindri, they are certainly inspired by him. With its burbling synths and new-agey sighs, "One Day" is a hope-filled lullaby delivered from mother to son, a product of the encircling haze of Björk's maternal daydream.

Containing a first line that sounds like it's being sung through a grin, "One Day" spills over with forlorn anticipation and unbridled excitement. Björk's assured forecast of what life has in store for Sindri speaks to her liberal parenting philosophy; her willingness to imagine adult success for her six-year-old echoes the autonomy she too was granted at an early age.

The stock library baby noises heard at the beginning aren't the only samples in "One Day"; a small portion nipped from the tail end of the Fatback Band's "Put Your Love in My Tender Care" can be heard looping at roughly the 1:47 mark.

**OVERTURE > From *Selmasongs***

Lars Von Trier's original film edit of *Dancer in the Dark* began with this song, played in its entirety, without any accompanying visuals whatsoever. His intention was for movie theaters to slowly raise their curtains on the film's opening scene just as the song concluded. These plans were abandoned after the film's North American distributor informed Von Trier that most American cinemas didn't have curtains. Since four minutes of darkness was not an advisable compromise, Von Trier assembled a visual montage of paintings done by Danish painter Pers Kirkeby, who also happened to be the husband of the film's producer, Vibeke Windeløv.

**OXYGEN > From *Her Greatest Hits*** (Evelyn Glennie)

The second of the Björk-Glennie collaborations to get an official release is only available on the Scottish musician's 1998 *Her Greatest Hits* album. With its slow rumblings, pregnant pauses and desolate vocals, "Oxygen" most immediately recalls the Elgar Sisters' "Stigdu Mig." Like all the compositions the pair forged together, it also made good use of Glennie's offbeat percussion collection.

"There were songs that included the UDU drum, steel drum . . . 'My Spine' uses tuned car exhaust pipes, 'Oxygen' employs the marimba, I used bass kalimba on another," she says. "We knew instantly when something was working and when an idea was not so we knew how to pace things. It's hard to describe an encounter like this because one is dealing with such inner feelings but yet such openness. We both had to be completely exposed and honest with our creativity."

**PAGAN POETRY > From *Vespertine***

As the second single from *Vespertine*, "Pagan Poetry" and its courageous video confirmed the emerging paradox at hand; Björk's increased withdrawal from the public spectrum was coinciding with the most fiercely personal work of her career.

Directed by Me Company's Nick Knight, the candid video for "Pagan Poetry" furthered the album's already-established themes of sexuality, body, and union by reclaiming a subset of suggestive or uneasy imagery as something pure, sensual. Nudity, nipple piercings, and finally a moment of uneasy candor, the words "I love him" offered *a capella* and repeated over and over again like a mantra.

**PLAY DEAD > From *Play Dead* CDS**

Composer David Arnold commissioned "Play Dead" for the Harvey Keitel film *Young Americans*, and the sweeping song was issued on the heels of *Debut*'s release in 1993. Recorded with a 60-piece orchestra as well as bassist Jah Wobble, the song features lyrics inspired by the film. "It was actually fun because the character in the film was suffering and going through hardcore tough times and at the time I was at my happiest," Björk later said. "It was quite liberating to sit down after writing a whole album and write from someone else's point of view."

In spite of being relatively difficult to find, "Play Dead" has remained a fan favorite through the years — Björk resurrected it for parts of her *Vespertine* tour while fans earmarked it for inclusion on the 15-track *Greatest Hits*.

**PLUTO > From *Vespertine***

Borne out of an impromptu jam session with Mark Bell in Spain's El Cortijo Studios, the squelching "Pluto" is *Homogenic*'s most violent song by far. Reminiscent of the digital hardcore emanating from German noiseniks such as Alec Empire (an acknowledged influence at the time), the techno throttle of *Homogenic*'s next-to-last song is the album's static-touched exorcism, the anguished tremor before the eventual rebirth of "All Is Full of Love."

"It's about getting plastered, that need to destroy everything so you can start over again," Björk said. "Having a lot in the planet Pluto, which I do, means you want to cut the crap, throw all the rubbish away. No extra baggage. It's death and birth."

**POSSIBLY MAYBE** > **From *Post***

The twinges of slide guitar heard in the background of "Possibly Maybe" were originally intended to be the song's focal point. Björk's initial instinct had been to strive for what she called an "ambient country" vibe, inspired by the heatwave desire of Chris Isaak's twangy "Wicked Game."

Although that tantalizing concept was eventually abandoned, it's not difficult to trace the existing connection between the two songs; both linger like apparitions in passion's purgatory, "Wicked Game" striving for a way forward, "Possibly Maybe" looking for a way out.

Because it documented the various stages of her ill-fated relationship with Stephane Sednaoui, disappointment and all, Björk struggled to claim "Possibly Maybe" as one of her own; for a long time, she thought it too self-indulgent and miserablist to release. "I would always write songs about happy things and keep my dirty laundry to myself," she said. "I was brought up so self-sufficient and happy and to never complain. Icelandic people are so furiously optimistic that it's aggressive. So for me to write songs that are not happy is a bit abhorrent. You feel ashamed about it . . . I was ashamed of writing a song that was not giving hope."

**SCARY** > **From *Bachelorette* CDS 1/2**

Co-written with Guy Sigsworth (who also provides the song's lone accompaniment), the harpsichord jaunt of "Scary" is an upbeat, fiery piece that spins a miniature drama around a female protagonist and her commitment-phobe partner. In some senses, it could be considered a sister song to the similarly disenfranchised "5 Years," except that "Scary" isn't as concerned with coercion as it is preoccupied with the perceived gap between men and women.

Granted, the "Men are from Mars, women are from Venus" sentiment is a bit facile, but Björk's sheer exuberance, combined with her genuinely clever turns of phrase is what makes this worthwhile.

**SCATTERHEART** > **From *Selmasongs***

The song that forms the narrative backbone of *Dancer in the Dark*'s dreamlike post-murder sequence, "Scatterheart" (originally titled "Smith & Wesson") begins with Selma's attempt to soothe herself and ends as she's consumed by creeping paranoia and out-of-body disbelief. Static-tickled, like a faded memory, the opening lullaby quickly descends into an unresolved mess of dissonant strings as her grief and despair overwhelm her.

Comprised of three discernible movements, wherein Selma's shift from imagination to reality coincides with the progression of digital to orchestral, it's probably one of her most ambitious compositions. At 6:39, it is also her longest.

**SHORT TERM AFFAIR** (w/ Tony Ferrino) > **From *Phenomenon*** (Tony Ferrino)
Obviously a riff on Neil Diamond at his most opulent and absurd, Portuguese lounge singer Tony Ferrino was one of of British comedian Steve Coogan's best-known characters — a greasy, hilariously overwrought cheeseball with a God complex and a string of "successful" albums under his snakeskin belt. So popular was Ferrino with Coogan's fans that an actual album spin-off was spawned; 1997's *Phenomenon* featured Ferrino's "greatest hits" as well as a few choice duets.

As a professed Coogan diehard, Björk was only too happy to lend a hand. She appeared on "Short Term Affair" as Ferrino's teenaged au pair — the song outlines the intimate, mostly hilarious details of their extra-marital fling. The duo performed the song live for a 1997 BBC Comic Relief showcase, with Bjork's barely suppressed giggles the obvious highlight.

**SIDASTA EG** > **From *Big Time Sensuality* CDS 1/2**
This is one of about 12 songs that Björk wrote and recorded with fellow Kukl bandmate Gudlaugur Ottarsson in the mid-1980s. Operating under the banner the Elgar Sisters, this side project gave both primary members an opportunity to flex the creative muscles they couldn't with Kukl. For Ottarson, it provided the opportunity to play something other than distended post-punk; for Björk, it was a chance to try her hand at writing slower, more considered compositions.

Of the two Elgar Sisters songs to be reborn as Björk b-sides, "Sidasta Eg" is probably the more essential. Whenever Ottarsson's agitated guitar line threatens to splinter like a bead of light in a hall of mirrors, Björk collects his notes under her sweeping refrain.

The subtle similarities between this 1986 composition and elements of *Vespertine* are slight, but nonetheless significant enough to warrant attention. For example, although 15 years separated, the unresolved harp line that punctuates the song's core is immediately reminiscent of the one that powers "Pagan Poetry."

**SO BROKEN** > **From *Joga* CDS 2/3**
Not only was the flamenco-inspired "So Broken" the first song that Björk wrote after receiving a mail bomb from Ricardo Lopez, it was also what ultimately led her to Trevor Morais' El Cortijo Studios in Spain. What was initially conceived as a brief jaunt to Spain (in order to work with famed flamenco guitarist Raimundo Amador) turned into an extended stay when she fell in love with the studio's picturesque environment.

Although "So Broken" was a highlight in the minds of many who worked on *Homogenic*, it was ultimately left off the album. Its stripped-down, guitar-led arrangement simply didn't fit in with the other songs that Björk was writing at the time, even though she was struggling desperately to find a way to make it work. "She was walking around San Pedro with a little tape recorder trying to pick up little sounds that we could incorporate into this piece," recalls Markus Dravs. "But I guess she never pulled it off."

**SOD OFF** > **From *Joga* CDS 2/3**

Björk's famous tendency to integrate local vernacular into her already skewed take on English is on full display here. "Sod off" is a British colloquialism meaning (more or less) go away, and it's got a peculiarly endearing currency coming from her trill Icelandic palette.

With its confrontational string arrangement and screamy delivery, "Sod Off" may be the most ferocious song to emerge from the *Homogenic* sessions. It was also a late contender for the album before being ultimately banished to b-sidedom.

**STIGDU MIG** > **From *Venus As a Boy* CDS 2/2**

The other of the two Elgar Sisters songs to subsequently surface on a Björk release, the sparse "Stigdu Mig" clocks in just shy of two minutes. It is, nevertheless, an uneasy pleasure. With Ottarsson's airy jazz chords unravelling behind Björk's tenuously connected melodies, it has the glint of a seabound vessel, cast adrift and moonlit.

**STRESSED OUT** (Remixes) > **From *Stressed Out* EP** (A Tribe Called Quest)

In an uncharacteristic reversal of roles, Björk authored three separate remixes of A Tribe Called Quest's single, "Stressed Out," for eventual inclusion on their 1997 *Stressed Out* EP. With an added horn line immediately reminiscent of Black Dog, not to mention her own overdubbed vocals, "Björk's Married to the Mob Mix" is the most experimental of the trio, forgoing beats in favor of atmosphere; "Björk's Dandelions Mix" reinstates the original's loping horn motif before submerging it in ambient sources, while the concluding "Björk's Say Dip Mix" is the most accessible of the bunch, stripping back some of the tracks but never to the point of making them unrecognizable. Although none are essential, these sturdy remixes confirm the suspicion that Björk's untapped potential extends to the sequencer and mixing board as well.

**SUN IN MY MOUTH** > **From *Vespertine***

Björk read a variety of different poets over the course of *Vespertine*, but it was the work of E.E. Cummings that best reflected her own impassioned state of mind. Featuring Cummings' poetry (the lyrics are borrowed from his work "Impressions") framed inside Björk's moon-dipped arrangements, "Sun in My Mouth" plays like some spectral duet.

"I think he's very interested in climaxes — in the divine and euphoric states," Björk said of Cummings. "But what is special about him is that he's always humble. It's very common for people who are really into peaks and crowns and euphoric states that they go really pompous and sort of Wagner-like. Which he never, ever, ever [does]. I guess that's something I found really curious — that you can go to the sharpest peak ever, but it's completely humble."

**SWEET INTUITION > From *Army of Me* CDS 1/2**

Boasting Black Dog's characteristically minimalist touches (imagine Steve Reich messing with *Analogue Bubblebath*'s sample banks) and a Bolshie performance from Björk, "Sweet Intuition" is a darkish slice of techno that valorizes instinct over reason.

Its striking lyrical similarity to "Bedtime Story" (the song Björk wrote for Madonna) also suggests that it was either inspired by or originally intended for same. With both songs containing many of the same lyrics it's possible that "Sweet Intuition" represents Björk's reclamation of this philosophy as her own.

While the Black Dog original merits investigation, a superior interpretation featuring Guy Sigsworth on pipe organ was later recorded at London's Royal Festival Hall. Released as "Sweet Sweet Intuition," this version is available on the first part of the single for *It's Oh So Quiet*.

**THERE'S MORE TO LIFE THAN THIS > From *Debut***

Inspired by a party in Iceland that Björk attended and then promptly sneaked out of, "There's More to Life than This" is one of *Debut*'s most critical tracks. With a portion of the vocals famously recorded in the toilets of London's Milk Bar while the backing tracks blared over the nightclub's house speakers, it marked the pinnacle of Nellee Hooper and Björk's experimental urges.

Largely because of that toilet stall interlude, the buoyant, housey thrash of "There's More to Life than This" evoked all the familiar details of a night out clubbing. It also reinforced the idea of Björk as questing independent, a person who occasionally celebrates the communal dance-floor throb of her favorite song by escaping to a place where her own conspiratorial voice is the only sound in earshot.

**TRAVESSIA > Currently unreleased**

Björk's adoration of this 1966 Milton Nascimento composition is quite well-documented. In 1996 she recorded a version of it for inclusion on David Byrne's AIDS awareness fundraiser album *Red Hot & Rio*. The song was intended to appear on the compilation right up until the eleventh hour, when she suddenly decided to pull it from the project.

Early statements out of the Björk camp suggested that she'd pulled the contribution because she was unhappy with the result. Later, in an interview with a

Brazillian newspaper, she claimed that her motivations were also political – in between the time she'd recorded it and the album's release, Eumir Deodato (who arranged Nascimento's original version) had explained to her that the song directly related to the military dictatorship that Brazil had suffered during the mid-1960s. Worried that her cover version might seem inauthentic and insensitive in context, she decided that it should never be released.

Nonetheless, as the song had already been recorded, it inevitably began doing the rounds on various bootlegs. While there's a novelty factor to hearing Björk grapple with Portuguese, the arrangements on this studio version are more than a little underwhelming, making it reasonable to assume that her reasons for quashing the song might be *both* artistically and politically motivated.

**UNDO > From *Vespertine***

"Undo" co-writer Thomas Knak reckons the best thing about this song was that it yielded a firsthand opportunity to marvel at the uninhibited manner in which Björk generously indulged her own curiosity and excitement about life. "To have [an idea] while she was there and [to] see her discover this new sound," he marvels. "Seeing her face and seeing her smile and everything – like an eight-year-old girl with a new toy – was so fantastic to experience."

Child's blood in its veins and gristly wisdom in its heart, "Undo" is a held hand, a reassuring reminder that anything can happen once you let it. If you are in pain, undo it, Björk suggests, no hint of disingenuousness in her voice, over climbing strings and a rising choir.

**UNISON > From *Vespertine***

"[It's] the only song I thought was a bit too self-indulgent," Björk originally said of *Vespertine*'s closing track. "I'm moaning a bit in that song. I'm not very proud of moaning."

Containing a refrain directly inspired by her experience with *Dancer in the Dark* and a healthy dollop of self-effacing humor evoked to counter the balance, "Unison" is an astounding album finale. Simultaneously playful and poignant, it searches for resolution before arriving, for a final time, at the doorstep of *Vespertine*'s prevailing message: love. "Let's unite tonight," Björk concurs, and suddenly she's minutes away from that hidden place. . . .

"Unison" contains a sample from Oval's "Aero Deck," a track found on 1996's *Systemich*. Oval – the alias of German artist Markus Popp – is widely cited as one of the originators of glitch.

**UNRAVEL > From *Homogenic***

Loping, sad, and true, the doleful "Unravel" is one of Björk's least recognized triumphs, a funereal lament for lost love that intermingles flashes of grief and hope with devastating poignancy.

"Unravel" is held spellbound by its own absence of resolution, whether in the way Guy Sigsworth's sonorous whale-call synth surrenders to an organ line played in memoriam or in the way Björk's bittersweet call-and-answer reverberates like a heart in flux. Perpetually lost then found, it's a graceful portrait of the negotiated state between fresh heartache and looming independence, compromised but perfect in every way.

**VENUS AS A BOY > From *Debut***

Conceived as a lyrical ode to the sensitivity of boyfriend Dominic Thrupp ("There's something very delicate and tender about him, but not in a sickly sort of woofty way" Björk once said), "Venus as a Boy" was directly influenced by the convergent cultures of London's bustling city center. With Talvin Singh lending his arranging talents and tabla playing to the proceedings, the end result came off all curling strings and tick-tock rhythms, an unlikely New Age/Bollywood pastiche.

The video for "Venus as a Boy" famously depicted Björk fondling and then frying an egg, an idea loosely inspired by a scene from one of her favorite books, Georges Bataille's hedonist text, *The Story of the Eye*.

The book, which Björk first discovered through Sjon Sigurdsson as a teenager, had included one particularly pornographic scene which featured a hard-boiled egg as a sexual prop. Wanting to somehow pay homage, Björk had encouraged director Sophie Muller to read Bataille's book prior to the video shoot, but Muller didn't get to it in time. The end result: a *fried* egg.

"[Sophie] kept going on about it being fried," Björk lamented. "I was saying, 'No way is that book about a fried egg! I'm sorry. Poached? Okay. Boiled? Okay. Raw? Okay. But *not* fried!'"

**VERANDI > From *Hidden Place* CDS 1/2**

Possessing a goosebump-inducing key change (see the 2:12 mark) and a garish, overblown arrangement that somehow works against all odds, the explosive "Verandi" owes its greatest debt to Bollywood composer Jolly Mukherjee. With Björk's original demo tape as guidance, Mukherjee composed and recorded the song's boozy string section with an orchestra in Bombay. Later, with the aid of Marius De Vries, Björk played off Mukherjee's heroic arrangements to startling effect.

While it's difficult to imagine any permutation of *Vespertine* in which the ferocious "Verandi" wouldn't seem hopelessly out of place, it's still a shame that this stunner had to be relegated to b-side status. It's handily superior to about a third of the album, and certainly ranks highly among Björk's castaways.

**VIOLENTLY HAPPY** > **From *Debut***

With a flurry of high-profile artists (Depeche Mode, Masters at Work, Nellee Hooper, Graham Massey, and Fluke among them) each customizing remixes of "Violently Happy" for a distinct strain of dance music, *Debut*'s fourth single was a dominating entity on the club circuit. Following on the heels of the previously issued "Big Time Sensuality," it served as the tail end of a potent one-two punch, providing unassailable proof that Björk was as viable a dance artist as she was an indie act, perhaps even more so.

"Violently Happy" is probably *Debut*'s least complex track, with its lone melody line, coruscating synths, and relentlessly thump-thump-thumping rhythms. As a club tune, it's special for precisely that reason. Implicit in the song's interest in dynamics over chord progressions is Björk's tacit understand of dance music; optimism best conveyed by brutal force, not subtlety.

**VÍSUR VATNSENDA-RÓSA** > **From *Chansons Des Mers Froides* LP**

Suzanne Vega, Jane Siberry, and Siouxsie Sioux are just some of the talents that French arranger Hector Zazou tapped for his album *Chansons des mers froides* (translation: "Songs of the Cold Seas"), a collection of traditional songs from countries with cold climates redone in his distinctly modernist style.

Björk's contribution, an Icelandic folk song named "Vísur Vatnsenda-Rósa," benefits nicely from Zazou's tearful, cinematic arrangements. With its slumbering melody, pensive instrumental break, and rousing conclusion, "Vísur Vatnsenda-Rósa" is indisputably one of the album's highlights; its standing as a fan favorite is well deserved.

**YOGA** > **From *Nearly God*** (Tricky)

As the concluding song on the wild growing thicket that is *Nearly God*, the gently percussive clatter of duet "Yoga" marks a fitting finale. Impenetrable, dense, and bustling with half-remembered phrases, "Yoga" put the lid on the album's inescapable glint of neurosis.

Björk's performance here is one-dimensional but strangely effective; she serves as the lithesome foil to Tricky's haggard mumblings by overwhelming his mutterings with her own quietly drawn out notes. On the whole, it's probably the weaker of her two contributions to *Nearly God*, but still well worth tracking down, if just for the fascinating vocal tensions between the two.

**YOU ONLY LIVE TWICE > Currently unreleased**

David Arnold originally produced Björk's sweeping rendition of John Barry's classic "You Only Live Twice" for inclusion on his own James Bond tribute album *Shaken & Stirred*, which featured Aimee Mann, Pulp, Iggy Pop, and other contemporary musicians trying their hands at classic 007 themes. Much like "Travessia," Björk struggled with the recording of this track, to the point where she eventually withdrew it from the compilation outright. "I learned the hard way that you should never cover your favorite tunes because they are good already," she said of the experience during a 1997 online chat. "Cover bad tunes and make them good."

Although it was never officially released, a high quality bootleg of the recording has since surfaced. Filled with spacey effects and strong orchestral flourishes, it's an unquestionably superb rendition, certainly strong enough to cause one to wonder where the perceived points of difficulty may have been.

**YOU'VE BEEN FLIRTING AGAIN > From *Post***

A drastically different version of this song (without strings) was recorded at Compass Point Studios in the Bahamas with Nellee Hooper at the helm; upon her return to London, Björk decided that she was unhappy with it and redrew the song on her own from scratch. The idea to do it strictly with a string section was a last-moment decision; with minimal guidance from Eumir Deodato, Björk arranged the strings herself. It marked the first time in her solo career that she'd endeavored to compose on such a huge scale.

As evidenced by its inclusion on Björk's list of personal favorite recordings (for a compilation packaged in the six-CD *Family Tree* box set), "You've Been Flirting Again" still has a very special place in her heart.

# Singles Guide

The sheer amount of unique Björk-related promotional items, singles, EPS, and albums — all impossibly compounded by subtle variances across countries — would make the process of definitive compilation worthy of a book in its own right. As such, what follows is in no way intended to be an authoritative or exhaustive Björk discography, but rather a rough guide to Björk's most commonly discussed CD singles and EPS.

**HUMAN BEHAVIOUR** > (June 1993)

1. Human Behaviour
2. Human Behaviour (Close To Human Mix)
3. Human Behaviour (Underworld Mix)
4. Human Behaviour (Dom T Mix)
5. Human Behaviour (Bassheads Edit)

Björk's first commercially released solo single ingratiated her to the dance crowd by offering up four remixes from some of the 1993's most viable electronic acts. Of the remixes offered here, Underworld's remains by far the most enduring, with Speedy J's "Close To Human Mix" coming a close second. Dominic Thrupp's "Dom T Mix" and the "Bassheads' Edit" are somewhat dated affairs and, therefore, for diehards only.

**VENUS AS A BOY 1/2** > (August 1993)

1. Venus as a Boy (Edit)
2. Venus as a Boy (Mykaell Riley Mix)
3. There's More to Life than This (Non-Toilet Mix)
4. Violently Happy (Domestic Mix)

Björk shifted to the two-part single format quite early on in her career, and "Venus as a Boy" suffers slightly from a lack of available resources. Mykaell Riley's dub-inflected, slightly askew treatment of the title track is an interesting excursion but not significantly replayable, the Björk/Hooper-produced "Non-Toilet Mix" of "There's More To Life Than This" veers off into cheese-house territory, and the "Domestic Mix" slows "Violently Happy" down to a confrontational, pipe-organ-led crawl.

**VENUS AS A BOY 2/2** > (August 1993)

1. Venus as a Boy (7" Dream Mix)
2. Stigdu Mig
3. The Anchor Song (Black Dog Remix)
4. I Remember You

This second component to "Venus as a Boy" is handily the better of the two singles. Surprisingly, with its more traditional percussion and warm synth pads, Mick Hucknall's (yes, he of Simply Red) swoony "7" Dream Mix" is arguably as good as the original, and certainly a reasonable substitute. Elsewhere, the burbling "Stigdu Mig" is happily resurrected from Björk's Kukl-era side project the Elgar Sisters, as is similarly the starry "I Remember You" from her pre-*Debut* demo sessions with harpist Corky Hale. Black Dog's Steve Reich–influenced loopfest on the strangely gorgeous Black Dog remix of "The Anchor Song" make this an absolutely essential pick overall.

**BIG TIME SENSUALITY 1/2** > (November 1993)

1. Big Time Sensuality
2. Sidasta Eg
3. Glora
4. Come to Me (Black Dog Remix)

The onslaught of singles in various formats resulted in the excavation of more fossils from Björk's past. As the only other Elgar Sisters song besides "Stigdu Mig" to see the light of day on a commercial release, the trembling "Sidasta Eg" marked an early career highlight. The sparse, instrumental flute piece "Glora," meanwhile, is an interesting (but not vital) curiosity. As ever, Black Dog's remix is well worthwhile; here, they set a sequence of minor key synth stabs against a droning tabla line to lovely effect.

**BIG TIME SENSUALITY 2/2** > (November 1993)

1. Big Time Sensuality (Fluke Minimix)
2. Big Time Sensuality (Dom T Big Time Club Mix)
3. Big Time Sensuality (Justin Robertson Lionrock Wigout Mix)
4. Big Time Sensuality (Morales Def Radio Mix)
5. Big Time Sensuality (Fluke Magimix)
6. Big Time Sensuality (Justin Robertson's Prankster's Joyride)
7. Big Time Sensuality (Fluke Moulimix)

Part Two of the "Big Time Sensuality" set sees *Debut*'s most remixable song get the red-carpet treatment from Fluke, DJ David Morales, Dominic Thrupp, and friend Justin

Robertson. While the sheer length of the remixes makes this good value for money, most of the rejigs here seem to be cut from the same cloth, relying on an unchanging 4/4 beat and peppering the builds by adding the swooshy synth histrionics of the day. Perhaps the most interesting work here belongs to Robertson, who seems to be the one most willing to experiment, even if it doesn't always yield the desired results (see the stomping squelch of his "Lionrock Wigout Mix").

**VIOLENTLY HAPPY 1/2** > (March 1994)

1. Violently Happy (Fluke Even-Tempered Mix)
2. Violently Happy (Graham Massey's Long Mix)
3. Violently Happy (Masters At Work 12" Mix)
4. Violently Happy (12" Vocal Mix) – Nellee Hooper
5. Violently Happy (Fluke Well-Tempered Mix)
6. Violently Happy (Graham Massey's Other Mix)
7. Violently Happy (Vox Dub Mix) – Nellee Hooper

About 25 of the nearly 40 minutes worth of "Violently Happy" strewn across these seven remixes is fairly forgettable stuff, either dated by way of their use of early '90s house swells, their unrelenting dullness, or a combination thereof. Of the remixers working here (Fluke, Graham Massey, Masters at Work, and Nellee Hooper), only Massey makes an attempt to bust the song out of its thump-thump-thump stronghold, by weaving looped sitar and clanging percussion around the song's relentless refrain. Elsewhere, by amping up the track with their own comically narcoticized bloops and rhythms, Fluke stay disappointingly true to form.

**VIOLENTLY HAPPY 2/2** > (March 1994)

1. Violently Happy (Fluke Even-Tempered Mix)
2. The Anchor Song (Acoustic Version)
3. Come to Me (Acoustic Version)
4. Human Behaviour (Acoustic Version)

Recorded almost 11 months before her benchmark *MTV Unplugged* appearance, these "acoustic" renderings of songs from *Debut* illustrate just how early on Björk had began to toy with the album's original arrangements. Although her accompaniment here is provided solely by Guy Sigsworth (on harpsichord), it's easy to see from these three tracks how the concept for doing something unplugged on a grander scale had been present from the very outset.

**PLAY DEAD** > (October 1993)

1. Play Dead (Tim Simenon 7" Remix)
2. Play Dead (Tim Simenon Orchestral Mix)
3. Play Dead (Tim Simenon 12" Remix)
4. Play Dead (Tim Simenon Instrumental)
5. Play Dead (Original Film Mix)

Featuring five different versions of the *Young Americans* theme, some which tweak the strings, others the rhythm section, but none of which differ significantly from the original, the *Play Dead* EP comprises a handy but hardly indispensable roundup of the various mixes that accompanied the single upon its release. Although it was once difficult to procure, the inclusion of "Play Dead" on 2002's *Greatest Hits* renders this EP necessary for the completist only.

**THE BEST MIXES FROM THE ALBUM DEBUT – FOR ALL THE PEOPLE WHO DON'T BUY WHITE LABELS** > (September 1994)

1. Human Behaviour (Underworld Mix)
2. One Day (Endorphin Mix)
3. Come to Me (Black Dog Mix)
4. Come to Me (Sabres of Paradise Mix)
5. The Anchor Song (Black Dog Mix)
6. One Day (Springs Eternal Mix)

This inconspicuously packaged, low-key EP served as the substitute to *Björk's Affairs*, the oft-delayed and eventually canceled remix album that Björk had intended to release as a complement to *Debut*. Packaged in a black cardboard slipcase featuring Björk's handwritten scrawl on the cover, *The Best Mixes* highlights some of *Debut*'s more noteworthy third-party contributions (Underworld's take on "Human Behaviour," Black Dog's unfussy reworkings) and includes a few rarities for good measure. The fresher material here comes solely from The Sabres of Paradise, whose three contributions were either previously unavailable (tracks four and six) or available in limited release (track two, via a cassette distributed with a January 1994 edition of the *NME*).

**ARMY OF ME 1/2** > (April 1995)

1. Army of Me
2. Cover Me
3. You've Been Flirting Again (Icelandic Version)
4. Sweet Intuition

The artwork to Björk's first single from *Post* saw her adapt well-known figures from the world of Japanese animation (namely, the jackbooted Astroboy) to her art aesthetic. Most of the artwork through *Homogenic* would continue in that trend, with much of it straddling the nature vs. technology divide by offering rendered versions of natural objects.

With its first two tracks lifted straight from *Post* and the third merely an Icelandic rendition (same arrangements) of another song from the album, the first part to "Army of Me" only really offers the Mark Bell–produced original "Sweet Intuition" as buyer's bait.

**ARMY OF ME 2/2** > (April 1995)

1. Army of Me (ABA All-Stars Mix)
2. Army of Me (Masseymix)
3. Army of Me (Featuring Skunk Anansie)
4. Army of Me (Instrumental ABA All-Stars Mix)

The famous "ABA All-Stars Mix" of "Army of Me" comes courtesy of none other than the Beastie Boys, whose version features a handful of choice hip-hop breaks and a mid-song meltdown laced with organ snippets and old-school sampledelica. Graham Massey runs Björk's vocals through a sawtooth filter to mixed results, while One Little Indian labelmates Skunk Anansie circumvent better judgment and re-envision "Army of Me" as a guitar-led screamer, inviting Björk's most uninhibited vocal ever.

**ISOBEL 1/2** > (August 1995)

1. Isobel
2. Charlene
3. I Go Humble
4. Venus as a Boy (Harpsichord)

With the mid-tempo strut of the enigmatic fan favorite "Charlene," the joyous techno strut of "I Go Humble," and the slowed-down chime of "Venus as a Boy," executed wonderfully with Guy Sigsworth on harpsichord, "Isobel" marks the finest of the *Post*-era singles, and certainly a nice refuge from the deluge of remixes that were to follow.

**ISOBEL 2/2** > (August 1995)

1. Isobel
2. Isobel (Eumir Deodato Mix)
3. Isobel (Siggtriplet Blunt Mix)
4. Isobel (Isobel's Lonely Heart — Goldie's Remix)

By pinching a rolling Latin drum groove and further deepening the song's thicket of rustling string parts, Eumir Deodato injects some Brazillian sensibilities into his "Isobel" mix; Sugarcube Siggi Baldursson tips his hand as a drummer with a percussive-heavy concept that succeeds as a rhythmic, vaguely ambient piece, and former beau Goldie delivers a laidback touch of jungle that weaves loping horns and lazy piano bits into the song's fabric with decent results.

**IT'S OH SO QUIET 1/2** > (November 1995)

1. It's Oh So Quiet
2. You've Been Flirting Again (Flirt Is a Promise Mix)
3. Hyper-ballad (Over the Edge Mix)
4. Sweet Sweet Intuition

Featuring two absolutely superb reconfigurations of prior songs, both of which required new vocals and arrangements to execute, Björk's dedication to the remix is fully on display here. First off is the stunning, self-produced "Flirt Is a Promise Mix" of "You've Been Flirting Again," which begins with an icy veil that slowly lifts to reveal an overpowering arrangement, courtesy of Eumir Deodato. Imposing and haunting, this version trumps its album counterpart in emotional gravity alone. Elsewhere, Björk's improvement on prior b-side "Sweet Intuition" (listed here as "Sweet Sweet Intuition") places the original against a backdrop of swirling accordions and twinkling organ bits that suit it nicely. The only misfire is "Hyper-ballad (Over the Edge Mix)," which sees sonic muckrackers Outcast bury the song in a muddle of obnoxious digital glop.

**IT'S OH SO QUIET 2/2** > (November 1995)

1. It's Oh So Quiet
2. Hyper-ballad (Brodsky Quartet Version)
3. Hyper-ballad (Girl's Blouse Mix)
4. My Spine

With twirling strings carrying out violinist Paul Cassidy's roughshod arrangement, Manchester's Brodsky Quartet give "Hyper-ballad" a rousing concert-like feeling here, pulling on the song's implicit drama for high effect. Next, former One Little Indian recording artists Outcast (Richard Brown and Beaumont Hannant) take the opposite route and deliver equally captivating results by completely stripping away the song's rhythmic element and drawing gloomy synth swirls behind the lead melodies for star-gazy effect. Finally, Björk's impromptu collaboration with Scottish percussionist Evelyn Glennie (who features on exhaust pipes) moves in joyous homemade strides.

**HYPER-BALLAD 1/2** > (February 1996)

1. Hyper-ballad (Radio Edit)
2. Hyper-ballad (Robin Hood Riding through the Glen Mix — Howie B)
3. Hyper-ballad (The Stomp Mix — LFO)
4. Hyper-ballad (The Fluke Mix)
5. Hyper-ballad (Subtle Abuse Mix — Outcast Productions)
6. Hyper-ballad (Tee's Freeze Mix — Todd Terry)

This mixed bag of healthy inspiration, middling mediocrity, and cheesebag house starts strongly but ends poorly. His agonizing penchant for synth hits aside, Howie B does fine work with "Robin Hood Riding through the Glen Mix," re-inventing the song's chord progression but never knocking it out of orbit; LFO's attempt to punch things up a bit with the syncopated "Stomp Mix" is inoffensive at best; Fluke turn in an uncharacteristically thoughtful remix with the nicely textured "Fluke Mix"; Outcast cue up a 4/4 beat and color round the edges with unmemorable flourishes on the "Subtle Abuse Mix," and house producer Todd Terry ingratiates himself with the cocktail set on the aimless "Tee's Freeze Mix."

**HYPER-BALLAD 2/2** > (February 1996)

1. Hyper-ballad (Radio Edit)
2. Isobel (Carcass Remix)
3. Cover Me (Plaid Mix)
4. Hyper-ballad (Towa Tei Mix)

Not so much a remix as it is a total facelift remade in their own image, heavy metal band Carcass' recut of "Isobel" may be one of Björk's most infamous collaborations to date. Although its clean strings and tribal rhythms were supplanted by the metallic squeals and deep pigskin thump of grindcore, the Carcass Remix didn't sacrifice any of the song's tunefulness, making it an unlikely fan favorite. Elsewhere, Plaid play with various levels of reverb and decay on their remix of the cavernous "Cover Me" and Deee-Lite graduate Towa Tei stretches "Hyper-ballad" into an eight-minute house excursion.

**POSSIBLY MAYBE 1/3** > November 1996)

1. Possibly Maybe
2. Possibly Maybe (Lucy Mix)
3. Possibly Maybe (Calcutta Cyber Café Mix)
4. Possibly Maybe (Dallas Austin Mix)

There's only two truly new tracks here (Mark Bell's "Lucy Mix" originally appeared on *Telegram*), but both of them are worth seeking out. The superb "Calcutta Cyber Café Mix" sees Talvin Singh tap into the song's inbuilt trance elements with a tabla-aided shudder that builds into a lovely rustle. Meanwhile, producer Dallas Austin (Madonna, TLC) garnishes his subtle remix with a more purposeful snare and a grab bag of lush accoutrements.

**POSSIBLY MAYBE 2/3** > (November 1996)

1. Cover Me (Dillinja Mix)
2. One Day (Trevor Morais Remix)
3. Possibly Maybe (Calcutta Cyber Café Dub Mix)
4. I Miss You (Photek Mix)

Trevor Morais dishes up seven minutes of gently shifting percussion on his fantastic take on "One Day," Talvin Singh tosses spaced-out drum shapes into the ether on his subtly rhythmic "Calcutta Cyber Café Dub Mix," and Goldie chum Photek (a.k.a. Rupert Parkes) takes his pincers to "I Miss You," where he sustains the washes of polite drama for over a minute before unleashing a typically muzzled-up break. Dillinja's definitive drum'n'bass remix of "Cover Me" is even better, but is more easily found on *Telegram*.

**POSSIBLY MAYBE 3/3** > (November 1996)

1. Big Time Sensuality (Plaid Mix)
2. Vísur Vatnsenda-Rósu
3. Possibly Maybe (Live)
4. Hyper-ballad (Over the Edge Mix) (Live)

Plaid lend their vintage IDM touches to an entirely resung version of "Big Time Sensuality," in turn confounding fans who thought that further versions of that oft-remixed song were no longer necessary. Next, the spectral tinge of Björk's standout contribution to Hector Zazou's *Chansons des mers froides* compilation makes a welcome return. Finally, the broody "Possibly Maybe" comes across as an imagined show-stopper in this Wembley Arena recording, whereas Björk's live rendition of

"Hyper-ballad," performed with Outcast's previously released "Over the Edge" remix as its template, isn't much of an improvement over the plodding studio version. Still good value overall, though.

**I MISS YOU 1/2** > (February 1997)

1. I Miss You
2. I Miss You (Dobie Pt. 2 Mix)
3. I Miss You (Darren Emerson Mix)
4. Karvel (Graham Massey Mix)

Björk continued to indulge her hip-hop fixation by commissioning a sturdy, beat-heavy remix from London Posse associate Dobie, who in turn tapped London Posse's own Rodney P for mic duties on this track. On the heels of its loping hip-hop beat, we're unceremoniously passed over to Underworld's Darren Emerson, who subjects "I Miss You" to a lengthy, house-driven workout that would've been better had it sounded more like Underworld. Finally, a nice surprise: "Karvel," the first Björk original to appear as a b-side in a long time, certainly a nice respite from an otherwise steady influx of hit-and-miss remixes.

**I MISS YOU 2/2** > (February 1997)

1. I Miss You (Dobie Pt. 1 Mix)
2. Hyper-ballad (LFO Mix)
3. Violently Happy (Live)
4. Headphones (Mika Vainio Mix)

Things really start to get dire here: "Dobie Pt. 1 Mix" is essentially "Dobie Pt. 2" without the hollowed-out hip-hop breaks, making it (depending on how you want to look at it), either the unmix of an existing remix or a remix of a previous remix. Either way, when combined with the rest of the offerings — a busy, almost trancey bit of new age fluff from LFO, a decent but wholly unnecessary live version of emerging dead horse "Violently Happy," and Mika Vainio's mix of "Headphones" that was released on *Telegram* a few months earlier — it's obvious that Björk's camp had completely exhausted themselves of b-side material by this point.

**JOGA 1/3** > (September 1997)

1. Joga (Howie B Main Mix)
2. Joga (String and Vocal Mix)
3. Joga (Buzz Water Mix)
4. All Is Full of Love (Choice Mix)

Björk's famous beats+strings methodology for *Homogenic* was anything but an exercise in brevity. As these mixes proved, the fewer elements a song had, the more it was sensitive to even the slightest tweak. As such, the three remixes of "Joga" offered here are each illuminating in their own way: "Howie B Main Mix" slightly more urgent, "String and Vocal Mix" more plaintive, "Buzz Water Mix" a sheen of white noise and disembodied melodies.

**JOGA 2/3** > (September 1997)

1. Joga
2. Sod Off
3. Immature
4. So Broken

This disc collects two outstanding b-sides from the *Homogenic* era (the full-out flamenco rush of "So Broken" and the furious stomp of "Sod Off") and matches them up with a sparse, utilitarian reworking of album track "Immature," making it a good bet for anyone immediately looking to get their hands on new material.

**JOGA 3/3** > (September 1997)

1. Joga
2. Joga (Alec Empire Mix)
3. Joga (Alec Empire Digital Hardcore Mix 1)
4. Joga (Alec Empire Digital Hardcore Mix 2)

Björk's musical dalliance with Germain punk noisenik Alec Empire has long been a point of contention for fans, many of whom resent the way he generally suffocates his source material with a giant cloud of distortion. That's a fair assessment of this disc too; unless you're already inclined towards the spiky thrash of Empire's hyper-accelerated techno punk, these abrasive and kinetic remixes aren't likely to impress.

**BACHELORETTE 1/3** > (December 1997)

1. Bachelorette (Radio Edit)
2. My Snare
3. Scary
4. Bachelorette (Howie "Spread" Mix)

Although probably not as good as the b-sides that appear on the "Joga" singles, the remaining two originals from the *Homogenic* sessions featured here are worth tracking down. The bounding "My Snare" (a.k.a. "Nature Is Ancient") and the sprightly "Scary" give a good view of what was happening on the peripheries of the album's beats+strings manifesto. Elsewhere, Howie B's "Spread Mix" of "Bachelorette" effectively eliminates the song's rhythm section and lower end, but not much else.

**BACHELORETTE 2/3** > (December 1997)

1. Bachelorette (Mark Bell "Optimism" Remix)
2. Bachelorette (Mark Bell "Zip" Remix)
3. Bachelorette (Mark Bell "Blue" Remix)
4. Bachelorette

The extent of Mark Bell's importance to the genesis of *Homogenic* is borne out by this disc, where Björk gives him ample room to fully indulge his various transpositions of "Hunter." To Bell's credit, all three remixes go trundling down completely different paths: the "Zip Remix" ends up a peppery slice of lethargic mid-tempo IDM, the "Blue Mix" a watery dollop of electro and syncopated rhythms, and the superior "Optimism Remix" a surging work-in-progress of whirlygigging synths and military drums.

**BACHELORETTE 3/3** > (December 1997)

1. Bachelorette (RZA Remix)
2. Bachelorette (Alec Empire "Hypermodern Jazz" Remix)
3. Bachelorette (Alec Empire "The Ice Princess and the Killer Whale" Remix)
4. Bachelorette (Grooverider "Jeep" Remix)

Wu-Tang's RZA may have obvious difficulties negotiating the slowish breakdowns of "Bachelorette," but when his rugged *36 Chambers*-style beats come skipping along behind the song's familiar verse motif, it's hard not to marvel at the gonzo appeal of this incongruous collaboration. Meanwhile, with its high-frequency pinpricks, analog belches, and busted-key synth noodlings, "Hypermodern Jazz" is probably one of the easiest Alec Empire remixes to parse. That, however, doesn't necessarily make it better. The white noise gush of the furious "Ice Princess and the Killer Whale" remix may spell eardrum havoc, but it's got a uniformity and drama that renders it the best of his two offerings here. Restoring a bit of order to the proceedings is London drum'n'bass mentalist Grooverider, whose serviceable "Jeep Remix" sees him pitch shift Björk's vocals up a few notches and slot a revolving assortment of breakbeats in underneath.

**HUNTER 1/3** > (October 1998)

1. Hunter (Radio Edit)
2. All Is Full of Love (In Love with Funkstorung Remix)
3. Hunter (u-Ziq Remix)

A mixed bag here: for starters, the "Hunter (Radio Edit)" basically just splices out a minute of the original, meaning it's more useful than a copy of the album track but certainly not essential or enlightening. Meanwhile, Funkstorung's "In Love with Funkstorung Remix" strips away the gravitas by hollowing out the song's center, leaving a brittle shell of vocals and beats in its space. By default, it is the worst of Funkstorung's "All Is Full of Love" remixes, but still recommended. Mike Paradinis' remix of "Hunter" puts its most salient elements through an extended aerobic lesson, turning Björk's vocals and strings against themselves to *Twilight Zonish* effect.

**HUNTER 2/3** > (October 1998)

1. Hunter
2. Hunter (State of Bengal Mix)
3. Hunter (Skothus Mix)

Only two tracks here to speak of, one of which is a stuttering, blue-cool jungle remix with nimbly skipping breakbeats and subtle sub-house flourishes (the excellent "State of Bengal Mix"), the other of which pinches Björk's most noncommittal vocal snippets and slaps them overtop a chugging, Roland-aided disco squelch to somewhat fruitless results (Gus Gus' "Skothus Mix").

**HUNTER 3/3** > (October 1998)

1. Hunter (Mood Swing Remix)
2. So Broken (DJ Krust Remix)
3. Hunter (Live)

Mark Bell emphasizes "Hunter"'s bolero strut to near absurdity on the "Mood Swing Remix," an aptly named mess of ideas that flits between orchestral pomp and circumstance, military flourishes, and a grab bag of twee organics. Surprisingly, it works well. Elsewhere, DJ Krust takes an unlikely drum'n'bass remix candidate in "So Broken" and aspires to give it a solid jungle workout; unfortunately, the end result is too crammed full of hollow gestures and mislaid inspiration to get this arranged marriage off the ground. Finally, recorded at Shephard's Bush, the live version of "Hunter" is tight, but hardly exciting for anyone already familiar with Björk's live treatment of the song.

**ALARM CALL 1/3** > (November 1998)

1. Alarm Call (Radio Mix)
2. Alarm Call (Rhythmic Phonetics Mix)
3. Alarm Call (Bjeck Mix)

Along with Mark Bell and Andy Bradfield's "Radio Mix" (which appears in the track's video), part one of the "Alarm Call" singles comes bundled with two fairly high-profile remixes. The "Rhythmic Phonetics" mix is not only significant for its mulched-up vocal sequence (wherein Björk's lyrics are spliced and syncopated, Prefuse 73-style over a clipping backbeat), but also because it marked Björk's first of many collaborations with San Francisco's Matmos, who spent days on the project. Elsewhere, professed superfan Beck turns in a serviceably spooky rejig that employs trebly harpsichords, clanging robo-beats, and B-movie theremins.

**ALARM CALL 2/3** > (November 1998)

1. Alarm Call (Potage du Jour)
2. Alarm Call (French Edit)
3. Alarm Call (French Dub)

The most dancefloor oriented of the three "Alarm Call" issues features the unrelenting stomp of Mark Bell's so-so "Potage du Jour" mix as well as two cuts from Alan Braxe and Ben Diamond. As two thirds of Stardust, a dance production crew fronted by Daft Punk's Thomas Bangalter, Braxe and Diamond stamp their signature elastic beats and rolling bass lines all over the boisterous "French Edit" and "French Dub," conjuring tantalizing images of what a proper Daft Punk/Björk collaboration might've sounded like.

**ALARM CALL 3/3** > (November 1998)

1. Alarm Call (Phunk You)
2. Alarm Call (Gangsta)
3. Alarm Call (Locked)

The strain of *Homogenic*'s remix overload peaked with this single, where it became evident that the demands of a three-single format had come at the expense of quality control. Mark Bell must have felt the pressure most — all three of these remixes are once again his. While none of them are particularly bad, they do suggest that his strengths as a remixer lie in more esoteric arenas; these tracks are half-warmed dance excursions, already trumped by Braxe & Diamond's superior cuts. That said, with its Mr. Oizo-on-speed vibe, the "Locked" mix deserves honorable mention.

**ALL IS FULL OF LOVE 1/2** > (June 1999)

1. All Is Full of Love
2. All Is Full of Love (Funkstorung Exclusive Mix)
3. All Is Full of Love (Strings)

Munich's typically austere Funkstorung expose their warmest side with the "Funkstorung Exclusive Mix," which swaps the song's smoothly paved undercarriage with a gravel road of skittish beats and gently hiccupping rhythms. As interesting as that is, it can't hold a candle to Björk's "Strings" mix — probably the finest "All Is Full of Love" remix available — which subtly infuses the song with a new glimmer of strings that exalts it to the very same place it breathlessly describes.

**ALL IS FULL OF LOVE 2/2** > (June 1999)

1. All Is Full of Love
2. All Is Full of Love (Plaid Mix)
3. All Is Full of Love (Guy Sigsworth Mix)

Two more brilliant reworkings here: Black Dog alumni Plaid strip the song down to its basest elements and then rebuild a typically sprightly set of gently bouncing synth bloops around it, in the process perfectly straddling the line between *Homogenic* and Plaid's *Not For Threes*. Elsewhere, the gutsy Guy Sigsworth eschews the song's cavernous orchestration in favor of a cheaply braying horn patch, which is just vaguely pitiable enough to resonate.

**HIDDEN PLACE 1/2** > (August 2001)

1. Hidden Place (Edit)
2. Generous Palmstroke
3. Verandi

The law of diminishing returns dictates that the first batch of singles from a new album should have the best b-sides, and the first "Hidden Place" issue is no exception. With the light (the gently resonate "Generous Palmstroke") and the dark (the charging Bollywood squeal of "Verandi") fully represented, it's hard to find fault with this opening salvo.

**HIDDEN PLACE 2/2** > (August 2001)

1. Hidden Place (A capella)
2. Mother Heroic
3. Foot Soldier

The *a capella* version of "Hidden Place" isn't a new vocal performance, but rather simply all the studio vocals (choir bits as well) sans accompaniment. The result – in-motion and far more thrilling than it sounds – further emphasizes the unprecedented importance of vocals on *Vespertine*. Combined with the nimble "Mother Heroic" and the sound dust cut-up of the gently percolating "Foot Soldier," this stands as one of the finer single packages from the album.

**PAGAN POETRY 1/2** > (November 2001)

1. Pagan Poetry (Video Edit)
2. Pagan Poetry (Matthew Herbert Handshake Mix)
3. Aurora (Opiate Version)

By *Vespertine*, Björk became notably more selective about the amount and quality of remixes that she was commissioning. Correspondingly, both of the recuts offered here scream quality control and are of exceptional merit. Matthew Herbert's "Handshake Mix" coaxes "Pagan Poetry" through a handful of warm, glitchy micro-house conceits but never strays too far from its original song form; meanwhile, Thomas Knak's take on "Aurora" unburdens the song of its considerable weight and sets it fluttering aloft on a wing of rhythmic harp drones and ambient crunches.

**PAGAN POETRY 2/2** > (November 2001)

1. Pagan Poetry
2. Domestica
3. Batabid

Mid-tempo and slumberous, outtakes "Domestica" (wherein Björk frets woozily over the loss of her keys) and "Batabid" (a swooshy instrumental) serve each other well and further reinforce the notion of the *Vespertine* era as one of creative tranquility. On a strict value-for-money scale, however, the fact that these two songs clock in at less than six minutes cumulatively may be reason enough to stay away.

**COCOON 1/2** > (March 2002)

1. Cocoon
2. Pagan Poetry (Music Box)
3. Sun in My Mouth (Recomposed by Ensemble)

The "Music Box" rendition of "Pagan Poetry" continues in the deconstructionist spirit of the *Vespertine* b-sides (see "Hidden Place (A capella)") by reducing the song to its most salient point — the gently twisting melody at its core, here resurrected via the pacified tinkling of a music box. The real highlight here, however, is Rephlex artist Ensemble's reworking of "Sun in My Mouth," which plays like a time-lapsed sunset by flitting busily from warmly mulched strings to gently cooing tones.

**COCOON 2/2** > (March 2002)

1. Cocoon (Radio Edit)
2. Aurora (Music Box)
3. Amphibian

With potential b-side material drying up, the last single release from the album offers barely a minute of new work — that in the form of the admittedly lovely instrumental chime of "Aurora," which is fleetingly recreated on a music box before concluding after a mere 68 seconds. Elsewhere, the presence of the seminal but previously available "Amphibian" and a hardly essential radio edit of "Cocoon" should rank this low on the list of *Vespertine* priorities.

**IT'S IN OUR HANDS 1/2** > (November 2002)

1. It's In Our Hands
2. Cocoon (Retangled by Ensemble)
3. All Is Full of Love (Live)

There's an intangible lovingness to all of these tracks that unexpectedly ties them together. Following the cushy caramel warmth of single "It's In Our Hands," Ensemble casts a gauzy, beatless spell over "Cocoon," ridding it of its rhythms so that it descends like a slow mist. As a finale, Björk's live version of "All Is Full of Love" (suitably re-arranged so as to accommodate her touring choir) is goosebump-inducing stuff, an old standard tweaked just enough so as to thrill once again.

**IT'S IN OUR HANDS 2/2** > (November 2002)

1. It's In Our Hands (Soft Pink Truth Mix)
2. It's In Our Hands (Arcade Mix)
3. So Broken (Live on Jools Holland)

With two of Björk's finest ever remixes (indeed, both Drew Daniel's "Soft Pink Truth Mix" and her own "Arcade Mix" have moments where they feel vastly superior to their source material) and a boisterous live rendition of an old fan favorite, it's difficult to go wrong here. Operating under his electro-inclined alter ago Soft Pink Truth, Daniel speeds up the track and then reroutes it to somewhere to the mid-'80s, where it settles nicely against a garbled-up acid bass line and a flurry of vocal snippets. Not to be outdone, Björk tapped both members of Matmos for input on the storming "Arcade Mix," which is built around a thick elastic drumbeat and a jet stream of syncopated rhythms. Recorded on the *Later with Jools Holland* television show in 1998, the inclusion of the infrequently played "So Broken" serves as an especially nice treat for fans.

# Sources


**INTRODUCTION**

*South Bank Show*. "Björk." Episode 21-4. Originally aired: November 9, 1997.

**CHAPTER 1**

Davis, Andy. "Secret History of Björk." *Record Collector*. March 1, 1994.
Eshun, Ekow. "Björk Free." *Face*. November 1993.
Garðarsson, Jónatan. Interview with author. March 6, 2002.
Gislason, Bjorgvin. Interview with author. March 4, 2002.
Gunnarsson, Guðmundur. Interview with author. March 7, 2002.
Gunnarsson, Thorsteinn. "Björk." *i-D*. May 1, 1993.
Harding, Louette. "Björk – Success and the Solo Mother." *You*. November 12, 1995.
Heath, Chris. "Björk From Ork." *Details*. July 1994.
James, Mandi. "Björk Again." *Face*. June 1, 1993.
Jónsson, Ásmunder. Interview with author. March 8, 2002.
Masuo, Sandy. "The World According to Björk." *Option*. October 9, 1995.
Matthíasson, Árni. Interview with author. March 6, 2002.
Melax, Einar. Interview with author. March 6, 2002.
Phillips, Dom. "Björk." *Mixmag*. November 1993.
Smith, Andrew. "Björk – An International Word." *Raygun*. June 1995.
Udovitch, Mim. "Björk – Thoroughly Modern." *Rolling Stone*. July 13, 1995.

**CHAPTER 2**

"Kukl – Holidays in Europe." Promotional material. January 1986.
"Kukl Concert Review." *NME*. October 6, 1984.
"Kukl Concert Review." *Sounds*. October 13, 1984.
"The Somewhat Complete Bad Taste Saga." www.smekkleysa.net. June 1986.
Aston, Martin. "Ssshhh! Quiet Everybody! Björk's Talking." *Raw*. January 1996.
Broughton, Frank. "Björk's Big Night Out." *i-D*. April 1, 1994.
Eshun, Ekow. "Björk Free." *Face*. November 1993.
Friðriksson, Friðrik þór. Interview with author. March 5, 2002.
Garðarsson, Jónatan. Interview with author. March 6, 2002.
Geirhardsson, Kormákur. Interview with author. March 6, 2002.
Gibson, Robin. "Sweet Sensation." *Sounds*. September 1, 1987.
Gislason, Bjorgvin. Interview with author. March 4, 2002.
Gunnarsson, Guðmundur. Interview with author. March 7, 2002.
Heath, Chris. "Björk from Ork." *Details*. July 1, 1994.
Hilmarsson, Hilmar Örn. Interview with author. March 3, 2002.
Hjálmarsson, Gunnar. Interview with author. March 5, 2002.

Johansson, Eyjólfur. Interview with author. March 5, 2002.
Jónsson, Ásmunder. Interview with author. March 8, 2002.
Matthíasson, Árni. Interview with author. August 26, 2002.
Matthíasson, Árni. Interview with author. March 6, 2002.
Melax, Einar. Interview with author. March 6, 2002.
Ottarsson, Gudlaugur. Interview with author. January 16, 2002.

**CHAPTER 3**

Bailie, Stuart. "Lock Up Your Gudmundsdóttirs." *NME*. December 25, 1993.
Eshun, Ekow. "Björk Free." *Face*. November 1993.
Fox, Paul. Interview with author. June 19, 2002.
Frith, Mark. "Bjonkers?" *Smash Hits*. November 24, 1993.
Garðarsson, Jónatan. Interview with author. March 6, 2002.
Hilmarsson, Hilmar Örn. Interview with author. March 3, 2002.
Gunnarsson, Guðmundur. Interview with author. March 7, 2002.
Hjálmarsson, Gunnar. Interview with author. March 5, 2002.
Jónsson, Ásmunder. Interview with author. March 8, 2002.
Keene, Nietzchka. Interview with author. June 2002.
Matthíasson, Árni. Interview with author. August 26, 2002.
Matthíasson, Árni. Interview with author. March 6, 2002.
Ottarsson, Gulli. Interview with author. January 16, 2002.
Snow, Mat. "World Domination or Die!" *Q*. November 1989.
Teller, Juergen. "Björk." *Index*. June 2001.
Tility, Jennifer. "Freaky Momma." *Bust*. Fall, 1996.

**CHAPTER 4**

Fox, Paul. Interview with author. June 19, 2002.
Gardner, Elysa. "In a Björk State of Mind." *Rolling Stone*. June 1, 1993.
Gondry, Michel. Interview with author. January 30, 2002.
Gunnarsson, Thorsteinn. "Björk." *i-D*. May 1, 1993.
Hale, Corky. Interview with author. January 4, 2002.
Hjálmarsson, Gunnar. Interview with author. March 5, 2002.
James, Mandi. "Björk Again." *Face*. June 1993.
Jónsson, Ásmunder. Interview with author. March 8, 2002.
Lake, Oliver. Interview with author. January 13, 2002.
Massey, Graham. Interview with author. November 27, 2001.
Matthíasson, Árni. Interview with author. March 6, 2002.
O'Brien, Lucy. "Call of the Child." *Vox*. October 1995.
St. Steingrímsson, Guðmundur. Interview with author. March 4, 2002.
Walker, Netty. Interview with author. June 22, 2002.

**CHAPTER 5**

Arab, Leila. Interview with author. March 2002.

Bailie, Stuart. "Lock Up Your Gudmundsdóttirs." *NME*. December 25, 1993.

Eshun, Ekow. "Björk Free." *Face*. November 1993.

Hajari, Nisid. "Cool Eccentric." *Entertainment Weekly*. July 1995.

Harding, Louette. "Björk — Success and the Solo Mother." *You*. November 12, 1995.

Lake, Oliver. Interview with author. January 13, 2002.

Matthíasson, Árni. Interview with author. March 6, 2002.

O'Brien, Lucy. "Call of the Child." *Vox*. October 1995.

Palmer, Tamara. "Björk Comin' On Strong." *UHF*. November 1995.

Savage, Jon. "The Always Uncjorked Björk." *Interview*. June 1995.

Walker, Netty. Interview with author. June 22, 2002.

**CHAPTER 6**

"Björk's Scanner in the Works." *Melody Maker*. July 17, 1995.

"Court Clears Björk of Copyright Theft." *Wire* reports. June 24, 1995.

"Scanner: It's in the Post." *Melody Maker*. June 24, 1995.

Aston, Martin. "Ssshhh! Quiet Everybody! Björk's Talking." *Raw*. January 1996.

Dalton, Stephen. "Trick 'N Mix." *Vox*. September 1995.

Dravs, Markus. Interview with author. June 29, 2002.

Gondry, Michel. Interview with author. January 30, 2002.

Hack, Jefferson, and Paul Smith. "Björk Calling Jefferson." *Dazed & Confused*. January 1996.

Hellegar, Jeremy, and John Griffiths. "Out of the Shadows." *People*. September 25, 1995.

Jónsson, Ásmunder. Interview with author. March 8, 2002.

Massey, Graham. Interview with author. November 27, 2001.

Micallef, Ken. "Home Is Where the Heart Is." *Raygun*. September 1997.

Savage, Jon. "The Always Uncjorked Björk." *Interview*. June 1995.

Smith, Andrew. "Björk — An International Word." *Raygun*. June 1995.

Udovitch, Mim. "Thoroughly Modern." *Rolling Stone*. July 13, 1995.

Walker, Netty. Interview with author. June 22, 2002.

**CHAPTER 7**

"The Bomb Changed My Life." *Blah*. December 1996.

Arab, Leila. Interview with author. March 2002.

Björk. "Björk Meets Karlheinz Stockhausen." *Dazed & Confused*. August 1996.

Gunnarsson, Guðmundur. Interview with author. March 7, 2002.

Hjálmarsson, Gunnar. Interview with author. March 5, 2002.

Marcus, Tony. "Love Bites — Björk & Goldie." *i-D*. June 1996.

Micallef, Ken. "Home Is Where the Heart Is." *Raygun*. September 1997.

Patterson, Sylvia. "Goldie." *NME*. March 16, 1996.

Patterson, Sylvia. "Lunatic Ginge." *NME*. July 20, 1996.

Robinson, John. "G! Christ! Superstar!" *NME*. November 1, 1997.
Walker, Netty. Interview with author. June 22, 2002.

**CHAPTER 8**

"Björk Interview." *Spin Online*. February 1997.
"The Bomb Changed My Life." *Blah*. December 1996.
Chaplin, Julia. "Army of She." *Paper*. September 1997.
Doerschuk, Robert L. "Saga You Can Dance To." *Musician*. December 1997.
Dravs, Markus. Interview with author. June 29, 2002.
Elliot, Paul. "Who the Hell Does Björk Think She Is?" *Q*. November 1997.
Fern, Rob. "Björk, Don't Run." *Mixmag*. September 1997.
Gunnarsson, Guðmundur. Interview with author. March 7, 2002.
Micallef, Ken. "Home Is Where the Heart Is." *Raygun*. September 1997.
Van Meter, Jonathan. "The Outer Limits." *Spin*. December 1997.

**CHAPTER 9**

"Causing the FX." *Sunday Times*. March 13, 1999.
Anthony, Ross. "Press Conference Interview with Björk, David Morse, and Catherine Deneuve." Rossanthony.com. September 2001.
Arab, Leila. Interview with author. March 2002.
Basham, David. "Björk Talks Cinematic Affair with Dancer in the Dark." *MTV Online*. October 5, 2000.
Friðriksson, Friðrik Þór. Interview with author. March 5, 2002.
Gunnarsson, Guðmundur. Interview with author. March 7, 2002.
Hilmarsson, Hilmar Örn. Interview with author. March 3, 2002.
Karan, Donna. "Björk." *Interview*. September 2001.
Kenny, Glenn. "Björk's Big Adventure." *Premiere*. October 2000.
Kirkland, Bruce. "Björk Wins, Then Quits." *Toronto Sun*. May 22, 2000.
O'Brien, Lucy. "Cash For Questions." *Q*. October 2000.
Reich, J. Sperling. "Shedding Light on Dark." *Reel.com*. September 28, 2000.
Von Trier, Lars. "Making Dancer in the Dark." Promotional material. May 2000.
Windeløv, Vibeke. Interview with author. October 13, 2002.

**CHAPTER 10**

"An Exclusive Björk.Com Interview With Valgeir." *Björk.com*. June 2001.
Anthony, Ross. "Press Conference Interview with Björk, David Morse, and Catherine Deneuve." *Rossanthony.com*. September 2001.
Arab, Leila. Interview with author. March 2002.
Bell, Donald. "Matmos Interview." *TapeOp Magazine*. May 2001.
Beller, Thomas. "Into the Light." *Spin*. October 2001.
Crossfield, Paula. "Matmos." *Envy13.com*. May 2001.
Duerden, Nick. "Lovefool." *Q*. February 2002.

Friðriksson, Friðrik Þór. Interview with author. March 5, 2002.
Gretschmann, Martin. Interview with author. April 2001.
Gunnarsson, Guðmundur. Interview with author. March 7, 2002.
Hack, Jefferson. "Björk Versus Reality." *Dazed & Confused*. May 2002.
Harris, John. "Behind the Mask." *Q*. Summer 2001.
Karan, Donna. "Björk." *Interview*. September 2001.
Kenny, Glenn. "Björk's Big Adventure." *Premiere*. October 2000.
Knak, Thomas. Interview with author. March 2002.
Lagambina, Gregg. "Look Back in Wonder." *Filter*. September 2002.
LeMay, Matt. "Matmos." *Pitchfork Media*. May 2001.
Mulvey, John. "The Twilight World of Björk." *NME*. August 11, 2001.
Palmer, Tamara. "A Different Sort of Bird." *Urb*. September 2001.
"The Piercing Sound of Björk." *NME.com*. October 19, 2001.
Pozo, Carlos M. "Matmos Interview." *Angbase Magazine*. September 1999.
Raczynski, Bogdan. Interview with author. January 2001.
Teller, Juergen. "Björk." *Index*. June 2001.
Toop, David. "As Serious as Your Life." *Wire*. September 2001.
Yago, Gideon. "Björk: In Focus." *MTVASIA.com*. March 2001.

**SONGBOOK/DISCOGRAPHY**

Björk. "Chat Transcript." *Sonicnet.com*. October 16, 1997.
Bitzer, John. "Bjork's Newest Vision." *CDNOW*. August 21, 2001.
Chaplin, Julia. "Army Of She." *Paper*. September 1997.
Curtis, Natalie. "Bjork." *Feedback*. February 1996.
Dravs, Markus. Interview with author. June 29, 2002.
Eshun, Ekow. "Björk Free." *Face*. November 1993.
Fricke, David. "Domestic Alliances." *Mojo Collections*. Summer 2001.
Geirhardsson, Kórmakur. Interview with author. March 6, 2002.
Glennie, Evelyn. Interview with author. April 8, 2002.
Gondry, Michel. Interview with author. January 30, 2002.
Gretschmann, Martin. Interview with author. April 2001.
Hale, Corky. Interview with author. January 4, 2002.
Heath, Chris. "Björk from Ork." *Details*. July 1994.
Hemingway, David. "Björk." *Record Collector*. September 2002.
Hilmarsson, Hilmar Örn. Interview with author. March 3, 2002.
Knak, Thomas. Interview with author. March 2002.
Lagambina, Gregg. "Look Back in Wonder." *Filter*. September 2002.
Lanham, Tom. "Björk." *Pulse*. July 1995.
Micallef, Ken. "Home Is Where the Heart Is." *Raygun*. September 1997.
Mulvey, John. "The Twilight World of Björk." *NME*. August 11, 2001.
Savage, Jon. "The Always Uncjorked Björk." *Interview*. June 1995.
Walker, Netty. Interview with author. June 22, 2002.

# Index